Beside the Still Waters

Vision Publishers, Inc.
Harrisonburg, Virginia

ISBN: 0-9717054-4-5

All Scripture references are from the
King James Version of the Holy Bible.

Published by Vision Publishers, Inc.
Harrisonburg, Virginia

Cover Design: Lonnie D. Yoder

For additional copies or comments write to:
Vision Publishers, Inc.
P.O. Box 190
Harrisonburg, VA 22803
Fax: 540/432-6530
e-mail: visionpubl@ntelos.net
(see order form in back)

Still Waters Ministries is supported by tax-free donations.
The bi-monthly devotional booklets are
distributed free of charge.

For more information on Still Waters Ministries, write to:
Still Waters Ministries
270 Antioch Road
Clarkson, KY 42726
Phone: 270/242-0459
Fax: 270/242-3529

A royalty payment from the sale of these
books will go to Still Waters Ministries.

Introduction

Is it possible to develop close relationships without communicating? Of course not! Communication is the very foundation of all relationships. There can be no fellowship without communication.

Sincere Christians desire a close relationship with their Lord. It is impossible to live the Christian life without knowing God. Only as we draw near to Him can we begin to understand the real meaning of life.

We must communicate with God if we are to have a good relationship with Him. We cannot expect to grow close to Him if we are unwilling to spend time with Him. But how can we communicate with God? We can't meet him face to face and discuss the issues of life. We might dial 1-800-CALL-GOD, but we will not connect with heaven. As amazing as the postal service is, they don't offer service to the Throne, and God doesn't have an e-mail address. Yet there is a way to communicate with Him. We are accustomed to fast, worldwide communication, but we must use a different method to speak with our Lord.

God has made His side of the conversation available to us through His Word, the Bible, and through His indwelling Holy Spirit. However, before we can hear Him, we must listen. A daily time of listening to God by meditating on His Word is essential to the victorious Christian life. We complete our part of the conversation by speaking to Him in prayer.

We hope this book will help you to come daily into the presence of God and to communicate with Him there.

The writings in this book were selected from the first three years of *Beside the Still Waters* (1996-1998), a bi-monthly, dated devotional booklet published by Still Waters Ministries. Writers from a variety of Amish and Mennonite churches from the United States, Canada, and other countries submitted the material that is used in this book.

We wish to express our heartfelt appreciation to all those who took time from their busy schedules to contribute to this project without receiving monetary benefits. May you be blessed with abundant spiritual blessings.

We also extend our thanks to the publisher for investing extensive time and effort to prepare the book and to publish it.

And we thank you, the reader, for selecting this book. We hope you will enjoy it.

Henry Yoder, Editor
Still Waters Ministries

A God of Beginnings

In the beginning God. . . .
Genesis 1:1

Notice that the Bible begins with God, not with a philosophical argument for His existence. God always was, and God always will be. He is the Alpha and the Omega, the beginning and the end. The Bible says it, that settles it, and I believe it.

Although God had no beginning Himself, He is a God of beginnings. The entire creation began with God. All life begins with a miracle that only He can perform. We can list many things that God has begun.

God is present when one becomes a living soul and begins life on the earth. Consider the life of a Christian. Our Redeemer rejoices with the angels when a person commits his life to Him and begins his walk as a Christian. Those of us who are married probably began our wedded lives in a ceremony performed by the Lord's ministers, in the Lord's house, and with the Lord's blessing. God has been with us through various beginnings; but best of all, He will be there to hold our hand as we cross the river and begin eternity with Him.

Since God is so experienced in beginning things, perhaps we should allow Him to have more say when we begin something. Every day, week, month, or year; every project, plan, or ambition—all should begin with God.

Begin this year with God. Lay all your plans at the feet of Jesus and allow the Master of beginnings to take care of them for you.

Henry Yoder, Clarkson, KY

Bible Reading: Genesis 1
One Year Bible Reading Plan:
Matthew 1
Genesis 1, 2

In the beginning God. . .
. . . and, behold, it was very good.
—Genesis 1:1, 31

5

Bread of Life

I am that bread of life.
John 6:48

We enjoy fresh whole wheat bread, right out of the oven. Ah-h-h, the aroma is so inviting, and the warm soft bread is so satisfying!

Bread is a widely eaten food. It provides a large share of many people's energy and protein, and is often called the "staff of life." Research shows that people who consume a reasonable amount of "daily bread" have less trouble with colon afflictions.

Bread is a complete food. Consider the manna that God gave the children of Israel. Moses said to them, "This is the bread which the LORD hath given you to eat" (Exodus 16:15). This manna was a complete food. It gave the people the nutrients they needed to face life in the desert. God was faithful to send the manna for forty years.

We need a daily portion of the Bread that comes from heaven. We are not satisfied to have only breakfast, skipping lunch and supper. Neither should we be satisfied to hastily read a portion of the Word of God and quickly scan a devotional booklet, and think that we have gathered all we need.

Do we have a good appetite for the Bread of Life? "And the Word was made flesh, and dwelt among us" (John 1:14). This is the Bread of God that will satisfy us and give us the spiritual strength we desperately need.

Bible Reading: John 6:26-51
One Year Bible Reading Plan:
Matthew 2
Genesis 3–5

Merl Beiler, Abbeville, SC

_____

Your spiritual health depends on your daily diet.

Who Is This?

And when he was come into Jerusalem,
all the city was moved, saying, Who is this?
Matthew 21:10

As Jesus rode into Jerusalem on a donkey, a multitude ran before him. There was excitement in the air. The whole city was moved. The question, "Who is this man?" caused perplexity and discussion.

To some, He was the son of a poor carpenter. To some, He was an interesting and charismatic teacher. To a few, He was an illegitimate son of a peasant girl. To others, He was a threat to their position and authority. Only a few loved Him and followed Him. Yet He was a person whom they could not ignore.

Two thousand years have passed. Jesus is still a person whom we cannot ignore. The many prophecies concerning His birth, life, death, and resurrection have been fulfilled in minute detail. Prophecies of events leading to His second coming are being fulfilled. This man's impact on the world has been unmatched by any other. No one has influenced the course of history like this "carpenter's son."

He was born of an exclusive people, in a remote Jewish village. Yet this person's life and influence have crossed oceans, nationalities, and racial barriers, and changed the lives of those who let Him.

Bible Reading: Matthew 21:1-11
One Year Bible Reading Plan:
Matthew 3
Genesis 6–8

Who is Jesus to you? The Son of God? The Savior and Lord? Make Him that today!

Jim Yoder, Leitchfield, KY

Neither is there salvation in any other: for there is none other name
under heaven given among men whereby we must be saved.
Acts 4:12

Hearing the Word

Take heed therefore how ye hear.
Luke 8:18

Because of my job, children often are thrilled to see me drive up. Their faces light up, and they smile big smiles as I unload and set up their swing set.

This summer I delivered a swing set to a home where the mother and an eight or nine-year-old son came out to meet me. The mother told me where she wanted the swing set up, and told me the boy had been deaf from birth. Because it was a very warm afternoon, the mother soon went back into the house, where it was cooler.

The boy stayed. He watched every move I made as I was assembling the set. As I was drilling holes and putting in bolts, I handed the boy some nuts and washers, and you should have seen his face. He raised his eyebrows, and a big smile came across his face. He got the message loud and clear, helping me whenever he could to set up the swing set.

When I had almost completed the job, the boy took off running toward the house. Because I could not communicate with him, I didn't know what I had done to offend him. (Maybe he had just grown weary of the sun's heat.) A little later he came out and handed me a large, cold drink, and I was very touched by his act of kindness.

On my way home, I had to think, "This little boy could not hear, yet he got the message." How do we respond to the voice of the Lord? Are we hearing the Lord, or are we so preoccupied with worldly things that we don't hear when He speaks to us? When we do hear the Lord, do we respond like the little boy, full of energy and ready to do the Master's will?

Only then can we carry out Luke 8:15: ". . . having heard the word, keep it, and bring forth fruit with patience."

Bible Reading: Luke 8:1-18
One Year Bible Reading Plan:
Matthew 4
Genesis 9–11

Menno Yoder, Monticello, KY

He that hath ears to hear, let him hear.

The Christian's Rest

Come unto me, . . . and ye shall find rest unto your souls.
Matthew 11:28-29

Hard work, sweat, fatigue, tired muscles, and aching bones. After a strenuous day of exerting brain and brawn, how sweet are home, family, and rest. After we have rested, we can return to work. We work with rest in view.

Even Scripture tells us, "Let us labour therefore to enter into that rest." Hebrews 4:3 says that not everyone will be able to enter the rest that God offers. Heaven will offer rest only to those who have labored faithfully. We look forward with anticipation to those mansions that Jesus has gone to prepare for those who love and obey Him.

Jesus said, "Come unto me, all ye that labour and are heavy laden, and I will give you rest." Rest is the prerogative of all who come to Jesus. It is given to us here and now, while we labor and toil, in mission work or in carpentry. Jesus is our rest. He invites sinners and saints to come to Him and receive rest for their souls.

Bible Reading: Hebrews 4
One Year Bible Reading Plan:
Matthew 5:1-26
Genesis 12–14

Eli Kauffman, Montezuma, GA

The idle man does not know what it is to enjoy rest.

Separated Stuff

Wherefore come out from among them, and be ye separate, saith the Lord, and touch not the unclean thing; and I will receive you.
2 Corinthians 6:17

Joshua had instructed the Israelites, "Keep yourselves from the accursed thing" (Joshua 6:18). Earlier, God had given the commandment, "Thou shalt not covet" (Exodus 20:17).

Achan disobeyed both of these commands. He took some of the banned things and buried them in his tent among his own stuff. He had no doubt seen and heard of the mighty works of God: the parting of the Red Sea, the water from the rock of flint, and the giving of manna and quail. God had separated Israel from the other nations to be His people, set apart, but apparently, Achan did not want to be quite as separated as the others. He eyed a Babylonian garment and some gold and silver, and took them for his own. The Israelites, and Achan's family, suffered greatly because of his sin.

When separated believers of Christ look to the world and covet its goods, are we not doing what Achan did? Why would we—as sanctified, separated, blood-bought believers—want the accursed things that the world has to offer?

As strangers and pilgrims, we do not need to mix worldly treasures among our own stuff. "For where your treasure is, there will your heart be also" (Matthew 6:21). Friend, whose stuff do you treasure—God's or the world's?

Bible Reading: Joshua 7:1-21
One Year Bible Reading Plan:
Matthew 5:27-48
Genesis 15–17

Terry Lester, Montezuma, GA

Heavenly treasures are more valuable than worldly stuff.

Slothfulness

Yet a little sleep, a little slumber, a little folding of the hands to sleep.
Proverbs 6:10

The effects of slothfulness in a person's physical life arouse us to pity.

But are we slothful in our spiritual lives? Let us examine ourselves. Am I struggling spiritually? Do I have a carefree, indifferent attitude about my spiritual welfare? Am I folding my hands? Am I satisfied to hear Sunday's message, but forget the truth as I go on my way through the week? Do I make a feeble, half-hearted attempt in my personal study of God's Word?

"The soul of the sluggard desireth, and hath nothing: but the soul of the diligent shall be made fat" (Proverbs 13:4). "Strive to enter in at the strait gate" (Luke 13:24). *Strive* means to make a great effort.

"Go to the ant, thou sluggard; consider her ways" (Proverbs 6:6). Let's take a lesson from the ant and likewise prepare ourselves so that we can live. We cannot afford to sit back and fold our hands. We must put forth much effort to study God's Word, to commune with God, to meditate, to listen and allow God to talk to us, so that we may experience a close, intimate relationship with God.

Let us strive to build spiritual stamina and to become more like Christ. Praise God for the strength we can experience as we walk with Him.

Marvin Yoder, Belvidere, TN

Bible Reading: Proverbs 6:6-11; 2 Peter 1:3-10
One Year Bible Reading Plan:
Matthew 6
Genesis 18, 19

The Lord wants not just our spare time, but our precious time..

Forever Free

And ye shall know the truth, and the truth shall make you free.
John 8:32

President Lincoln wrote the Emancipation Proclamation, which went into effect on the first of January, 1863. It declared "forever free" all residents of the United States. Yet, many slaves remained with their masters, even after the war ended. Either they were ignorant of their freedom, or they didn't know how to appropriate it, even though the President and Congress signed the Proclamation, and many Union soldiers laid down their lives to enforce it.

Many Christians, like those slaves, either choose to ignore or don't know how to appropriate the "freedom" won by Christ's death on the cross and His resurrection. Many are still in bondage to their old master (Romans 6:16) and can't, or won't, accept the victory won for us by the finished work on Calvary.

Here are three reasons why this is so: 1) Ignorance. Many Christians are unaware of the liberty Christ purchased for them through His redemptive work on the cross. They do not see that the benefits of the cross are now available to us. They do not grow in grace and the knowledge of Jesus Christ. 2) Inconvenience is another reason. Following Christ is not always a trouble-free, comfortable experience. It is a life of self-denial, discipline, sacrifice, and service. 3) Fear is another hindrance. Many believers are afraid of change. Like the emancipated slaves, they are afraid to venture out into a new world.

The cross of Christ is our Emancipation Proclamation. We can experience release from every form of bondage. But we must trust Christ and depend on Him for His deliverance. We do not have to live as captives to our past, to our emotions, or to our circumstances. Thank God we can be "forever free!"

Rudy Overholt, Russellville, KY

Bible Reading: John 8:31-59
One Year Bible Reading Plan:
Matthew 7
Genesis 20–22

If the Son therefore shall make you free,
ye shall be free indeed.

The Potter and the Clay

O LORD, . . . we are the clay, and thou our potter.
Isaiah 64:8

I stood watching a potter working with a lump of clay. He took the clay and put it on the potter's wheel and began to shape it. He worked on the clay until gradually it took the shape of a vessel. When it was finished, he set it back to dry.

After it is dry, the potter will put it into the fire and slowly raise the heat to about 1900° Fahrenheit. Later, he will glaze it and put it in the fire again. It will come out a beautiful vase.

Without the fire, the vase would be useless.

God is the potter. He wants us to be clay that He can mold in His own way. Sin has deformed us, but God wants to remold us for His glory. When we go through the fires of trials and temptations, they temper us and make us ready for the Master's use. How would the potter feel if the clay complained or refused to go into the fire?

This potter told me that he dislikes too much "makeup" (designs, paint, etc.) on his pots, because it draws attention to the pot, rather than to the potter. In the same way, God wants us to be vessels that are meek, humble, modest, and holy, so that we draw attention to Him—the Potter of our lives.

Sam Nisly, Cullman, AL

Bible Reading: Isaiah 64:6-12; Jeremiah 18:2-6
One Year Bible Reading Plan:
Matthew 8
Genesis 23, 24

When we rob God, we also cheat ourselves.

Garbage in Our Salad

Abstain from all appearance of evil.
1 Thessalonians 5:22

Do you ever find yourself trying to justify the places you go, the books you read, or of the music you listen to? I have. Often we think that a little bad won't hurt.

One day as a mother was scraping and peeling vegetables for a salad, her daughter came to ask her permission to go to a worldly center of amusement. On the defensive, the daughter admitted it was a questionable place, but said that all the girls were going. They did not think it would actually hurt them.

As the girl talked, she suddenly saw her mother pick up a handful of discarded vegetable scraps and throw them into the salad. In a startled voice, she cried, "Mother, you're putting the garbage into the salad!"

"Yes," her mother replied, "I know, but I thought that if you did not mind garbage in your mind and in your heart, you certainly would not mind a little in your stomach."

Thoughtfully, the girl removed the offending material from the salad, and with a brief "thank you" to her mother, went to tell her friends that she would not be going with them.

The Bible tells us, "Love not the world." We must be on our guard.

If you have spiritual indigestion and a sick testimony, maybe it is because you have allowed too much garbage in your salad.

Bible Reading: 1 John 2:12-17; Philippians 4:4-8
One Year Bible Reading Plan:
Matthew 9:1-17
Genesis 25, 26

Mark Webb, Hicksville, OH

The mark of the Christian is not perfection but consecration.
—Westcott

Walk Worthy of the Vocation

That ye might walk worthy of the Lord . . .
Colossians 1:10

We are not all called or gifted in the same way, but we may be sure that as we walk in the way of the Lord, He will use our individual talents. The Lord will provide opportunities to exercise these talents as we yield ourselves to His will. Furthermore, if we willingly obey our calling in little things, God will promote us to greater things. It is most important that we act when God calls us.

Gideon was called to a great work, but he was busy in the work before he became a great leader and worker in God's plan.

God is interested in our well-being. He will not ask us to do more than we can do. He will give us the grace and strength with which to work.

If we look around us, we will soon find things to do that will be of use to someone.

Abner Overholt, Auburn, KY

Bible Reading: Colossians 1:1-14
One Year Bible Reading Plan:
Matthew 9:18-38
Genesis 27, 28

Little is much if God is in it.

How Will Jesus Find You?

When the Son of man cometh, shall he find faith on the earth?
Luke 18:8

There was a man who was passionately fond of yellow. The walls and ceiling of his room were painted yellow. The wall-to-wall carpet was yellow. The draperies, the bedspread, and even his pajamas were yellow.

One day the poor man was stricken with yellow jaundice. His wife sent for the doctor and waited outside the room until the doctor had examined her husband. In a moment, the doctor came out looking puzzled. "How is he?" asked the wife. "I don't know," replied the doctor, "I can't find him."

Often there is so little difference between those who call themselves "Christians" and those who do not, that one can hardly tell them apart. Their lifestyle blends so well with the secular background that they are hard to find.

What does Jesus want to find in the life of His child when He returns? Wealth, fame, popularity?

Jesus asked, "Will I find faith?" Will He find a faith that has made a difference and continues to make a difference in your life; a faith that has separated you from the world and its system; a faith that overcomes the world, the lust of the flesh, the lust of the eyes, and the pride of life?

Will Jesus be able to find your faith when He returns to the earth?

Bible Reading: 1 John 2:15-17; 5:1-5
One Year Bible Reading Plan:
Matthew 10:1-23
Genesis 29, 30

Mervin Graber, Auburn, KY

_____

A faith that will save you is a faith that will change you.

Walk With the Lord

Walk before me, and be thou perfect.
Genesis 17:1

Perfection means nothing less than a full commitment to God's commandments.

As God's children, we are no less responsible to walk according to God's will than Abraham was. Walking perfectly with God is a beautiful way of life, with promises to look forward to at the end of the road.

God promised Abraham that if he would walk perfectly before Him, there would be no end to the blessings he would receive. We stand in line for the same promise.

We travel one of two roads, and we need to think seriously about where the road we are on will lead.

A wise man will not only think of what he is doing today, but also where his actions will lead him. What effect will today's actions have on our future and on the future of our children? Abraham obeyed. What will we do?

Abner Overholt, Auburn, KY

Bible Reading: Genesis 17:1-11, 23-27
One Year Bible Reading Plan:
Matthew 10:24-42
Genesis 31, 32

Wicked men obey out of fear,
good men out of love.
—Aristotle

Living in the Spirit

If we live in the Spirit, let us also walk in the Spirit.
Galatians 5:25

We hear much preaching and teaching about the Spirit. People are sometimes confused about the Spirit-filled life.

Before He returned to heaven, Jesus said that He would send the Comforter, who is the Holy Spirit. He said that this Spirit of Truth would glorify Him. If the things we do are not glorifying God, we are not following the Spirit. We need to live so that people can see our good works and glorify our Father in heaven (Matthew 5:16).

Ask yourself: Is the fruit of the Spirit apparent in my life? Do I have joy, peace, an even temper, goodness, faithfulness, humility, and self-control? Others can see these qualities (or the lack of them) even when we are not aware of them ourselves.

If we find ourselves lacking in these attributes, God will give us His Spirit if we ask Him.

Bible Reading: John 14:16-20
One Year Bible Reading Plan:
Matthew 11
Genesis 33–35

Abner Overholt, Auburn, KY

Let us walk in love.

The Renewed Mind

And be renewed in the spirit of your mind.
Ephesians 4:23

According to a syndicated news release, the most celebrated brain of the 20th century resides in Apt. 13 on the second floor of a nondescript apartment building in Lawrence, Kansas. Bathed in formaldehyde and cut into about 100 chunks and slices, the brain of Albert Einstein is contained in three glass jars owned by Thomas Harvey of Lawrence.

Dr. Harvey, who was asked to perform an autopsy on the 75 year old scientist in 1955, says that his goal has been "to discover some physical evidence of intellectual brilliance in the brain of one of humanity's greatest intellects."

Probably the greatest natural gift God has given to man is the mind. Life itself is perceived and experienced through the mind. God reminds us in His Word that we can know about Him in our natural mind (the intellect), but to know Him intimately requires a mind that has been renewed by God's Spirit. The mind that has been renewed and equipped with godly wisdom will have a far greater influence on the destiny of mankind than a genius who does not know God.

According to Philippians 2:5, we are to possess the mind of Christ. Perhaps this sounds unrealistic, and maybe even impossible; however, we can be assured that God reveals His will and character to us through the Holy Spirit and His word. As we grow in grace and knowledge, we are better able to understand God's desires and intents.

Bible Reading: Ephesians 4:17-29
One Year Bible Reading Plan:
Matthew 12:1-21
Genesis 36, 37

Phil Hershberger, Abbeville, SC

You are today where your thoughts have brought you;
You will be tomorrow where your thoughts take you.

*January 16*_____

Fountains or Cisterns

Out of his belly shall flow rivers of living water.
John 7:38

Water is important for our existence. How wonderful it is, when we are hot and thirsty, to come to the well for a refreshing drink! We can come to Jesus for a spiritually refreshing drink. He said, "The water that I shall give him shall be in him a well of water springing up into everlasting life."

Jeremiah 2:13 laments a people who forsake the fountain of living waters to build cisterns, broken cisterns that do not hold water.

Cisterns catch rainwater from roofs. They can give only what is put into them, and even then, a cistern usually needs to be pumped out. A cistern often gets stale and lukewarm. Do you drink from a spiritual cistern, or do you come daily to the fountain, God and His Word?

God wants us to become fountains of living water. Let us keep a fresh relationship with God, so we can refresh others. The world is longing for a good drink. Will you bless someone today by your refreshing walk with Jesus?

Bible Reading: John 4:1-15
One Year Bible Reading Plan:
Matthew 12:22-50
Genesis 38–40

Sam Nisly, Cullman, AL

_____

A fountain flows freely, but a cistern needs to be pumped.

The Living God

For therefore we both labour and suffer reproach,
because we trust in the living God.
1 Timothy 4:10

Life is a characteristic of God. No less than thirty times, the Bible describes God as *living*.

Jeremiah chapter 10 speaks of the cunning customs of heathen workmen. They were skilled craftsmen, able to make beautiful things. They cut trees from the forest and carried them to another place. There they nailed them in place with nails and decked them with silver and gold.

Our God is completely different. He is not a dead object; He is the living God. Jesus called God the living Father (John 6:57). Peter confessed later that Jesus is the Christ, the Son of the living God.

Paul was able to say wholeheartedly, "For this reason we labor and endure reproach, because we trust in the living God." Paul believed that godliness is profitable not only for the future, but also for the present, and his life showed that his trust was not in dead objects, but in the God who is alive.

It would be well for us to check our lives from time to time to see where our trust really is. Is it in dead objects or in the living God?

LaVerne Yoder, Woodburn, KY

Bible Reading: Jeremiah 10:1-16
One Year Bible Reading Plan:
Matthew 13:1-32
Genesis 41

If you want a secure present and future, trust in the living God.

Giving

Every man according as he purposeth in his heart, so let him give; not grudgingly, or of necessity: for God loveth a cheerful giver.
2 Corinthians 9:7

A man complained to his pastor, "It is getting to be just one continuous give, give, give." The pastor replied, "You have just given one of the best descriptions of Christianity that I've ever heard." So it is in the Christian's life. We give, and give, and give some more, till it hurts.

The Christian gives his money, his time, his self, his possessions, and what the world calls his *personal rights*. We give it all for the sake of Jesus, who said, "It is more blessed to give, than to receive."

How do we react when someone takes our good deeds for granted, and expects more from us? Do we keep giving? We should. Paul reminds us not to be "weary in well doing: for in due season we shall reap, if we faint not. As we have therefore opportunity, let us do good unto all men, especially unto them who are of the household of faith" (Galatians 6:9-10). Do not give in hope of receiving. As another has said, "If we bestow a gift or a favor and expect a return for it, it is then not a gift, but a trade."

Kevin Miller, Auburn, KY

Bible Reading: 2 Corinthians 9
One Year Bible Reading Plan:
Matthew 13:33-58
Genesis 42, 43

We make a living by what we get.
We make a life by what we give.

Ambassadors

Now then we are ambassadors for Christ.
2 Corinthians 5:20

Are you not amazed that the King of Kings has called you to be His ambassador? An ambassador is the nation's highest-ranking diplomat. Yes, we were born on this earth, and we still live here, but when Christ reconciled us to God, we were born citizens of a heavenly kingdom. Since Christ has come to earth to bring us to God, we are no longer part of this earthly kingdom.

The ambassador has no rights in the country where he serves. He may not vote, campaign, receive benefits, or march to get his way. As God's ambassadors, we have no rights in this earthly kingdom, either. We are here to tell the world the message of our King, Jesus. His will is that all be saved and become a part of His kingdom.

> **Bible Reading:** 2 Corinthians 5:14-21
> **One Year Bible Reading Plan:**
> Matthew 14:1-21
> Genesis 44, 45

Dear friends, can our King count on us to be faithful ambassadors for Him today?

Sam Nisly, Cullman, AL

If Jesus is not Lord of all, He is not Lord at all.

Lost—Do You Care?

And of some have compassion, making a difference.
Jude 22

Once I was attending a street meeting where a preacher was preaching a "hell-and-damnation-without-Christ" sermon. He stood facing the oncoming traffic. As the traffic drove around the square, each would hear a little preaching. I wondered how much good the brother was doing, until I heard a young man tell his friend, "I am hell-bound, and I love it. . . ." I could not believe my ears! Did he really mean it? Or was he trying to cover his guilt?

Maybe this man did not care that he was lost, but praise God, there was a man who did care. He was out there preaching, and although these men did not hear a long sermon, they heard enough to remind them that they were lost. That is where our part comes in. Maybe they do not care—but do we? You never know what may take place when you share a word for the Lord. The man who said he loves being hell-bound may never come to Christ, but his blood is no longer required of that preacher. So many of us say we care, and pretend we care, but do very little warning, pleading, or praying.

Let us lend a comforting or encouraging word to the struggling and help others find the Lord through kindness, showing them that we care.

> **Bible Reading:** Jude
> **One Year Bible Reading Plan:**
> Matthew 14:22-36
> Genesis 46–48

Kevin Miller, Auburn, KY

The world has more winnable people than ever before;
let us not come out of the ripe field empty-handed.

Time

But the end of all things is at hand; be ye therefore sober.
1 Peter 4:7

A year of 365 days holds 8,760 hours. Here is how we might have spent last year: 1,272 hours for worship, fellowship, and rest on Sundays; 2,184 hours of sleep, if we slept an average of seven hours per night; 468 hours eating, if we ate one and one-half hours per day; 3,120 hours working, if we worked ten hours per day; 156 hours for midweek services. We still have a balance of 1,560 hours.

We are accountable for the time that the Lord has allotted to us. Ephesians 5:16 tells us to redeem the time, to buy it back! It is not the number of years we live, but what we do while we are living, that determines the weight of our lives.

You cannot recall time. What is done, is done. Youth cannot be relived; it can only be remembered.

A limited time is allotted to each of us. "My days are swifter than a weaver's shuttle" (Job 7:6). "It is even a vapour, that appeareth for a little time, and then vanisheth away" (James 4:14). "So teach us to number our days, that we may apply our hearts unto wisdom" (Psalm 90:12).

Bible Reading: Romans 13
One Year Bible Reading Plan:
Matthew 15:1-20
Genesis 49, 50

What did you do with the last 1,560 hours?

Andy Miller, Malta, OH

You cannot kill time without injuring eternity.
—Henry David Thoreau

Kindness

And be ye kind one to another.
Ephesians 4:32

In my young years, Ephesians 4:32 became fixed in my mind. As I grew older, I saw kindness exemplified in the life of Joseph.

When Joseph was a teenager, his brothers sold him to some Ishmaelites for thirty pieces of silver. Their willingness to sell their brother to strangers came from hearts of jealousy and hatred. They could not even speak peaceably or politely to their brother.

Joseph was taken from his family and thrust into slavery. Then came an extreme test of his righteousness and moral purity. He did not succumb to sin. For that, he was rewarded with a prison sentence.

He was forgotten in prison. He had plenty of time to stew over his cruel mistreatment by his brothers. He had plenty of time to plan revenge once he got out of prison.

Joseph chose neither of these. He went another way. He moved from the pit where his brothers threw him, to the throne of Egypt next to the king.

Then his brothers came and bowed down before him. Joseph had the opportunity to take full revenge. Joseph's brothers worried that Joseph would now pay back revenge, since their father had died.

Joseph responded instead with kindness and forgiveness. Unlike his brothers, who twenty years earlier could not speak kindly to him, forgiveness empowered Joseph to treat them with supreme kindness.

I need to exercise this kind of kindness. It takes more than kind words. It takes the work of God's Spirit in my heart. When God is allowed to do a work of contrition in me, kindness and forgiveness can flow from my life.

Bible Reading: Genesis 50:15-26
One Year Bible Reading Plan:
Matthew 15:21-39
Exodus 1–3

Simon Schrock, Fairfax, VA

Happy will be your recollection of injuries forgiven, rather than revenged.

The Family of God

*But as many as received him, to them gave he power to become
the sons of God, even to them that believe on his name.*
John 1:12

Today many children will be born into the world. Sadly, many will not have Christian fathers. They will never know what it is like to be a son or daughter in a Christian home. They will never realize the blessings of love, joy, and happiness that a home is meant to have. They probably will not even know that anything like that exists.

However, anyone may choose to become a child of God. God desires that all men would be His children. John 1:12 says, "But as many as received him, to them gave he power to become the sons of God." God is no respecter of persons, and He will receive anyone who receives Him, if we allow Him to be the Lord and Savior of our lives.

I thank God that I can be His child and that I can belong to the richest and most loving Father in the world. Our Father has the power to see us through each situation, no matter what difficulty, struggle, or temptation we may face. There are many times that I go about my daily work without really thinking that I am a child of God. We need to thank God daily for allowing us the privilege of being His children. Even throughout the day, we ought simply to thank God that we can be a part of His family.

It cost Christ a great price to make it possible for us to be a part of His family. It cost Him more than we can ever comprehend. Yet sometimes we live as if it were not that great a price. Take time today to thank the Lord that you can be a part of His family.

Bible Reading: Romans 8:12-28
One Year Bible Reading Plan:
Matthew 16
Exodus 4–6

Stephen Mast, Caneyville, KY

---

*Being born makes you physically alive and places you
in your parent's family. Being reborn makes you
spiritually alive and puts you in God's family.*

Only a Little Step

Take us the foxes, the little foxes, that spoil the vines:
for our vines have tender grapes.
Song of Solomon 2:15

Because of all the added activity, I knew that the bluebirds had hatched. After a week, I decided to check the box. Opening the front, I observed the healthy little bluebirds, then delicately lifted the nest and peered underneath. Sure enough, under the nest were quite a few worms. Knowing that the worms could kill the little birds, I removed the nest and meticulously cleaned out the worms. I then fashioned a new nest of soft grass and put the babies back again.

On the surface all might appear to be well, but we must continually be on guard for the worms. Tigers we can handle because we can see them, but worms? They are so small, and it seems they are incapable of doing much harm. They seem so insignificant. They just take a little nibble here and a little nibble there.

Little attitudes, a little playing around, a little carelessness, a little looseness of the tongue, a little loving of the world, all seem so trivial. "Evil and sin abound," we rationalize. "A little evil is so much better than a lot," we reason, "so a little sin is so much better than a big one." Why not sin a little? It is such a little step.

Be aware that the first little step to sin is the biggest step towards hell that you can take. There is only one step that separates us from God. That is the "little" step of sin. We call it a step; God calls it a stairway. We call it a small second step; God calls it a landing. We call it little; God calls it a decision.

Bible Reading: Psalm 1
One Year Bible Reading Plan:
  Matthew 17
  Exodus 7, 8

Alvin Mast, Millersburg, OH

Sin causes the cup of joy to spring a leak.

The Witness of the Conscience

*Their conscience also bearing witness, and their thoughts
the meanwhile accusing or else excusing one another.*
Romans 2:15

I build pallets, and because of the difference in size, I sometimes have extra to send on a given load. Nearly two years ago we
had one of those "high count" loads, and the driver needed two
extra straps. We lent them to him, and he promised to return them.
We had nearly forgotten the incident until one day he came by. His
first comment was, "I have two straps that belong to you." Though
the straps had faded from my mind, his conscience had kept them
in the forefront of this driver's mind.

Another incident illustrates the burden of a guilty conscience.
Several Amish boys decided to have some fun with an old man's
buggy. One evening, they filled Old John's buggy with rocks. Hiding around a corner of the barn, they waited to see what the old
man would do. Their gleeful anticipation was short lived. Old John
quietly unloaded the buggy of its heavy burden, hitched up his
horse, and left for home.

Not a word of the incident was ever heard in the community,
and many years passed, perhaps twenty-five. Then, one day a young
father came to Old John and asked, "Do you remember that night
when you came out to your buggy, and it was full of rocks?" Without waiting for an answer he rushed on, "I was one of those that
did it, and I'm very sorry."

The old man, with eyes full
of compassion said, "I gladly forgive you," and then softly added,
"I had those rocks for one night,
but you have carried them for
twenty-five years."

Jerry Yoder, Auburn, KY

Bible Reading: Romans 2:1-15
One Year Bible Reading Plan:
Matthew 18:1-20
Exodus 9, 10

*Conscience warns us as a friend
before it punishes us as a judge.*
—Stanislas

January 26_____

More Than Conquerors

Be not overcome of evil, but overcome evil with good.
Romans 12:21

Usually in a conflict or a contest, the defeated party does not celebrate their defeat. They've been conquered. They've lost, and with the loss, come bitterness and jealousy.

Paul tells us in Romans that we can be more than conquerors.

A sheep farmer in Indiana was troubled by his neighbors' dogs, who were killing his sheep. Sheepmen usually counter that problem with lawsuits, or barbed wire fences, or even shotguns; but this man had a better idea. To every neighbor child he gave a lamb or two as pets. In due time, all his neighbors had their own small flocks, and began to tie up their dogs. That put an end to neighborhood dogs killing his sheep.

This man was more than a conqueror. There were no feelings of defeat, bitterness, or anger.

We need the wisdom of God to know how to respond to confrontations that come our way because of people's thoughtlessness or simply because they don't care about the unpleasantness they may cause another person. We have the weapons we need to be more than conquerors. Let's use them, and make the other party feel good about it too.

Ivan Hershberger, Due West, SC

> **Bible Reading:** Romans 12:1-21
> **One Year Bible Reading Plan:**
>   Matthew 18:21-35
>   Exodus 11, 12

------

*The most glorious victory over an enemy
is to turn him into a friend.*

Is There Anyone I Cannot Forgive?

But I say unto you, Love your enemies, bless them that curse you,
do good to them that hate you, and pray for them
which despitefully use you, and persecute you.
Matthew 5:44

A Turkish soldier had beaten a Christian prisoner until he was only half conscious. While he kicked him, the soldier demanded, "What can your Jesus do for you now?" The Christian quietly replied, "He can give me strength to forgive you."

When Christ was on the cross, He responded to the spitting, bloodthirsty scoffers' jeers and mocking, by crying, "Father, forgive them, for they know not what they do."

What is our response when someone mistreats us? Do we love to the point that Christ commands in John 15:12-13, as He has loved us? Do we pray for those who despitefully use us? Jesus prayed for His accusers, and He loved and forgave them.

We must forgive others, if we would be forgiven ourselves. As Jesus says in Matthew 6:15, "But if ye forgive not men their trespasses, neither will your Father forgive your trespasses." "And this commandment have we from him, That he who loveth God love his brother also" (1 John 4:21).

Kevin Miller, Auburn, KY

Bible Reading: Matthew 5:38–6:15
One Year Bible Reading Plan:
Matthew 19:1-15
Exodus 13–15

If you are suffering from a bad man's injustice,
forgive him; lest there be two bad men.

"Would Be" Disciples

And why call ye me, Lord, Lord, and do not the things which I say?
Luke 6:46

The Gospel, as presented in much of Christendom today, is an easy Gospel. Books are written insisting that if Jesus is Savior, He must be Lord. Others are written to refute such a severe position, teaching that since salvation is free, no strings are attached. We do well to ask: "What saith the Scriptures?"

For reasons not given, the "certain man" in our Bible reading wanted to follow Jesus. Perhaps he had heard of the free bread distributed to the five thousand earlier in the chapter. Jesus reminded him that true followers must be willing to endure the hardship of poverty. Many Christians endure poverty because of persecution and exile.

Another, whom Jesus called to preach the kingdom of God, revealed his reluctance with his "after-my-father-dies-I-will," attitude. Perhaps his father was not favorably inclined to his son being a disciple, and especially not a preacher.

The third "would be" follower had nice things to say about following Jesus, but revealed where his heart was with his "let-me-first" request.

Jesus' reply to these three is still valid. The Gospel plow will not plow properly if the one who is plowing is hoping for something easy, or is fearful of what others might think, or is allowing something to take precedence over following Christ.

Bible Reading: Luke 9:57-62
One Year Bible Reading Plan:
Matthew 19:16-30
Exodus 16–18

Eli Kauffman, Montezuma, GA

For my yoke is easy, and my burden is light.
—Matthew 11:30

Grace in the Wilderness

*Thus saith the LORD, The people which were left of the
sword found grace in the wilderness; even Israel,
when I went to cause him to rest.*
Jeremiah 31:2

We are on a journey through life. We cherish the times that our
trek takes us through lush fertile valleys where life is pleasant and
rewarding. However, every Christian will at times travel through a
"wilderness"—a barren time of soul-testing affliction and trial. Feelings of loneliness, discouragement, doubt, sorrow, or confusion may
accompany these wilderness experiences.

Usually we enter a wilderness not knowing its confines. We
may never fully know God's purposes in taking us through the wilderness. The wilderness may even be nameless—a trek that seemingly no one has traveled before.

O wilderness-sick soul, take heart! There is grace in the wilderness! You need not succumb to the pressure and become one of the
skeletal statistics that litter the way through the wilderness. Your
Savior is at this moment with you, though He may—for reasons
known only to Him—seem removed from your view. He has traveled this road before you, and His grace is sufficient for the
moment—He promised it! Boldly depend on it! His grace will bring
you through this wilderness vic-
toriously!

"Let us therefore come
boldly unto the throne of grace,
that we may obtain mercy, and
find grace to help in time of
need" (Hebrews 4:16).

Bible Reading: Psalm 107:1-21
One Year Bible Reading Plan:
  Matthew 20:1-16
  Exodus 19–21

Ken Kauffman, Falkville, AL

He has grace for my need; I have need of His grace.

What Are You Drinking?

And whosoever will, let him take the water of life freely.
Revelation 22:17

How long will they hold out? This question was on the minds of many Babylonian soldiers in 588 B.C., as they stood in their positions surrounding Jerusalem. Nebuchadnezzar's army had surrounded Jerusalem, cutting off all the inhabitants' food and supplies. How long could this small city survive? One month went by; then two. A whole year passed, and the people of Jerusalem still held their own! How could they?

Their main secret was their abundant water supply. Outside the city walls was an excellent spring. Previously, it had been very vulnerable to invading armies, but King Hezekiah solved this problem by having a 1,777 foot tunnel cut through solid rock. This amazing tunnel passed beneath the city walls into a reservoir inside Jerusalem called the Pool of Siloam. Without this life source, Jerusalem would have succumbed very soon to the enemy.

Over 2,500 years have passed. Again, the enemy is surrounding Jerusalem. This Jerusalem is the church of Jesus Christ. Again, the question in the enemies' minds is, "How long will they hold out?" Once again, the deciding factor is the water supply!

Where are Jerusalem's occupants drinking to satisfy their thirst? There is an abundant supply of the pure water of life available through Jesus Christ. (Read John 4:13-14.)

Some are actually venturing outside the city walls and sipping from the reservoirs of the enemy! At an extreme danger to their spiritual health, they are forfeiting the pure water of life for the disease-laden puddles of Satan.

Oh, let us remain within Jerusalem's secure walls with its watchful, caring leaders and its protecting standards! Yes, and let us drink often from the pure, untainted Fountain of Living Water.

Bible Reading: Isaiah 55
One Year Bible Reading Plan:
Matthew 20:17-34
Exodus 22–24

Joshua Yoder, Clarkson, KY

How long will you survive?
It depends on what you are drinking.

The Unity of the Spirit

By this shall all men know that ye are my disciples,
if ye have love one to another.
John 13:35

In Ephesians 4, the apostle Paul beseeches us to a worthy walk and to maintain the unity of the Spirit. I fear there are still too many Diotrephes (3 John 9) who will go down in infamy for their hard speeches and love of preeminence. How much better when members of Christ's body, with all lowliness and meekness, "esteem others better than themselves" (Philippians 2:3). Those who tarry for the Spirit and depend on His leading will be directed to the meek and lowly ways of the Lord Jesus. Oh, that the world, as it looks into the church, would only be able to see men and women, young and old, whose hearts are filled with love for God and for one another.

The unity that the Holy Spirit brings into a congregation does not necessarily assure that everyone will be exactly alike. However, it will grace the members of that congregation with hearts that forbear one another in love (Ephesians 4:2). The Spirit of Christ enables those in whom He dwells to live in peace (2 Corinthians 13:11), and to strive together for the faith of the gospel (Philippians 1:27).

Disunity grieves the Spirit of God (Ephesians 4:30); therefore, it behooves the members of the body of Christ to "be . . . kind one to another, tenderhearted, forgiving one another, even as God for Christ's sake hath forgiven you" (4:32).

Bible Reading: Ephesians 4
One Year Bible Reading Plan:
Matthew 21:1-22
Exodus 25, 26

Eli Kauffman, Montezuma, GA

Great peace have they which love thy law:
and nothing shall offend them.
—Psalm 119:165

_____

Grace That Works

For by grace are ye saved through faith;
and that not of yourselves: it is the gift of God.
Ephesians 2:8

The great heart of God, moved with compassion for sinning humanity, devised an effective plan under which men could both be saved from condemnation, and live out the rest of their lives for His good pleasure.

The grace of God is offered to all men. As far as the effects of sin reach, so far does God's offer of grace and forgiveness reach. Oh, that all men would reach out in faith and receive this grace, which effectively changes the hearts and lives of its grateful recipients. Grace teaches us to do God's will. Grace guides our feet heavenward and away from the paths of worldliness. Divine grace makes saints of sinners and gives them purpose for living in this present world.

The goodness of God leads us to repentance (Romans 2:4). Grace, the unmerited favor of God, is freely given to those who are poor in spirit (Matthew 5:3). Grace is given through our Savior Jesus Christ. Those who truly receive Him are redeemed and purified. Grace lays claim to a peculiar people, set apart to be light and salt in a dark and perishing world (Matthew 5:13–16). Those who have tasted the marvel of divine grace look forward with glad anticipation for that blessed hope, the glorious appearing of our great God and Savior, Jesus Christ, when He will come to be glorified in His saints, and to be admired by all them that believe.

Eli Kauffman, Montezuma, GA

Bible Reading: Titus 2
One Year Bible Reading Plan:
Matthew 21:23-46
Exodus 27, 28

_____

When he giveth quietness, who then can make trouble?
—Job 34:29

Strive for Excellence

That ye may approve things that are excellent; that ye may
be sincere and without offence till the day of Christ.
Philippians 1:10

Christians too often are satisfied with the meager offerings of average Christianity, rather than striving for and achieving the "excellency of the knowledge of Christ" (Philippians 3:8).

God is an excellent God. "He is excellent in power" (Job 37:23), and greatness (Psalm 150:2). He "hath done excellent things: this is known in all the earth" (Isaiah 12:5). His dealings with men are characterized by His excellent lovingkindness, and the recipients of it pray that it may continue (Psalm 36:7, 10). Those who have experienced these aspects of God's excellency declare with the Psalmist, "O Lord our Lord, how excellent is thy name in all the earth" (Psalm 8:1)!

Our Lord Jesus, having completed His "more excellent ministry" (Hebrews 8:6) of procuring our complete salvation, "obtained a more excellent name than they" (Hebrews 1:4).

The supreme excellency of the Godhead motivates us to speak of excellent things (Proverbs 8:6) and, as Daniel, to be of an excellent spirit (Daniel 6:3; Proverbs 17:27). We will also live in the "more excellent way"—the way of self-sacrificing love (1 Corinthians 12:31).

Finally, if we are faithful to "approve [discern, test, and demonstrate] things that are excellent" (Philippians 1:10), it will be our privilege to hear Jesus' voice from "the excellent glory" (2 Peter 1:17), "Come, ye blessed of my Father . . ." (Matthew 25:34).

Bible Reading: Job 37
One Year Bible Reading Plan:
Matthew 22:1-22
Exodus 29, 30

Ken Kauffman, Falkville, AL

Good, better, best—never let it rest
till the good is better, and the better, best.

The Man of the New Covenant

*This is the covenant that I will make with them after
those days, saith the Lord, I will put my laws into
their hearts, and in their minds will I write them.*
Hebrews 10:16

The man of the new covenant is saved by grace and has the indwelling Spirit of God to direct his steps, enabling him to keep the moral law. In Christ he is a new creature; old things are passed away, and all things are become new. He walks in newness of life. He is dead unto sin and alive unto God. He is a servant unto righteousness, obedient from the heart. He is risen with Christ and seeks those things above. He has a heart of compassion, meekness, longsuffering, forgiveness; and the peace of God rules in his heart. He walks in the light and has fellowship with God and his fellow Christians. The power of God has transformed his life, and he lives as peaceably as possible with all men. He does not avenge himself. He renders to no man evil for evil. If his enemy hungers, he feeds him. He overcomes evil with good. His life bears the fruit of the Spirit: love, joy, peace, longsuffering, kindness, goodness, faithfulness, meekness, and self-control. He knows that the salvation that the prophets sought after and searched for diligently is now here. He girds up the loins of his mind to live a life separated unto God.

Bible Reading: Hebrews 8:1-13
One Year Bible Reading Plan:
Matthew 22:23-46
Exodus 31–33

Andy Miller, Malta, OH

---

*The Christian finds victory only as
he starves the old nature and feeds the new.*

Beauty Or Danger?

Lest Satan should get an advantage of us:
for we are not ignorant of his devices.
2 Corinthians 2:11

It was all in a normal day's work—cutting beautiful orchids and selling them. Seeing a beautiful orchid out on a tree limb, Horace decided to climb the tree and take the flower down. With a knife in his hand, he reached for the orchid.

As his hand closed around it, he felt a terrible sting in his arm: the orchid was not only an object of physical beauty, it was also the home of a poisonous snake! What had looked so pretty, also contained enough poison to send him to an early grave. Only by being rushed to the hospital was Horace's life spared.

Satan offers many beautiful "orchids." Sometimes the danger is obvious, but more often, the danger is well concealed. Who would hold a colorful coral snake, even though it is beautiful?

Satan, the master deceiver, carefully conceals his traps behind a shield of temporary pleasure. Who, by looking at the advertisements, could imagine that cigarettes would reduce a healthy man to a near invalid, surviving with only forty percent of his lung capacity? Who would think that the car for which you are longing would bring with it a sting of pride? The sensual magazine will surely inject its venom, but how about the sports section in other magazines? You cannot place those sports figures on a pedestal, without your devotion to Christ being affected.

The orchids are many and diverse. Name the ones in your life, and determine never to touch them.

Michael Overholt, Isabella Bank, Belize

Bible Reading: Genesis 3
One Year Bible Reading Plan:
Matthew 23:1-22
Exodus 34–36

Beware of the poisoned meat in the choice china.

Trust Me

*Naked came I out of my mother's womb, and naked shall I
return thither: the LORD gave, and the LORD hath taken away;
blessed be the name of the LORD.*
Job 1:21

Most of us have experienced some of the same things Job suffered, but not as many serious attacks as he received, one right after the other. We have been jolted by financial setbacks, sent reeling after hearing the news from the doctor that we have a serious health problem, or felt crushed when we lost a loved one.

What keeps us from giving up? What sustained Job in his dark hours?

The answer is found in our key verse, Job 1:21. The word *naked* not only implies zero possessions, but also means utter helplessness.

When we came into this world, we had absolutely no choice when or where we were to be born, and we were totally dependent on forces greater than ourselves to provide for us. When we leave this world, we will have no say in the matter, either. We will stand utterly helpless before Almighty God, who will usher us into eternity.

So why not trust Him in this short life? We have no control over the things that life throws at us. The only thing we can control is our response. We can choose to curse God and wish we were dead, like Job's wife; find someone else to blame, like Job's friends; or trust God to see us through our problems, as Job did.

It is far, far better to let Him choose the way that we should take. If only we will leave our lives to Him, He will guide without mistake.

Bible Reading: Job 1
One Year Bible Reading Plan:
Matthew 23:23-39
Exodus 37, 38

Melvin Troyer, Leitchfield, KY

---

*The suffering man may curse and blame—
or child-like, call on the Father's name.*

The Necessity of Love

He that loveth not knoweth not God; for God is love.
1 John 4:8

One of England's monarchs tried an experiment. At his command, a number of orphaned children, the great majority of them infants, were picked off the streets and placed in a special orphanage. The nurses in charge of the orphanage were given detailed instructions as to how they were to treat the children. They were told to clothe and feed their charges, and to take care of all their physical needs, but never in any way to show them any love. They were never to hold, cuddle, smile, or speak a kind word. Over half of the children in the experiment died, not because they were denied the physical necessities of life, but because they were denied one of humanity's basic needs—to love and be loved in return. Thus they lost the will and desire to live.

Imagine a world without love. A world where no kind words are ever spoken. A world devoid of caring, encouragement, forgiveness, and pity. A world where every man thinks only of himself and cares nothing for the misfortunes of others. A world without God, for God is the very essence of love. Oh, perish the thought of such a black, miserable existence!

The Bible has much to say about love. John 3:16 pictures God's marvelous demonstration of love, the gift of His only begotten Son. His Son, in turn, has given us a new commandment in John 13:34, "A new commandment I give unto you, That ye love one another; as I have loved you, that ye also love one another."

Craig Eicher, Grabill, IN

> **Bible Reading:** 1 Corinthians 13
> **One Year Bible Reading Plan:**
> Matthew 24:1-22
> Exodus 39, 40

God is Love, and He wants us to love.

What Is That in Thine Hand?

Whatsoever thy hand findeth to do, do it with thy might.
Ecclesiastes 9:10a

God asked this question of Moses in order that he might gain a new perspective of something completely common to him. The rod was as common to Moses as a hammer is to a carpenter, or a trowel to a mason. However, God took this common thing and used it for an uncommon purpose.

In verse 17, God told Moses to take the rod with him when he led the people out. By verse 20, it had become the "Rod of God." What an evolution! From a simple shepherd's rod to the "Rod of God."

God longs to use common everyday experiences and talents to do something special in His kingdom. Imagine what would have happened if Moses' reply to God would have been something like this: "A rod, Lord, . . . but it's really nothing fantastic. Wait, I'll fetch a sword. It's a lot more useful." What a blessing he would have missed; and yet, that is often the way we respond to the talents God has given us! Many times we compare ourselves with those around us and become covetous of what God has given to them, instead of being content with the gifts God has given to us.

Accept the calling with which God has called you. He has a special purpose for each of us, and has given us everything we need to fulfill this purpose and calling. Let us be faithful in thanking Him for the talents He has given us, and let us exercise them for His glory. It may be that He will grant further talents and callings as we are faithful in each step of the way. Remember, it is not necessarily the most talented people who best serve God, but the dedicated ones. May our prayer be that every talent in our life becomes the "Talent of God" for the work of God.

Bible Reading: Exodus 4:1-23
One Year Bible Reading Plan:
   Matthew 24:23-51
   Leviticus 1–3

Jay Mast, Belgium

Burying one's talent is a grave mistake.

No Tracts, Thank You

. . . and the prisoners heard them.
Acts 16:25

Paul and Silas had been cast into prison for doing the Lord's work, but the grace of God allowed them to escape from prison. While in prison, they did not complain or threaten retaliation. They only praised God. The other prisoners heard them. Another rendering of Scripture says, "The prisoners _listened._" They listened because they heard something contrary to human nature coming from the apostles' cell.

The other prisoners were choked with hatred and inner misery. The sounds of singing stirred their curiosity. What made these two men sing? What was in their hearts that bubbled out even in adversity?

We, too, have an unseen audience listening. Most of the people we meet are prisoners of sinful desires. Sinful habits fetter them. The shackles of their carnality bind them in their misery.

What do they hear from us? Do the songs that come from our lives stir a curiosity to know the secret of our joy?

A church was being established in a new neighborhood. The congregation decided to distribute gospel tracts one afternoon. The first man they spoke to refused the literature with this comment, "No tracts for me, thank you, until I observe your tracks for a while."

Bible Reading: Acts 16:22-34
One Year Bible Reading Plan:
Matthew 25:1-30
Leviticus 4–6

Jim Yoder, Leitchfield, KY

God, may my walk of life create a curiosity to know you.

God's Exalting Program

Humble yourselves in the sight of the Lord, and he shall lift you up.
James 4:10

"Yes, Lord, I'll be humble if you exalt me." Have you ever told God that? Maybe not, but far too often our reason for wanting to be humble is so that others will look up to us as a strong spiritual person.

Far too often I want humility on my own conditions. God says, "Humble yourself," "commit thy way unto the Lord," and "make yourself of no reputation." Often, I am willing to be humble only as long as it doesn't hurt my reputation, and others still think highly of me.

The Bible says, "Draw nigh to God, and he will draw nigh to you." Our focus must be on God. When we have a proper focus, we can lay our reputation at the feet of Jesus. We no longer will be so worried about what others think. We will strive to please God alone.

True humility makes us esteem others better than ourselves, and look out for their good. When someone does a job well, we want to compliment them. Humility loves to see others exalted and do well.

In order to have this victory, we must submit everything to God. We must give Him every part of our life. When God calls you to do something, even though it may seem insignificant, do it to the honor and glory of God. As we prove ourselves faithful, God will call us to greater things.

"Humble yourselves therefore under the mighty hand of God, that he may exalt you in due time" (1 Peter 5:6).

Bible Reading: James 4:5-10; Philippians 2:1-11
One Year Bible Reading Plan: Matthew 25:31-46 Leviticus 7–9

Titus Miller, East Rochester, OH

A great man is measured by his love of serving others.

Let Your Light Shine

Let your light so shine before men, that they may see your good works, and glorify your Father which is in heaven.
Matthew 5:16

Looking out over the fields as twilight is falling over the land, I notice a security light shining in the distance. As I look again and observe the light some more, I see that there are branches of a bush obscuring some of the light from my view.

When we accept Christ as our Savior, we become a shining light for Jesus. God loved us so much that He sent His Son to die on the cross for our sins. We in turn are to reflect His love to those around us who are lost in sin.

Are you shining for Jesus? Is your light so clear and bright that those who observe your life know that you are a Christian? Or are there "branches" in your life that are making your light dim? Sin in your life can make your light go out. Even "small" sins that you think are hidden, or that no one knows about, will extinguish your light. Keep your life free of "branches," and your light will shine.

If you have been washed in the blood of Jesus and have God's love abiding in you, your light should be shining clear and bright. Do not be ashamed of your light; let it shine for Jesus!

Marlin Stoll, Leitchfield, KY

Bible Reading: Philippians 2:1-18
One Year Bible Reading Plan:
Matthew 26:1-19
Leviticus 10–12

The light that shines farthest shines brightest at home.

God's Way

Commit thy way unto the LORD; trust also in him;
and he shall bring it to pass.
Psalm 37:5

A couple of boys were driving a tractor to a friend's house to help with some work. On the way over, the tractor got off the road, overturned, and the driver was killed.

My niece was a normal, healthy girl, till one day it was discovered that she had cancer. The next two years of her life were filled with pain and hospitalizations.

We look ahead and plan our lives. But things come up. Calamities, sickness, failures, and disappointments arise, shattering our hopes and dreams!

We wonder why these things happen. At times, we may even be tempted to wonder if God is being fair.

God is the Master Designer. He sees the future, while we see only the present. Only as we submit to the Lord's plan, will our lives be useful. Even though we do not understand the reasons for all that God allows, they will be clear someday.

Luke Schwartz, Sparta, TN

Bible Reading: Isaiah 43:1-21
One Year Bible Reading Plan:
Matthew 26:20-54
Leviticus 13

Man sees the present. God sees the future.

A Little Push

A word fitly spoken is like apples of gold in pictures of silver.
Proverbs 25:11

I was stuck. Solid, rock hard, stuck. My son-in-law came to my rescue with a green, no-nonsense John Deere tractor. He eased up to the trailer, and with only a low sigh of the engine, pushed me forward and out of the sticky mud. It was just a little push, but it was all I needed.

My son was in tears, for the task before him seemed monumental. The buckets of milk were so cumbersome, and it was going to take so long. I picked up two buckets and carried them with ease. When I carried those buckets for him, his whole countenance changed. It was an easy task for me, but it was an awesome job for a little boy.

I was overwhelmed with weariness, for the assignment before me was enormous. I shared my concern with a brother, and he gave me a spiritual push. To him it was only a small push, but to me, it was sufficient. That push was all it took to give me confidence to carry out the task before me.

Paul was not superhuman; he also needed a little push at times. One day some brethren came, and Paul acknowledged that the encouragement they gave him was exactly what he needed (1 Corinthians 16:17, 18).

God uses brethren in the church to provide pushes. Wouldn't you like to be one whom God uses to encourage others? Look for an opportunity to encourage someone today. Be sensitive to the Spirit of God, and He will put you in the right place at the right time.

Bible Reading: Hebrews 10:19-25
One Year Bible Reading Plan: Matthew 26:55-75
Leviticus 14

Alvin Mast, Millersburg, OH

The best cure for depression is to encourage someone else.

The Seven Pillars of Wisdom

Wisdom hath builded her house,
she hath hewn out her seven pillars. .
Proverbs 9:1

The book of Proverbs personifies Wisdom as a mother who builds her house with seven supporting pillars. After the construction is complete, she prepares a feast and sets the table with fine dishes (verse 2). She then sends her maidens out with invitations, while she herself goes to the high point of the city to call out her invitation (verse 3). Who does she invite? The simple ones and those who lack understanding (verse 4)! A number of folk come to her house to dine on her bread and wine (verse 5). As they file into the house, each person walks among the seven large, hand-hewn pillars at her entrance.

James 3:17 lists the seven attributes of divine wisdom, which are the pillars of Proverbs 9. Wisdom, James says, is: pure, peace-loving, gentle, easily-entreated (approachable and open), full of mercy and good fruits, impartial, and sincere. These seven pillars of divine wisdom stand in stark contrast to the seven pillars of worldly wisdom: earthly, sensual, devilish, envying, strife, confusion, and evil works (verses 14-16).

As you hear Wisdom's invitation to her house, stop and study her seven pillars. Are these attributes characteristic of your life? Is Wisdom building her house in your life?

Bible Reading: Proverbs 3:13-20; 9:1-12
One Year Bible Reading Plan:
Matthew 27:1-31
Leviticus 15–17

Ken Kauffman, Falkville, AL

Knowledge is awareness of facts;
wisdom is knowing how to use knowledge for its most noble purpose.

Serve the Lord in Sincerity

Now therefore fear the LORD, and serve him in sincerity and in truth.
Joshua 24:14a

In today's Bible reading, Joshua exhorts the children of Israel to serve the Lord in sincerity and truth, and to put away the gods that their fathers served (verse 14).

In verse 15, Joshua asks the Israelites to make a choice. "Choose you this day whom ye will serve." He then speaks for himself, saying, "but as for me and my house, we will serve the LORD."

The people responded to Joshua in verse 18: "Therefore will we also serve the LORD."

But Joshua told them, in verse 19, "Ye cannot serve the LORD: for he is an holy God; he is a jealous God." In verses 23-24, he explained to them that they could not come to God until they put away their strange gods and were totally willing to obey Him.

We cannot serve God in sincerity and truth unless we totally yield our lives to Him. God is a holy and jealous God. If we want His blessings, we must live holy lives in total commitment to Him alone.

As you go about today's duties, whatever they may be, lay aside anything that is hindering you from serving God in true sincerity.

Raymond Yoder, Vinemont, AL

Bible Reading: Joshua 24:14-28
One Year Bible Reading Plan:
Matthew 27:32-66
Leviticus 18, 19

---

*If we want to spend eternity with a
holy God, we must live holy lives.*

The Love of God

A new commandment I give unto you, that ye love one another;
as I have loved you, that ye also love one another.
John 13:34

Years ago, sickness entered the home of Princess Alice, daughter of Queen Victoria. Her little boy, the prince, was very ill with diphtheria. The doctor warned the mother of the danger of inhaling the breath of her child. As she stood by the bedside, watching him, she laid her cool hand upon his feverish brow. The touch seemed to revive him for a few moments, and he whispered, "Kiss me, Mother." The mother's love yielded, and she kissed the child, but it was death for her. Oh, what great love is a mother's love! Love stops at no peril or sacrifice.

Christ loved us even to the death on the cross. "Greater love hath no man than this, that a man lay down his life for his friends" (John 15:13). "But God commendeth his love toward us, in that, while we were yet sinners, Christ died for us" (Romans 5:8).

What is your response to such wonderful love? Should it not constrain us to surrender our lives to the blessed Master?

Christ's command to us is that we should love one another. How is our love one to another? Do we love only in word or in prayer, or do we also love in deed? 1 John 3:18 says, "My little children, let us not love in word, neither in tongue, but in deed and in truth."

Bible Reading: 1 John 4
One Year Bible Reading Plan:
Matthew 28
Leviticus 20, 21

Sylvan Yoder, Windy, KY

By this shall all men know that ye are my disciples,
if ye have love one to another.
—John 13:35

A Childlike Faith

Abraham believed God, and it was
counted unto him for righteousness.
Romans 4:3

As I look back over my life, I recall times when the mountains seemed so high that I could not possibly get over them. So I turned them over to God, and in a matter of time, He removed them for me. Jesus said in Matthew that if we have even the smallest amount of faith, we would be able to remove mountains.

God told Abraham that he must take his son, his only son Isaac, and go to a place that He would show him, and offer him as a sacrifice. Abraham might have thought to himself, How can this be, and how can God ever fulfill His promise that my seed would be like the sands of the sea?

Abraham did not question God. He simply trusted Him. He had faith that even if he offered up Isaac, God would raise him up again. This was a real test for Abraham—and surely he was tempted all the way to just give up the whole thing. But he remained faithful and was obedient to the end. Then God said, "Now I know that thou fearest God, seeing thou hast not withheld thy son, thine only son from me" (Genesis 22:12).

Jesus took a little child and said, "Except ye be converted, and become as little children, ye shall not enter into the kingdom of heaven" (Matthew 18:3). We must have a childlike faith in a great God.

Abner Overholt, Auburn, KY

Bible Reading: Romans 4:1-12
One Year Bible Reading Plan:
Mark 1:1-22
Leviticus 22, 23

When you say a situation is hopeless,
you slam the door in the face of God.

A Sorghum Mill Lesson

For our light affliction, which is but for a moment,
worketh for us a far more exceeding and eternal weight of glory.
2 Corinthians 4:18

Standing at the sorghum press, pushing cane stalks through the press rollers, I noticed something interesting. Sorghum stalks and human beings share a common tendency. They moan when you "put the squeeze" on them.

Psalm 23 begins with a comfortable setting: green pastures, plenteous water, and security. But it isn't until verse 4 introduces the valley of the shadow of death that the relationship becomes deeply intimate: "Though I walk through the valley of the shadow of death, . . . thou art with me; thy rod and thy staff they comfort me. Thou preparest a table." It was the "valley experience" that caused the Psalmist to sense his great need of drawing closer to God. As unpleasant as it seemed, it was for his good!

There is good even in seemingly unpleasant circumstances! God uses the valleys to draw us closer to Jesus, to conform us more to His image, to enable us to comfort others (2 Corinthians 1:4), and to be a glowing witness of the grace of God while under pressure.

A school principal informed four naughty boys that they were to be soundly spanked at the end of the day. The most experienced of the young lads shared a nugget of wisdom with his terrified friends: "When he paddles, don't pull away—he'll wear you out. When he swings, move in as close to him as you can. He can't get much leverage when you are close, and it won't hurt so bad."

When in the valley, we are tempted to fret, to grow bitter, and even to draw away from God. But that only intensifies the pain. Move closer and receive comfort from intimacy with the good Shepherd.

Bible Reading: Psalm 23;
2 Corinthians 4:16-18
One Year Bible Reading Plan:
Mark 1:23-45
Leviticus 24, 25

Jim Yoder, Leitchfield, KY

God has one Son without sin, but He never had a son without trials.
—Spurgeon

No More Strangers

_Now therefore ye are no more strangers and foreigners, but fellow
citizens with the saints, and of the household of God._
Ephesians 2:19

The Gentile believers addressed in our text verse no doubt rejoiced in this authoritative assurance from the apostle Paul. We likewise rejoice in this promise because it is, by extension, given to us.

Having been estranged from God, "[we] who sometimes were far off are made nigh by the blood of Christ" (Ephesians 2:13). By this same act of grace, we also are made strangers and pilgrims to the world and its value system. We are always strangers—either to the household of God by being a friend of the world (James 4:4), or to the world, by being a friend of God (2 Corinthians 6:14–18).

Being no more a stranger to God means that I no longer feel condemned in His holy presence. Rather, I feel a kinship and bond with Him, whereby I cry "Abba, Father" (Galatians 4:6). By the same token, this "no-more-a-stranger" relationship with God makes me keenly aware of the sharp enmity between God and the world. A "strangers and pilgrims" perspective toward the world and its citizens makes me feel comfortable being uncomfortable when associating with a worldly person, because I know to Whom I belong.

Let us rejoice in our "no-more-a-stranger" relationship with God and practice a faithful "stranger" relationship with the world. May God help us to this end.

Bible Reading: Ephesians 2:8-22
One Year Bible Reading Plan:
Mark 2
Leviticus 26, 27

Ken Kauffman, Falkville, AL

_With You, Lord, a stranger no longer;
but with the world a stranger yet stronger._

*February 19*_____

What Is the Reason for
Our Gathering Together?

*And upon the first day of the week,
when the disciples came together . . .*
Acts 20:7

A certain governor once asked his slaves why they always wanted to go to church in order to sing and pray together, when they could do so privately at home.

They were standing by a fire, and one woman answered, "Dear Master, separate these coals of fire, and they will soon die out, but see what a nice fire they give when they all burn together!"

Christians gather together for many reasons, but the reason that I would like to mention is that when we gather, we receive warmth and fellowship one from another.

The brotherhood is like a wagon wheel, with Christ as the hub. The closer we get to the hub, the closer we get to each other. Born-again believers are one in Christ!

When we feel a coldness toward our brothers and sisters in Christ growing in our hearts, let us draw near to Jesus with a heart full of faith and assurance.

Bible Reading: Psalm 122
One Year Bible Reading Plan:
Mark 3:1-21
Numbers 1, 2

David Lee Yoder, Auburn, KY

---

*There is no name other than the name of Jesus
to unite a body of believers.*

Stones for Evidence

What mean ye by these stones?
Joshua 4:6

It must have been exciting to be in the camp of Israel on that eventful day when God's people were miraculously led through the Jordan River on dry ground.

God, knowing man's forgetfulness, immediately commanded Joshua to return to the middle of the river and locate twelve stones, which were brought out and placed on a pile for a memorial.

God's instructions were probably given to benefit the children who would in later years discover God's supernatural work. Not only are we forgetful, but, perhaps more importantly, we often fail to transmit to the coming generation the truths which we have been taught. It is sobering to think that we might be only one generation away from blending with a godless society.

When Satan brings doubt about our salvation experience, or a feeling of defeat, we can with comfort and confidence point the deceiver to the Word of God and say, "There is my memorial, and it stands."

Though we may not have the tangible evidence Israel witnessed, we do have the blessing of the Holy Spirit, who quietly reminds us of our covenant with God.

Bible Reading: Joshua 4:1-9
One Year Bible Reading Plan:
Mark 3:22-35
Numbers 3, 4

Let us remember today, and remind our children of the eternal, loving God and His memorial in the Scriptures.

Phil Hershberger, Abbeville, SC

The greatest memorial man can display
is a life totally yielded and surrendered to God.

The Lamp and Light

Let the word of Christ dwell in you richly in all wisdom.
Colossians 3:16

The impact of God's Word on a person's life is indeed greater than we many times realize.

A man in our community often made sneering remarks about Christians. He seldom went to church, because he thought Christians were mostly hypocrites. One Sunday morning, however, as I taught Sunday school, I noticed him sitting on a back bench listening intently. As I continued speaking, I thought I saw his eyes fill with tears of emotion.

Later in the week we met, and soon we were talking about spiritual things. He told me, "You see, Roger, they all have a lot of things to say, and we end up following a man. But as you were talking on Sunday," again his eyes were glossy, and he spoke with feeling, "you were reading to us from the Bible. What you said came straight from the Word of God. We need to hear what the Bible says."

God has used that incident many times since then to speak to me. Where do we go for our main source of inspiration in morning devotions—the songbook, the storybook, the devotional book; or do we go to the Word of God? "Mine eyes fail for thy word," the psalmist wrote, "O how love I thy law! it is my meditation all the day" (Psalm 119:82, 97). In our services, what do we hear the most? Is it some great author, philosopher, or commentator; or is it the Word of God? "Behold, I will make my words in thy mouth fire, and this people wood, and it shall devour them" (Jeremiah 5: 14).

I want God and His Word to show me the path of life today, because in His presence there is fullness of joy, and at His right hand there are pleasures forevermore.

Roger Rangai, Lott, TX

Bible Reading: Psalm 19
One Year Bible Reading Plan:
Mark 4:1-20
Numbers 5, 6

"Thy word is a lamp unto my feet, and a light unto my path."
—Psalm 119:105

Friends

Then Jonathan and David made a covenant,
because he loved him as his own soul.
1 Samuel 18:3

When was the last time you stopped to thank God for those special people in your life you call friends: a sibling, or a brother or sister in Christ, or your spouse? What is it that separates them from the rest and makes them special to you?

Jonathan and David were true friends. Two promising young men on a collision course to the throne. Jonathan was the rightful heir to the throne after his father Saul. And David had been anointed by God to succeed the king. They had everything to lose by being friends, for only one of them could reign.

They could have become suspicious and jealous of each other. They could have plotted to destroy each other, in order to gain the throne. But they did not. Neither young man was interested in promoting himself. Jonathan risked his life several times to help David, despite his father's warning that his throne would never be established as long as David was alive (1 Samuel 20:31). And David risked his life many times fighting the Philistines, in order to help Saul and Jonathan establish their kingdom.

Bible Reading: 1 Samuel 18:1-15
One Year Bible Reading Plan:
Mark 4:21-41
Numbers 7

That is what being friends is all about—being primarily concerned for the well-being of the other, regardless of the cost to myself. That is love.

Melvin Troyer, Leitchfield, KY

A man went out to look for some friends and could not find any.
Another man went out to be a friend and found lots of them.

God's Delight

Praise ye the LORD. *Praise the* LORD, *O my soul.*
Psalm 146:1

What a mighty God we serve! Psalm 147 is a psalm of praise to an almighty God, a God in whom we can put our complete trust.

I am sitting here in the hospital with my twenty-two-year-old son, who was in a motorcycle accident in the Dominican Republic. He was there helping to construct a house for our new mission. Now he is recovering from his third surgery in the past three weeks to stabilize his back, which was broken. After this surgery, he will go through a rehabilitation program to help him learn how to live in a wheelchair, since he was paralyzed from the waist down by his injury.

You may ask, "How can you praise the Lord in a situation like that?" Well, we can count the blessing that his life was preserved. And we are assured that the same God whom David praises in this psalm is in control of what has happened to our son. We know that we can continue to praise our almighty God, and that God will be glorified even in our infirmities.

The tenth verse of this psalm caught my wife's attention the other day while she was having her daily devotions: "He delighteth not in the strength of the horse: he taketh not pleasure in the legs of a man." Praise God that we can still delight in "the LORD, [that] taketh pleasure in them that fear him, in those that hope in his mercy" (verse 11).

Bible Reading: Psalm 147:1-11
One Year Bible Reading Plan:
Mark 5:1-20
Numbers 8–10

Joe Miller, Auburn, KY

When the world around you is crumbling,
God is the Rock on which you can stand.

Ask, Seek, and Climb

And he sought to see Jesus who he was; and could not
for the press, because he was little of stature.
Luke 19:3

There are many people today who long for the peace and joy that Christians have, but they do not know how to find it. They do not realize that they have no joy because they do not have Jesus in their hearts.

John 1:12 says, "But as many as received him, to them gave he power to become the sons of God, even to them that believe on his name." Without receiving Him, we cannot receive peace or joy.

How do we find Jesus? The Word of God says we must ask, seek, and knock (Matthew 7:7).

Zacchaeus was a man who meant business with the Lord. Zacchaeus was desperate to see Jesus, but he was so little that he could not get next to Him. So he thought about how he could work things out. He spied a tree out ahead, and he climbed up into it. Now he had a bird's-eye view of Jesus. He could see Him walk and hear Him talk. When Jesus came to the tree, He looked up and said, "Zacchaeus, make haste, and come down; for to day I must abide at thy house" (Luke 19:5). Zacchaeus gladly received Jesus. Notice how quickly his spirit was revived. He had joy and peace! Why? Because he was with Jesus! The secret of his success was that he sought hard after Jesus. Even though he was an important man, he was willing to "climb a tree" if that was what it took. Zacchaeus confessed his sins and found life eternal.

Humble yourself before the Lord, and He will lift you up.

Abner Overholt, Auburn, KY

Bible Reading: Luke 19:1-10
One Year Bible Reading Plan:
Mark 5:21-43
Numbers 11–13

If you are too proud to climb a tree,
then you the Lord will never see.

Intercessory Prayer

I pray for them . . . which thou hast given me.
John 17:9

When our congregation meets for midweek prayer meeting, someone often requests prayer for "each other." I am sure this request is given with noble intentions, but I often think this is a rather impersonal way to pray for the brotherhood. Granted, we might not pray for each person in our prayer group by name because there are certain rules of conduct we should follow, such as considering our allotted prayer time and allowing others in our group to have enough time for prayer, also. How then should we pray for "each other"? In John 17 we see Christ praying to the Father for his disciples (and for us). His prayer provides guidelines we do well to follow.

In John 17:15, Christ prayed that His followers would be kept from evil. Every Christian faces temptations to sin. We must intercede for others, so that they can also be kept from the results of those temptations.

In verse 21, He prayed that we would have unity, as He had with the Father. Since disunity hinders our walk of faith and our witness to the unsaved, we must pray for unity among the brotherhood.

Other New Testament passages give us more guidelines for praying for each other. Ephesians 5:20 tells us to give thanks always for all things, and we certainly ought to thank God for each of our brothers and sisters in Christ.

James 5:14 tells us to pray for each other's healing: physical, spiritual, and emotional.

Finally, James 1:5 tells us to pray for wisdom, and this is a request we should make not only for ourselves, but for each member of the brotherhood.

Marcus Yoder, Grove City, MN

Bible Reading: John 17
One Year Bible Reading Plan:
Mark 6:1-32
Numbers 14, 15

Prayer changes things!
Prayer changes us!

Seek the Lord

Seek the LORD, and his strength: seek his face evermore.
Psalm 105:4

The men from the East in Matthew 2 were wise in many ways. God spoke to them for their salvation, and they listened. These men had plenty of this world's wealth, but there was a vacuum in their hearts. Only God could fill that vacuum.

The wise men seemingly were acquainted with the prophesies of the Bible. They knew that a baby boy was to be born, and that He was to be King of the Jews (Matthew 2:1, 2).

When God told them to follow the star that appeared in the sky, they got on the road. We do not know how many people were traveling together, but they had one thing in mind—to find the baby Jesus, and to worship Him. They took the most expensive gifts they had to give to Jesus.

I can almost see the camels and the wise men coming over the hills and the sandy desert. Nobody know how far they came or how long they were on the road. They were seeking their Redeemer.

How much effort do we put forth to seek the Lord?

Abner Overholt, Auburn, KY

Bible Reading: Matthew 2:1-11
One Year Bible Reading Plan:
Mark 6:33-56
Numbers 16, 17

It is a wise man who knows that he isn't.

God's Holiness—Our Response

*Holy, holy, holy, is the L*ORD *of hosts:*
the whole earth is full of his glory.
Isaiah 6:3

The familiar account in 2 Chronicles 26 of King Uzziah's trespass in the temple and his consequent leprosy reminds us that God's holiness must be held in high regard by His people. In the opening verse in Isaiah 6, we see that the young prophet Isaiah was greatly affected by God's vengeance upon King Uzziah. Shortly thereafter, God reinforced for Isaiah the truth of His absolute holiness with this remarkable vision. Isaiah's response to the vision can teach us some noteworthy lessons about our response to God and His holiness.

Our first observation is that Isaiah saw himself from a different perspective after viewing God's holiness. As a prophet, he was accustomed to pronouncing woe upon others. (See the six woes pronounced in the previous chapter.) But now he pronounces the woe upon himself! His eyes had seen the King, and his sense of personal holiness completely unraveled.

Secondly, he recognized the sinfulness of the people around him. In contrast to the holy God, his friends and neighbors now appeared to be "people of unclean lips."

Thirdly, this vision of God's holiness stirred within him a missionary zeal. Upon hearing of the need, Isaiah promptly responded, "Here am I; send me."

Let us candidly evaluate ourselves. Have we personally obtained a keen sense of God's holiness? As we do, we will, like Isaiah, keenly sense our basic sinfulness and unworthiness, we will be burdened with the sinfulness of our society and have a motivating missionary zeal.

Bible Reading: Isaiah 6
One Year Bible Reading Plan:
Mark 7:1-13
Numbers 18–20

Ken Kauffman, Falkville, AL

It is one thing to acknowledge God's holiness;
quite another thing to practice it.

Bring in the Candles

Wherefore the rather, brethren, give diligence to make your calling and election sure: for if ye do these things, ye shall never fall.
2 Peter 1:10

On May 19, 1780, the "horror of great darkness" descended over New England. Without warning, midday became midnight. Men prayed, women wept, and children clung to their parents in fear. Surely the great judgment day had come.

In the Connecticut State House, a motion was made to adjourn. Abraham Davenport stood and responded to the motion saying, "This may well be the day of judgment which the world awaits; but be it so or not, I only know my present duty and my Lord's command to occupy until He comes. So at the post where He set me in His providence, I choose, for one, to meet Him face to face—no faithless servant frightened from my task, but ready when the Lord of Harvest calls; and therefore, with all reverence I would say, Let God do His work, we will see to ours. I move—bring in the candles!"

Often, we meander through life, not giving much thought to our purpose for living. So we tend to have wrong purposes, to get our priorities wrong, and to take our eyes off the goal.

What should be our focus? What is your goal? Developing the character of Christ, spoken of in 2 Peter 1:5-7, should be our purpose. To grow from faith to virtue, from virtue to knowledge, from knowledge to self-control, and on in Jesus' character until we are mature in godly love. If we diligently strive for these goals, we "shall never fall" (v. 10).

If our purpose is clear, when darkness comes, when opposition arises, or the way gets rough, we will be ready to bring in the candles, and continue on with our work.

Tim Stoltzfus, Harrison, AR

Bible Reading: 2 Peter 1:1-15
One Year Bible Reading Plan:
Mark 7:14-23
Numbers 21, 22

Trying times are no time to quit trying.

Has the Cock Crowed?

And immediately the cock crew.
Matthew 26:74

Do you know Jesus? Do you *know* Him? How many times have we denied knowing Jesus, just as Peter did when he was in hostile company? Vehemently he declared, "I do not know Him!" Can you imagine the look of compassion in Jesus' eyes, as he witnessed Peter's denial? How it tore at Peter's heart as he fled! Why, oh why, had he done it? He loved Jesus, and yet he had denied Him.

You may say, "Oh, Peter! Such shallowness! What was wrong with you? How could you deny Jesus, your own Master?"

Wait, my friend! Have you done this? Peter, although without excuse, had not yet received the power of the Holy Spirit. That was Peter's problem. What is ours? After Pentecost, Peter was a different man. He boldly proclaimed Jesus, as his heart was filled with the Spirit. All fear of man was gone. In Acts 2:36, he was the first to confess Jesus both Lord and Christ.

My friend, is there evidence of the Holy Spirit in your life? Do you struggle with the problem of no power? Sometimes we are critical of Peter, Judas, Thomas, and the Pharisees, for their lack of faith, insight, and commitment. But Jesus said, if our righteousness does not exceed that of the Pharisees, we shall in no case enter into the kingdom of heaven. There are many people today just like these Pharisees, of whom Jesus said, "This people draweth nigh unto me with their mouth, and honoureth me with their lips; but their heart is far from me." Oh, let us not have only lip service! Let our lives be living proof that we know Jesus.

Bible Reading: Matthew 26
One Year Bible Reading Plan:
Mark 7:24-37
Numbers 23, 24

Kevin Miller, Auburn, KY

If we love Christ, our devotion will not remain a secret.

Condemned or Forgiven?

There is therefore now no condemnation to them which are in Christ Jesus, who walk not after the flesh, but after the Spirit.
Romans 8:1

Have you ever had trouble sleeping, lying awake at 2:00 A.M. with several things on your mind, bothering you? Maybe it is a little worry about something that happened on the job, or maybe there is something in your spiritual life that concerns you.

Just this morning I lay awake like that. Finally, rising around 3:00, I went to my desk to have a little quiet time. Being somewhat troubled, I found it difficult, as I bowed my head to pray, to know just what I had to be thankful for. But as I prayed, all of a sudden a verse came to my mind—Romans 8:1.

Yes, there it was! How could I not be thankful to the Lord Jesus for that wonderful reality that there is "no more condemnation" after we have repented and forsaken the sin that we had lived in so long! Praise the Lord, I have been forgiven!

My heart goes out to those who are still living in sin. Since God has sent His Son to die on the cross, shedding His precious life blood so that our sins have been forgiven, we no longer have to live under condemnation. No matter what troubles we may face, that realization should cause a fountain of thanks to spring up in our hearts.

Bible Reading: Romans 8:1-14
One Year Bible Reading Plan:
Mark 8
Numbers 25–27

Joe Miller, Auburn, KY

Man remains lost because he refuses God's remedy for sin.

March 2

Samson's Pitfalls

Can a man take fire in his bosom, and his clothes not be burned?
Proverbs 6:27

The story of Samson has always intrigued me. He did not seem to learn from his mistakes. (Remember the riddle?) He permitted himself to be deceived and mocked, over and over as he pursued what he wanted in life.

The same things happen to people today, who are made of the same material as Samson was. If we do not stay on our guard and stay close to God, we, too, will be deceived. We are no stronger than Samson was.

It amazes me how God used Samson. God used the hardships Samson brought on himself to bring judgment on the Philistines (see Judges 14:4). God's ways are so much higher than our ways. His will is often (perhaps we should say always) fulfilled in spite of us.

How can we guard against the pitfalls that Samson fell into? 1) Stay close to God through prayer and Bible reading. 2.) Choose godly companions. 3) Flee temptation. 4) Resist the devil.

Samson lost his eyes, his freedom, and even the Spirit of the Lord for a time, when he allowed himself to be deceived. May God help us to learn from the life of Samson.

Bible Reading: Judges 16:1-31
One Year Bible Reading Plan:
Mark 9:1-29
Numbers 28, 29

Mark Webb, Birmingham, AL

Whatsoever a man soweth, that shall he also reap.
—Galatians 6:7

Take It to the Lord in Prayer

Fear ye not, stand still, and see the salvation of the LORD.
Exodus 14:13

In 1939-1940 Admiral Richard E. Byrd headed an expedition into Sulzberger Bay, trying to penetrate the ice of that bay farther than any vessel had reached before.

But their little ship, the *USS Bear*, became locked in the ice, and they were not able to move forward or backward. They could not use their sails, and their 600 horsepower auxiliary diesel engine was not powerful enough to free them. After he had studied their case, Admiral Byrd told his lieutenant and navigator that they would need to exercise patience. "What we need in the Antarctic is patience to wait and let the wind and the tide have a chance to change." And that is what happened. The wind changed, the ice loosened, and they were able to go on.

Sometimes situations arise in our lives—they may be personal, in our families, or in our congregations—and we feel stuck. We cannot see any way through our problem. All our frustrations and struggles do not seem to help. In fact, they may even hinder us and get us in deeper.

> **Bible Reading:** Exodus 14:8-20
> **One Year Bible Reading Plan:**
> Mark 9:30-50
> Numbers 30, 31

But we need not give up. We can wait, and with patience and prayer leave our affairs in the hands of the Lord. He sees our difficulties and hears our prayers. And He is able to get us on the right track again.

Abner Overholt, Auburn, KY

Patient waiting is often the highest
way of doing God's will.
—Jeremy Collier

The Blessedness of Forgiveness

Blessed is he whose transgression is forgiven, whose sin is covered.
Psalm 32:1

When was the last time you thought about your debt of sin? Who is responsible for that debt? Could you ever "work off" that debt? Has it been paid? What have you done about it? Are you still guilty before God, or are you free?

Praise God, the price has been paid! What a blessing! What a privilege! We could not ever pay off our debt of sin. Never! But the blood of Jesus takes away that sin and sets us free to serve Him.

Psalm 32:9 instructs us to not be as the horse or mule, with no understanding. God desires a willing sacrifice of ourselves and our wills—a complete surrender.

Verse 11 says, "Shout for joy, all ye that are upright in heart." Where is our rejoicing? Is it being heard? What is our testimony? Are we shouting with the upright?

Friends, has God blessed His people? Indeed He has! Let us trust in the Lord and be glad in Him. Then our hearts and lives can overflow with His blessing.

Bible Reading: Psalm 32
One Year Bible Reading Plan:
Mark 10:1-31
Numbers 32, 33

Chris Beiler, Auburn, KY

Life has taught me to forgive much,
but to seek forgiveness still more.
—Otto von Bismarck

The Power of God

God is my strength and power: and he maketh my way perfect.
2 Samuel 22:33

Recently we went to help in the cleanup after a tornado. Arriving at our destination, we found large trees lying all over the yard; some were three feet in diameter. In the afternoon, we helped a farmer clean debris out of his bean field. We found an assortment of objects, from pictures to logs, scattered over the field.

When the day was finished, I stood in awe as I thought of the power revealed in the tornado. I felt so small and insignificant as I looked at what God's power can do. His power has no limits. Thinking back over the day, I had to ask myself, "Who am I, that I would dare to stand against this mighty, wonderful, powerful God who can at any moment move mountains if He wishes?" Friends, we are the losers if we in any way resist God.

There is another power of God—the power to save lost souls through Jesus Christ. This power becomes available to us as we surrender to Him. Have you experienced the thrill of being one with Him in Christ? Have the big trees and debris been removed from your life? Do you feel His power moving through you?

Bible Reading: Job 38:1-19
One Year Bible Reading Plan:
Mark 10:32-52
Numbers 34–36

Larry Baer, Auburn, KY

Is the power of God moving in your heart?

God's Ways Are Not Always Our Ways

Wherefore, if God so clothe the grass of the field,
which to day is, and to morrow is cast into the oven,
shall he not much more clothe you, O ye of little faith?
Matthew 6:30

If you think you can control the future, think again.

Once there was a family in a financial bind, and the father thought that if he would work more hours, they could get ahead. They prayed about his plan, and he promised that things would be different in the near future.

God heard their prayers, but He answered differently than they expected. The father had an accident. He suffered a broken leg and torn ligaments, which resulted in his being unable to work for four months.

What would the family do now? God's people provided for them in all areas, and God received the praise. When payments came due, the exact amount was there, and more food came in than they normally had to eat.

Both the family and the church received God's blessings. And His promise was kept to "never leave [us], nor forsake [us]." So let us trust in Him for our everyday needs, whether large or small. Give God the glory He deserves, and He will bless you for it.

John Hostetler, Auburn, KY

Bible Reading: Matthew 6:19-34
One Year Bible Reading Plan:
Mark 11:1-19
Deuteronomy 1, 2

_____

Providence knows better what we need than we ourselves.
—Fontaine

A Might-Have-Been

Whosoever shall humble himself as this little child,
the same is the greatest in the kingdom of heaven.
Matthew 18:4

Jesus called Judas Iscariot to be one of His closest disciples. Judas followed Jesus for three years, but failed in his commitment to his Master. Looking only for a good life on this earth and freedom from Roman rule, when he realized this wasn't going to happen, Judas went out and hanged himself. What a tragic might-have-been!

What is a might-have-been? A might-have-been is someone who has the potential to do something for God but fails to allow God to work through him. All of us have the potential of contributing to God's kingdom, but a might-have-been is a great disappointment to God and others.

How can one avoid being a might-have-been? Jesus said that even the one who merely provides a child with a cup of cold water, would not lose his reward—or, become a might-have-been. A mother caring for her children and a father bringing up his children in the nurture and admonition of the Lord escape becoming might-have-beens. The boy or girl who learns to be obedient to parents and to God is *someone* in the Kingdom of God. You do not have to be a might-have-been. You can, by God's grace, be someone fit for the Master's use.

We are not all called to do a conspicuous work, but we are all called to an important work. At the end of time, God will recognize those who are faithful in His kingdom. We do not have to become might-have-beens.

Mark Webb, Hicksville, OH

Bible Reading: Matthew 27:1-10
One Year Bible Reading Plan:
Mark 11:20-33
Deuteronomy 3, 4

Choice, not chance, determines your destiny.

Thy Word Have I Hid in My Heart

I have esteemed the words of his mouth
more than my necessary food.
Job 23:12

The Bible is more accessible to us today than ever before! We can study it in thousands of languages and hundreds of translations. Computer Bible programs allow us to do in minutes word studies and searches that previously took hours to do by hand.

H. A. Ironside once visited a godly Irishman, Andrew Frazer, who had come to southern California to recover from a serious illness. Though quite weak, Frazer opened his worn Bible and began expounding the deep truths of God in a way that Ironside had never heard before. Ironside was so moved by Frazer's words that he asked him, "Where did you get these things? Can you tell me where I might find a book that would open them up to me? Did you learn them in some seminary or college?"

The sickly man gave an answer that Ironside said he would never forget. "My dear young man, I learned these things on my knees on the mud floor of a little sod cottage in the north of Ireland. There with my open Bible before me I used to kneel for hours at a time and ask the Spirit of God to reveal Christ to my soul and to open the Word to my heart. He taught me more on my knees on that mud floor than I ever could have learned in all the seminaries or colleges in the world."

God still wants to speak directly to our hearts through His Word! Do not let the glitz of electronics short out the still small voice of the Holy Spirit!

Bible Reading: Psalm 119:9-24
One Year Bible Reading Plan:
Mark 12:1-27
Deuteronomy 5–7

Laverne Miller, Hicksville, OH

A Bible that is falling apart usually belongs to a person who isn't.

Peace

Peace I leave with you, my peace I give unto you:
not as the world giveth, give I unto you.
Let not your heart be troubled, neither let it be afraid.
John 14:27

People all around us long for peace. They seek it through sports and vacations, drugs and alcohol, but only find greater turmoil than before.

Peaceful settings are enjoyable. How peaceful to relax beside a stream and listen to the water running across the rocks! We enjoy that. Watching a herd of cattle graze in a nice lush pasture calms us. Looking out from a mountain overlook and feeling a slight breeze as we view the beauty of a plain before us is peaceful, too.

But in our reading today, we find Jesus resting in a storm! Was He unaware of the danger? No! He was trusting His Father completely.

We can be in a peaceful setting and still not experience peace. Or, like Christ, we can be in the heart of a storm—whether physical or spiritual—and still have peace. That is the nature of the peace God gives.

We can have this peace only as we place all on the altar, and Jesus is Lord of our lives. Then peace will be found within, no matter what the circumstances without.

Bible Reading: Mark 4:35-41
One Year Bible Reading Plan:
Mark 12:28-44
Deuteronomy 8–10

Stephen Beachy, Huntland, TN

Peace is not having all things in control,
but knowing Him who controls all things.

Zacharias and Elizabeth

And they were both righteous before God, walking in all the
commandments and ordinances of the Lord blameless.
Luke 1:6

The lives of Zacharias and Elizabeth provide a clear, definite picture of the true saint of God. They believed God and did that which was right. They walked in the commandments and ordinances of the Lord. Daily, they walked with God. Their lives were blameless.

We should walk before God in the same manner. We are commanded to do so: "That ye may be blameless and harmless, the sons of God, without rebuke, in the midst of a crooked and perverse nation, among whom ye shine as lights in the world; holding forth the word of life" (Philippians 2:15, 16).

To be blameless does not mean that we are without faults, or that we do not make mistakes. However, it does mean that when we do have faults or make mistakes, we are willing to correct them and make amends. It is this willingness to correct our errors that makes us blameless before God.

Are you a Zacharias or an Elizabeth? Their lives challenge us to walk faithfully before God and the world, "holding forth the word of life."

LaVerne Yoder, Woodburn, KY

> **Bible Reading:** Luke 1:5-25
> **One Year Bible Reading Plan:**
>   Mark 13:1-13
>   Deuteronomy 11–13

_____

To make mistakes is human; to be blameless is godly.

Oil in Our Vessels

Watch therefore, for ye know neither the day
nor the hour wherein the Son of man cometh.
Matthew 25:13

The parable of the ten virgins teaches us that on the day the Lord returns, there will be those who appear to be ready to go with Him, but have no oil in their vessels, which disqualifies them from going with the bridegroom. Since this oil was the factor dividing the wise from the foolish virgins, what should we do today to be among the wise virgins when Christ returns?

We must know Him (verse 12). And when we know Him, He gives us all things that pertain unto life and godliness (2 Peter 1:3). His Spirit dwells in us and fills us with His fruit (Galatians 5:22-25). In this manner, Christ gives us the oil that we must possess at His coming. There are affections and lusts that deplete one's oil supply. Galatians 5:24 cautions, "They that are Christ's have crucified the flesh with the affections and lusts."

We also glean from the parable that the day of the Lord will come at a time when we are not expecting it. Verse 10 says that when the bridegroom comes, those who were ready went in with Him, and the door was shut. The note of finality that rings from that firmly closed door urges us toward carefulness in this life, that we may be ready to go with Him into the next life.

If His presence fills us today, we will be ready to meet Him, our vessels filled with a goodly supply of oil.

1. The Lord will return in an hour when we least expect Him.
2. Watch, therefore.
3. Be ready.

Paul Beiler, Huntland, TN

Bible Reading: Matthew 25:1-13
One Year Bible Reading Plan:
Mark 13:14-37
Deuteronomy 14–16

Prepare to meet thy God.
—Amos 4:12

The Tongue

Let the words of my mouth, and the meditation of my heart, be acceptable in thy sight, O LORD, my strength, and my redeemer.
Psalm 19:14

God has given us a very versatile tool in the tongue. In the tongue lies a tremendous power. It has the power to tear down or to destroy. It has the power to build and to save. It has the power to cut, and it has the power to heal. What are you doing with your tongue?

In the Bible reading for today, James tells us that no one can control the tongue. The tongue of itself will speak the things of the carnal man, or the tongue of a new man will speak the things of God.

Someone has said, "Our words are the window to our heart." Matthew 12:34 says, "Out of the abundance of the heart the mouth speaketh." Our words, then, are a revelation of our heart's condition.

Is my tongue, out of a love for Christ, singing the songs of Zion? Is it encouraging others and telling the lost about Christ? Or is it tearing others down and spreading gossip?

We are told in the Word of God that we must give an account of all the words that we speak. Let us let Christ control our tongues by allowing Him to have full possession of our hearts.

Mark Yoder, Whiteville, TN

Bible Reading: James 3:1-12
One Year Bible Reading Plan:
Mark 14:1-25
Deuteronomy 17–19

Make your words sweet—someday you may have to eat them.

The Value of the Scriptures

*For ever, O L*ORD*, thy word is settled in heaven.*
Psalm 119:89

Why are the Scriptures so valuable?

The Scriptures are valuable because they are inspired by God. In 2 Peter 1:21 we read, "For the prophecy came not in old time by the will of man: but holy men of God spake as they were moved by the Holy Ghost." Our Bible reading for today says the Scriptures are profitable for doctrine. They teach and instruct us in that which is true. They show us the plan of salvation and tell us of our perfect example: Jesus Christ.

It also says the Scriptures are profitable for reproof or correction. Through the preaching of the Scriptures, we are convicted and reproved when something in our lives is amiss. The last part of 1 Corinthians 1:21 says, "It pleased God by the foolishness of preaching to save them that believe." It is through receiving and applying the teachings of the Scriptures that we can be saved.

The Scripture is profitable for instructing the saints toward perfection. The man of God is fed by the Scripture. It is a perfect rule of faith and practice.

O, that we would love the Holy Scriptures more! May they grow more precious every day as we daily feast on them!

Timothy Allgyer, Xenia, IL

Bible Reading: 2 Timothy 3
One Year Bible Reading Plan:
Mark 14:26-50
Deuteromony 20–22

Let your Bible be your owner's manual.

Rash Words

Be not rash with thy mouth, and let not thine heart be hasty
to utter any thing before God: for God is in heaven,
and thou upon earth: therefore let thy words be few.
Ecclesiastes 5:2

Jephthah's rash words brought him to a very sad time in life. He made a very wrong vow, because of hastiness and thoughtlessness.

Perhaps Jephthah's poor companions (Judges 11:3) influenced his thoughts and set him up to make his rash statement. The Bible tells us that evil communications (companions) corrupt good manners (morals). By the same token, we also know that good companions help build strong character qualities.

In Jephthah's vow to God, he said, "If thou shalt without fail deliver . . . then it shall be, that . . . I will . . . " Jephthah bargained with God. He promised to do something for God, if God gave him the victory. And yet, it appears that God had already promised Jephthah the victory, and that He had laid out the conditions for that victory. Jephthah would have been much wiser to accept God's promise and to give thanks.

We can learn from Jephthah's example and put into practice what the Bible teaches: not being rash with our mouths, but being slow to speak.

Bible Reading: Judges 11
One Year Bible Reading Plan:
Mark 14:51-72
Deuteronomy 23–25

LaVerne Yoder, Woodburn, KY

Our speech should be like a carpenter's work —
measured twice and sawed once.

Garden Meditations

*And the L*ORD *God took the man, and put him into*
the garden of Eden to dress it and to keep it.
Genesis 2:15

After a number of years of less than satisfactory results from her garden, my good wife turned the gardening over to me. Although I am not much of a gardener, I am a compulsive weed puller. While my hands (and my hoe) may be busy, working in the garden gives opportunities to meditate. It occurred to me that gardens are like people's minds. Some gardens are clean and well-tended. It is obvious that much effort goes into enriching the soil. Things are well-watered, and everything looks lush and green. The rows are straight and neat. Weeds are kept to a minimum. Every effort is made to ensure a good harvest.

So should be the minds of those assuming the name of Christ: clean and well-tended. It is enriching to converse with saints like this. Their outlook is optimistic and uplifting. They keep "weeds" to a minimum by filling their minds with good things. They are careful to read only uplifting or inspiring material. Their music inspires, and honors the living God. They look forward to everlasting life as their harvest. Your imagination can picture the other type of garden.

Let us tend the gardens of our minds as carefully as we tend the gardens in our yards.

Joe Schmucker, Haven, KS

Bible Reading: Mark 4:3-20
One Year Bible Reading Plan:
Mark 15:1-26
Deuteronomy 26, 27

To cultivate a garden is to walk with God.
—Christian Nestell

Opportunities for the Furtherance of the Gospel

*The things which happened unto me have fallen out
rather unto the furtherance of the gospel.*
Philippians 1:12

Paul had no idea what would take place when he responded to the Macedonian call (Acts 16:9). But, being led by the Spirit, he was willing to accept whatever happened and to be ready to turn every incident into an advantage for furthering the Gospel. The stopover at Philippi started out as a pleasant experience in the furtherance of the Gospel, when the Lord opened people's hearts and they came to faith (Acts 16:15). However, as time went on, things happened which grieved Paul. Because he obeyed as the Spirit led him, both he and Silas ended up in prison (Acts 16:16-24). Still being led by the Spirit, and wanting to magnify the Lord, Paul and Silas spent their first night in prison praying and singing praises unto God. We can imagine how the hearts of the prisoners who heard them were touched by the Gospel message, which they had never before heard.

After the earthquake which shook the foundation and opened the doors of the prison, another opportunity for the furtherance of the Gospel presented itself, and Paul seized it, too. The jailer, who was intending to commit suicide, became a believer instead, and received baptism, along with all that were in his house (Acts 16:25-32).

Several years later, when Paul wrote the letter to the Philippians, he was again imprisoned, this time at Rome. He undoubtedly took advantage of every opportunity in Rome to further the Gospel as he testified to prison guards and to everyone he met.

May you and I turn the happenings in our lives into opportunities for the furtherance of the Gospel.

Moses Gingerich, Middlebury, IN

Bible Reading: Philippians 1:8-20
One Year Bible Reading Plan:
   Mark 15:27-47
   Deuteronomy 28

"Only let your conversation be as it becometh the gospel of Christ."
—Philippians 1:27

Noises, or a Still Small Voice

*And after the earthquake a fire; but the LORD was not in
the fire: and after the fire a still small voice.*
1 Kings 19:12

We live in a world full of voices, and much noise. Along with these comes much confusion. God is not the author of this confusion.

Satan is the prince of the power of the air, and he is using his power over men's ears and eyes to influence and deceive people, and to drown out God's still small voice. Much of Satan's influence comes through contemporary music, television, radio, and videos.

Recently, a grandmother related how her grandson had made a nasty remark to a lady. He had picked up the phrase from a video they had watched. The grandson was told to go back to the lady and apologize. Perhaps it also would have been in order for the boy's parents to have apologized to their son for setting an evil thing before his eyes. How confusing it must be to children to be taught two opposing ideals!

Bible Reading: 1 Kings 19:9-19
One Year Bible Reading Plan:
Mark 16
Deuteronomy 29, 30

Returning to God, we must learn the beauty of quiet meditation alone with God, so we can hear His still, small voice.

Sam Hostetler, Linn, MO

---

*God is not in the fire of country music,
or in the earthquake of rock music.
God is in the still small voice.*

Walking or Sinking?

But when he saw the wind boisterous, he was afraid;
and beginning to sink, he cried, saying, Lord, save me.
Matthew 14:30

The life of Peter has been a real inspiration to me. It seems like Peter did everything with enthusiasm! It even got him into some tight places at times.

In today's reading, the disciples had just finished feeding the five thousand, when Jesus told them to get into the boat and go across the sea. The disciples, no doubt, were tired after the long day and ready for a time to relax. Jesus also needed time to be alone; He went into the mountains to pray.

The disciples were out on the sea and it became boisterous. In the middle of this situation, Jesus came to them walking on the water. When the disciples first saw Him, they cried in fear because they thought they were seeing a spirit; but Jesus called to them and told them, "Be of good cheer; it is I; be not afraid." Then we see Peter's response, "Lord, if it be thou, bid me come unto thee on the water." Jesus told him to come, and Peter stepped overboard and began to walk toward Jesus. On his way to meet Jesus, Peter was distracted by the waves around him and began to sink.

So often this happens to us. We take our attention off Jesus, and we end up sinking instead of walking with Him as we should.

The story does not end there, however. As Peter called out for help, the Lord reached down and pulled him up. That is what He wants to do for everyone. The next time you feel like you are sinking, call out to the Lord, and He will pull you out.

Bible Reading: Matthew 14:15-33
One Year Bible Reading Plan:
Luke 1:1-23
Deuteronomy 31, 32

Dwayne Beachy, Free Union, VA

It takes the storm to prove the real shelter.

Mighty Man of Valor

I can do all things through Christ which strengtheneth me.
Philippians 4:13

Gideon's account is an intriguing one, which has a lot to say to us today. I would like to highlight two characteristics of Gideon. Because of these qualities, God chose him to lead the children of Israel to victory over the Midianites.

First, Gideon was a brave man. We notice his bravery as he threshed wheat by the winepress, and hid it from the Midianites. We observe his bravery when he destroyed the altar to Baal, and then erected one to the Lord and offered a sacrifice on it. Later, we see him going against the multitudes of the enemy with only three hundred men. Truly, Gideon was a brave man.

Secondly, Gideon was a humble man. He considered himself poor and the least in his father's house. Gideon needed a sure sign that God would be with him. He recognized that in his own strength he could not face the enemy. Gideon demonstrated humility when he acknowledged that God was the One who would deliver Israel.

We need men, women, boys, and girls who are brave and humble—brave, in that they are willing to stand for right in a world that is bent on doing evil; humble, in recognizing that without God we are no match for the enemy. Remember, Christ is the victor! Bravely, but very humbly, go forward against the foe.

Mark Webb, Hicksville, OH

Bible Reading: Judges 6
One Year Bible Reading Plan:
Luke 1:24-56
Deuteronomy 33, 34

Be strong and of good courage . . .
—Joshua 10:25

One Drop Not Enough

Thou shalt love the Lord thy God with all thy heart,
and with all thy soul, and with all thy mind.
Matthew 22:37

A lawyer once came to Jesus tempting Him with a question, "Master, which is the great commandment in the law?" Jesus told him, "Thou shalt love the Lord thy God with all thy heart, and with all thy soul, and with all thy mind" (Matthew 22:36, 37). In reality, Jesus was saying, "Love the Lord with all of your desire, your will, and your understanding."

How do we do this? How do I know when "all" of my heart, soul, and mind are engaged in loving God? Can we know the "end" of our being?

I don't even know how much potential I have for love. How big is a heart? How big is love? How much less than all is still all? When is a glass full of water? I filled a glass, and there was room for more. I added a few more drops, but there was still room for more. Finally, the drops that I put in spilled out. It was full.

We don't know how much our hearts can hold, but if they are not full of God, let's start adding some drops. If you find more enjoyment in doing other things than you do in exercising godliness, add a few more drops. If you take more pleasure in researching earthly knowledge than heavenly knowledge, add more drops. Not adding that last drop might make an eternal difference.

When we add drops of commitment, God adds drops of joy. David added drops, and God added drops. If God would have withheld one drop, David's cup could not have run over (Psalm 23:5). How sad if we should have to hear God say, "You failed to add the last drop"!

Bible Reading: Deuteronomy 30
One Year Bible Reading Plan:
  Luke 1:57-80
  Joshua 1–3

Alvin Mast, Millersburg, OH

Tell me whom you love, and I will tell you what you are.

Light Or Weighty

This same Jesus, which is taken up from you into heaven,
shall so come in like manner as ye have seen him go into heaven.
Acts 1:11

At a construction site there were two light plastic bags blowing around in a slight breeze. Soon, one of them started floating upward. It continued its ascent as we watched, and soon it disappeared into the clouds.

I'm sure there is a scientific explanation for this, but it reminded me of what the Apostles saw when they watched Jesus Christ being "taken up, and a cloud received him out of their sight." The Scriptures promise that He is coming again in like manner as they saw Him go into heaven. When He returns, He will take up with Him all those who have been washed in the blood of the Lamb and are faithful to Him. They, too, will suddenly rise against the laws of nature and disappear into the heavens.

Remember, there were two bags; one rose up, and the other did not. The conditions were right with one, but not with the other. Hebrews 12 urges us to "lay aside every weight and the sin which doth so easily beset us." The weight of besetting sins will hold us down. We may spend too much time away from our family to gain profit in this world. We may live in pleasure, forgetting those who do not know where their next meal is coming from. We may spend too much time conforming to the world in order to bring honor to ourselves. Our lives may be so crowded with selfish interests that we skip midweek prayer meeting or forget that our neighbor is dead in his sins. Anything we put before the Lord's service may weigh us down when Jesus comes again.

If we keep our hearts focused on Jesus and consider what He has done for us, what He went through, and where He is now, the things of this world will not be so tempting, and we will rise on that great, glorious day and ascend with Him, out of earthly sight!

Bible Reading: 1 Thessalonians 4:16-18; Hebrews 12:1-10
One Year Bible Reading Plan:
Luke 2:1-24
Joshua 4–6

Freeman Miller, Franklin, KY

The price of a ticket to heaven is giving your heart and life to Jesus.

What Does Your Faith Do for You?

Ye should earnestly contend for the faith
which was once delivered unto the saints.
Jude 1:3

Hebrews 11 describes living faith, which empowers people to live as God would have them live. It carries them through times of trial as well as through times of prosperity.

People like Dirk Willems also embraced this faith. To them, a faith worth living for was a faith worth dying for. Under severe persecution they died triumphantly. Dirk Willems, after fleeing for his life, saw his pursuer fall through the ice on the lake. Dirk's faith carried him back to help the man who had been seeking his life. After helping the man out of the icy water, Dirk was arrested and sentenced to be burned at the stake. On the day of his execution, a strong east wind limited the flames to the lower part of his body and brought great pain to this faithful follower of Christ. His cries of "Oh God" were heard over seventy times in the nearby town of Leerdom. Finally, the bailiff made a quick end to his life. Dirk's faith not only brought him to that hour, but kept him faithful even through this great trial of being burned alive.

What does your faith do for you? Does it carry you through in times of trial? Does it cause you to love even your enemies? Is it strong enough to bring you to prayer meeting or to Sunday evening services? Is your faith worth dying for, as well as worth living for?

Bible Reading: Hebrews 11:1-16
One Year Bible Reading Plan:
Luke 2:25-52
Joshua 7, 8

Eugene Eicher, Grabill, IN

Faith focuses on God instead of life's problems.

Throw It Down

*And whatsoever ye do in word or deed, do all in the name
of the Lord Jesus, giving thanks to God and the Father by him.*
Colossians 3:17

Moses had to learn a lesson before God could use him to lead the Israelites out of Egypt.

Moses was born to Hebrew parents and was hidden by a godly mother, who dared to defy the king's orders that all Hebrew boys must be killed at birth. Later, he was placed in a basket by the river's edge and was found by Pharaoh's daughter, who gave him back to his own mother to be cared for as a baby. Finally, this young Hebrew boy was brought into the court of the king, where he received the best of Egyptian training.

At forty years of age, with all these experiences behind him, Moses felt ready to do the job that God had for him. He had all the credentials for leading his people out of bondage. But God was not ready to use him yet. What was he lacking?

After forty more years of training, this time in the desert herding sheep, God came to Moses and told him he was just the man He wanted to lead His people out of Egypt.

Moses no longer felt qualified for this responsibility. Herding sheep was his life, and the rod that he carried in his hand was the only credential that he now had. Moses was humble. He did not have much left, but God asked him to give that up, also. When Moses was willing to leave his sheep, to trust and depend on God, and to throw his rod down before God, then he was truly ready to be God's servant and to lead His people.

We, too, must be willing to leave our sheep, to trust and depend on God , and to throw down our rod (our abilities and our gifts). Only then can we be useful vessels for the Lord.

Merle Yoder, Whiteville, TN

Bible Reading: Exodus 3:1-14;
4:1-5
One Year Bible Reading Plan:
Luke 3
Joshua 9, 10

Give it up to God, and He will give back something better.

Walking With God

And Enoch walked with God: and he was not; for God took him.
Genesis 5:24

What are your thoughts when you wake up in the morning? What do you talk about after a church service? What dominates your thinking? Are you so busy with some hobby or with your job, that your mind does not have room to meditate on God? Walking with God is more than just quick devotions in the morning. It is constant communion with God. Throughout the day, meditate on some Scripture verse you have memorized. When you are tempted to speak angry words, or lust with your eyes, listen to God's Spirit as He convicts your conscience. Consult God's Spirit when you need to make a quick decision. Talk to God about everything. Talk to Him while you are driving, working, fishing, or whatever you find yourself doing.

In spite of all the evil that surrounded him, Noah walked with God and was a just man. By the grace of God, he was able to be victorious.

Enoch also walked with God. The Bible does not say Enoch was a king, a great leader, teacher, or evangelist; but we have this wonderful testimony— that he pleased God.

Let us glorify God in everything we do.

Bible Reading: Genesis 6:1-9
One Year Bible Reading Plan:
  Luke 4:1-32
  Joshua 11–13

Ivan Overholt, Auburn, KY

The man who walks with God gets to his destination.

Weapons for Spiritual Warfare

And the dragon was wroth with the woman, and went to make war with the remnant of her seed, which keep the commandments of God, and have the testimony of Jesus Christ.
Revelation 12:17

The outcome of a war depends in part on how well the soldiers are armed. Not only are weapons needed with which to fight—a sword, a bow and arrows, and a spear; but also means of protection are needed—a shield, a helmet, a coat of mail, greaves of brass for the legs (1 Samuel 17:5-7), and a girdle, from which the sword hangs when not in use.

Second Corinthians 10:4 tells us that the weapons of our warfare are not carnal, but mighty through God. And Ephesians 6 points out that the armor we need consists of seven weapons: having our loins girt about with truth, having on the breastplate of righteousness, being prepared to spread the Gospel, having the shield of faith, the helmet of salvation, the sword of the Spirit, and using the avenue of prayer. Besides these, we need perseverance, watchfulness, and steadfastness, if we are to overcome the wiles of the devil and the fiery darts of the wicked, with which we are constantly confronted. May we seek the Lord's direction in all things.

Moses Gingerich, Middlebury, IN

Bible Reading: Ephesians 6:10-20
One Year Bible Reading Plan:
Luke 4:33-44
Joshua 14, 15

And when the battle's over, we shall wear a crown.
—Isaac Watts

Time and Eternity

But the end of all things is at hand:
be ye therefore sober, and watch unto prayer
1 Peter 4:7

I glanced at the clock on the microwave oven to see what time it was. To my surprise, it said, "End." Obviously, someone had set the timer, and it had run out. It reminded me that someday, time will come to an end.

Time is a short interval within eternity. We are very time conscious. We have a time to get up, a time for devotions, a time to go to work, times to eat and to go to bed. The writer of Ecclesiastes says there is a *time* for every purpose under heaven (Ecclesiastes 3:1-8).

Our time-bound minds cannot comprehend eternity. Such phrases as "the ceaseless ages" or "throughout eternity" are the best that human language can do to describe what is beyond the realm of time, but they hardly do justice to the matter.

In Psalm 90, Moses speaks of the brevity of life. He follows with this prayer, "So teach us to number our days that we may apply our hearts unto wisdom." The New Testament teaches us to redeem the time, making the most of every opportunity. Wasted time can never be recalled. But time spent serving the Lord is actually invested in eternity. Our earthly lives at the longest are only like a vapor that soon disappears. How sobering to realize that what we make out of these fleeting moments has eternal consequences. Today let us make good use of our time. If we are faithful, we will someday be ushered into God's eternal kingdom, where time will be no more.

> **Bible Reading:** 1 Peter 4
> **One Year Bible Reading Plan:**
> Luke 5:1-16
> Joshua 16–18

John Glick, Gap, PA

Build your hopes on things eternal.

Feet Too Big or Shoes Too Small?

But speaking the truth in love.
Ephesians 4:15

A woman sat down in a shoe store to try on new shoes. The sales clerk fitting her shoes said, "Ma'am, your feet are too big for those shoes." The customer left in a huff and went to a store across the street. There she sat down to try on another pair and had the same problem. The second sales clerk said, "Ma'am, those shoes are too small for your feet." The woman happily tried on another pair, and the sale was made.

Speaking the truth does not require that we dispense with Christian courtesy. We cannot excuse blunt, tactless speech with the explanation, "I must stand firm for the truth," or, "Let the chips fall where they may—here's the truth."

In our interpersonal relationships within the church, or in discussions with non-Christian neighbors, truth must be served, but it must also be well garnished with courtesy and love. Love without truth is misleading, but truth without love is brutal and unappealing. We will hardly argue or debate someone into the kingdom of God. Speaking the truth does not dispense with courtesy.

> **Bible Reading:** Colossians 3:5-17
> **One Year Bible Reading Plan:**
> Luke 5:17-39
> Joshua 19, 20

"I'm sorry, Ma'am, those shoes are too small for your feet."

Jim Yoder, Leitchfield, KY

You will catch more flies with honey than with vinegar.

God Loves to Give

Fear not, little flock; for it is your Father's
good pleasure to give you the kingdom.
Luke 12:32

Too often we find ourselves floundering about, or even getting stuck, in the rut of trying to obtain favor with God by the good works we do. Maybe we are fearful of not entering into life eternal because of some unknown mistake in the past.

Dear Christian friend, if you are walking in those shoes, take heart. God has much more than such a life for you, if you will only let Him give it to you.

Ephesians 1:1-14 speaks of wonderful things—redemption through Christ's blood, forgiveness of sins, being chosen in Him, our adoption as His children, the good pleasure of His will, and the obtaining of an inheritance.

All these things are free gifts for us to enjoy, because Jesus has already paid for them. What we need to do is rejoice in these wonderful gifts, which God so delights in giving to us, and then out of grateful and humble hearts shall flow good works, obedience to His Word, and the praise of His glory that God desires of us.

Since God loved you, forgave you, and accepted you when you came to Him as a sinner, you can rest assured that He will continue to do so, as you continue in the same spirit of repentance that you had on that day.

Bible Reading: Ephesians 1:1-14
One Year Bible Reading Plan:
Luke 6:1-26
Joshua 21, 22

Merle Yoder, Whiteville, TN

Let go, and let God give.

Hard Lessons

I press toward the mark for the prize of the
high calling of God in Christ Jesus.
Philippians 3:14

What would life be like if we never experienced failures? No one has ever become a success without having his fair share of failures; nor has anyone become a failure without first refusing to learn from his mistakes. God wants us to achieve. He wants us to press toward the mark.

The first thing we must do when we fail is acknowledge our shortcomings. Confess them to God and admit them to others. If we come to this point, God can forgive us. "But where sin abounded, grace did much more abound" (Romans 5:20). If we refuse to face up to our failure, we will never be victorious in that area. It is only when we humble ourselves and confess our wrongs that Christ can make us victorious.

Secondly, we must learn from our mistakes. Failure is the opportunity to start over again, wiser than before. Failures are the lessons of life, and we are fools to reject their teaching.

Once you have admitted your failure and learned from it, you must move on. Do not dwell on your shortcomings. Philippians 3:13 says we are to forget those things which are behind and reach toward things ahead. Allow God to work in your life. If you are not open to growth, you will not grow. If you do not allow God's strength to surge through you, you will never be more than a weakling. Remember, there is no failure until you fail to keep trying. Press toward the mark!

Bible Reading: Philippians 3:1-14
One Year Bible Reading Plan:
Luke 6:27-49
Joshua 23, 24

Clair Kauffman, Ronks, PA

Past failures are guideposts for future success.

Come, Follow Me

Follow me, and I will make you fishers of men.
Matthew 4:19

We notice in today's reading that Jesus chose men who were at work. They had jobs. No doubt they had goals that they wanted to reach in life. Then Jesus came along and said, "Come ye after me."

How would I respond? Am I willing to follow Jesus as these men did?

To be a follower of Christ today requires the same commitment that Simon, Andrew, James, and John demonstrated when they dropped their nets and followed Him. When the Spirit prompts us to speak a word for God, what do we do? When there is work to do at the church house, schoolhouse, or for a brother, what do we do? Our number one goal should be to follow our leader, the One we say we love the most. When we love God with our whole heart, we want to follow Christ.

As we follow after Him, not pushing ahead nor lagging behind, but right after Jesus, we will not lose the way, because our Leader knows the way. Praise God!

Also, as we follow Jesus, we can be a good example to those who follow us. Someone is following us. Oh, to be able to say with Paul, "Be ye followers of me, even as I also am of Christ" (1 Corinthians 11:1). Let us lead others in the right direction.

Bible Reading: Mark 1:16-22
One Year Bible Reading Plan:
Luke 7:1-30
Judges 1, 2

Stephen Beachy, Huntland, TN

Arm me with zealous care,
As in Thy sight to live;
And oh! Thy servant, Lord, prepare,
A strict account to give.
—Charles Wesley

Thank You

Enter into his gates with thanksgiving, and into his courts
with praise: be thankful unto him, and bless his name.
Psalm 100:4

Recently I was asked to be a substitute teacher for a week. An incident happened that left an impression on me.

I told my students on Monday that on Thursday or Friday we would do something special to break the routine. As Thursday afternoon rolled around, I decided we would play some games and have some snacks. We all had an enjoyable time. Just before it was time to go home, one pupil came to me and said, "Thank you for all the fun we had." I am sure the rest of my pupils appreciated it, too, only their thanks were not spoken.

How do I respond when someone goes to extra effort to do something special for me? Do I just take it for granted, or do I express my gratitude by saying "Thank you"?

Thank God today for the plan of salvation, for His Word, His Spirit, for food, shelter, and clothing. . . . The list goes on.

Let us make an extra effort today to say "Thank you" to those around us; to our children, our spouse, our parents, and co-workers. They will appreciate it!

Robert Burkholder, Monticello, KY

Bible Reading: Psalm 148
One Year Bible Reading Plan:
Luke 7:31-50
Judges 3–5

Gratitude is an attitude.

Victory in Christ

Who is he that overcometh the world, but he
that believeth that Jesus is the Son of God?
1 John 5:5

Have you ever struggled with a temptation that kept returning? Or, maybe your struggle is with more than a temptation—maybe you are experiencing a lack of victory over sin itself. Try as you may, a true lasting victory seems impossible to win.

I would like to ask you a question that will reveal a vital point in your search. Where do you look for strength in times of struggle? If the answer is anything other than Jesus Christ and His Word, we are getting close to the root of the problem.

Even Christ was tempted, but He was victorious, and you can be, too. In His temptation, Christ relied on God and His Word for strength. We should follow His example. No temptation is stronger than Christ.

Why is it that so often we must exhaust all other resources before we turn to Christ? He alone can give us true, lasting victory in temptations and over sins. Do not go through life thinking that you are a match for the devil and his temptations, for that is pure folly.

Dear friend, bring your temptation to Christ. Claim the victory that is waiting for you. Any other recourse will cheat God out of the chance He is just waiting for, to deliver you.

It does not matter how large or small the temptation or sin— there is **victory in Christ**!

Peter M. Whitt, Montezuma, GA

Bible Reading: 1 John 5
One Year Bible Reading Plan:
Luke 8:1-21
Judges 6, 7

Christ is the first stop on the road to victory.

Have You Taken a Walk Today?

And Enoch walked with God: and he was not; for God took him.
Genesis 5:24

Enoch walked with God—what a statement! Before his translation, it is said that he pleased God—what a compliment!

Walking has gained popularity in our day, especially for those whose work keeps them behind a desk. Interestingly, many who walk for exercise have "walking partners," perhaps for security, or perhaps, just because they are good friends.

Why did Enoch walk with God? Do you suppose it was because Enoch enjoyed God's presence? While the Bible doesn't give us a direct answer to these questions, it seems safe to assume that Enoch and God enjoyed a mutual friendship.

Imagine taking a walk with God down a winding path through fields of wildflowers, then on into the shaded forest. As you are walking, God pauses occasionally to explain the marvel of the hovering hummingbird, the flitting butterfly, the soaring eagle, the flying squirrel, or the tree frog. The conversation turns to the deep mysteries of the kingdom of God, the wonders of His love, the fullness of His wisdom and understanding, the perfection of His plan for man, and the generosity of His grace and mercy.

Does not such a walk with God sound inviting? Indeed, God wants to walk with each of us each day, even as Jesus walked with two of His disciples after His resurrection. He opened to them the Scriptures and caused their hearts to burn within them, as a result of meaningful fellowship. A daily walk with God will restore your weary soul and inspire your faith. Have you taken your walk with God today?

Bible Reading: Luke 24:13-35
One Year Bible Reading Plan:
Luke 8:22-56
Judges 8, 9

Ivan R. Beachy, Free Union, VA

He who walks with God never walks alone.

Working Quietly

And thy Father which seeth in secret
himself shall reward thee openly.
Matthew 6:4

Charles Spurgeon and his wife sold the eggs their chickens laid, and refused to give any eggs away. Even close relatives were told, "You may have them, if you pay for them." As a result, some people labeled the Spurgeons "greedy and grasping."

They accepted the criticism without defending themselves. Only after Mrs. Spurgeon died was the full story revealed. All the profits from the sale of the eggs went to support two elderly widows. Because the Spurgeons were unwilling to let their left hand know what their right hand was doing, they endured the attacks in silence.

Jesus said, "Blessed are ye, when men shall revile you, and persecute you, and shall say all manner of evil against you falsely, for my sake. Rejoice, and be exceeding glad: for great is your reward in heaven: for so persecuted they the prophets which were before you" (Matthew 5:11, 12).

Have you experienced ridicule for Christ? What a blessing! And yet our old nature likes credit. He wants to be noticed. And, as always, the old man wants his reward now: praise, or if nothing else, a little recognition, so that others will think well of him, and he is elevated!

Jesus also said, "Do not sound a trumpet before thee, as the hypocrites do in the synagogues and in the streets, that they may have glory of men. Verily I say unto you, They have their reward. But when thou doest alms, let not thy left hand know what thy right hand doeth: that thine alms may be in secret: and thy Father which seeth in secret himself shall reward thee openly" (Matthew 6:2-4). Try keeping your good works a secret. You will love it!

Bible Reading: Matthew 6:1-4, 17-21
One Year Bible Reading Plan:
Luke 9:1-36
Judges 10, 11

Kevin Miller, Auburn, KY

_____

He who sings his own praises is seldom asked for an encore!

Today—A Gift From God

*This is the day which the L*ORD* hath made;*
we will rejoice and be glad in it.
Psalm 118:24

Today I will be a thankful person!
Today I will take time to pray and read the Word!
Today I will forgive as Christ has forgiven me!
Today I will do everything to God's glory!
Today I will be kind, compassionate, and helpful to my fellowmen!
Today I will think on lovely things!
Today I will remember, it is more blessed to give than to receive!
Today I will love without respect of persons, for God is love!
Today I will give all my time and talents for His kingdom's sake!
Today I will lock the door to the past—it is forever gone!
Today I will trust God for all my tomorrows!
Today may be my very last day, and I am now here by His grace!

Sam Hostetler, Linn, MO

Bible Reading: Psalm 118
One Year Bible Reading Plan:
  Luke 9:37-62
  Judges 12–14

We cannot change people or circumstances,
but we can change our attitude toward people and circumstances.

Small Things Grow

He that saith he is in the light, and hateth his brother,
is in darkness even until now.
1 John 2:9

The sin of bitterness sometimes starts in a small way. At first, it may seem as though it is not even a sin, and that it is not necessary to confess it. But there is no sin that may be overlooked, and if the Spirit of God convicts you of not forgiving something someone said or did against you, you will never regret freely forgiving that person. It might make the difference in your soul going astray.

Bitterness is like a cancer. Cancer starts in a small way, but if it is not dealt with, it soon spreads. In time, it will mean death. Bitterness will do the same thing to us spiritually.

My mother told me of a man who had become so bitter, that even on his deathbed he refused to forgive a brother who had wronged him. How sad! A little fire is easy to extinguish, but if it is not taken care of while it is small, or if it is given fuel, it will soon become uncontrollable.

In the Lord's Prayer we pray, "Forgive us our debts, as we forgive our debtors." God is simply telling us that in order to be forgiven ourselves, we must be willing to forgive others.

The peace and joy that comes from forgiving those who have hurt us is well worth anything it might cost us—like setting aside our pride. "I can do all things through Christ which strengtheneth me" (Philippians 4:13).

Abner Overholt, Auburn, KY

> **Bible Reading:** 1 John 2:1-12
> **One Year Bible Reading Plan:**
>   Luke 10:1-24
>   Judges 15–17

You cannot love God and hate your brother.

Where Is Your Closet?

He that dwelleth in the secret place of the most High
shall abide under the shadow of the Almighty.
Psalm 91:1

Where do we go when there is no place to go? Most of us have had an experience in which we felt like we were all alone in the world. It seemed like no one really cared, or if anyone did care, there was nothing anyone could do. Maybe we faced a severe testing, a trial, or a broken relationship that left us feeling like no one really understands. The days and weeks ahead looked like only mountains—big mountains that seem impossible to climb.

Many of the experiences a Christian encounters are impossible to face in our own strength. But we are never alone, because we have God as our Father. He does not expect us to travel life's pathway alone. He understands the trials and temptations, because Christ has gone that way before. There were times in Jesus' life when He faced weighty decisions or encountered very difficult persons or situations. During these times, He withdrew from the crowds and spent time alone with His Father. In His closet, He found strength to continue. In His closet, He found strength to face the demanding crowds that followed Him wherever He went.

Life places many demands on us and presents experiences that discourage us. At such times we need our closet, where we meet God and receive strength and direction for all of life's trials. We need daily time alone with God. This equips us to face even those most difficult experiences.

Steve Stoltzfus, Kennedyville, MD

Bible Reading: Psalm 91
One Year Bible Reading Plan:
Luke 10:25-42
Judges 18, 19

Lord, do not remove this mountain—just give me strength to climb.

*April 7*_____

Is It Seemly?

Doth not behave itself unseemly, seeketh not her own,
is not easily provoked, thinketh no evil.
1 Corinthians 13:5

Before I say anything, I should weigh my words. Is it seemly for a child of God to say? There are some places unseemly for a child of God to go. There are certain jobs and certain clothes which are unseemly for God's children.

I like the story of a sculptor shaping an elephant from a rough piece of granite. Each day, people stopped by to watch him work. When the sculpture was completed, one of his admirers commented, "I cannot see how you can take a rough piece of granite, and make such a perfect elephant."

The sculptor replied, "It is easy, I just chip away the part that doesn't look like an elephant."

This is what God seeks to do in our lives. He keeps chipping away those things which are not Christlike, those things which are unseemly. He seeks to conform us to the image and mind of Christ.

He is chipping away the unseemly inclinations to be provoked easily, to think ill of others, and to seek our own interests.

Thank God that through our conscience, by the written Word, and by those whom He sends into our lives, He keeps chipping, shaping, and molding us into the mind and image of Christ.

Bible Reading: 1 Corinthians 13
One Year Bible Reading Plan:
Luke 11:1-28
Judges 20, 21

Melvin Yoder, Gambier, OH

He is the potter, we are the clay.
Let us joyfully submit to His hand.

The Joy of the Lord

For this day is holy unto our Lord: neither be ye sorry;
for the joy of the LORD is your strength."
Nehemiah 8:10

What a privilege to live a truly joyful life! This joy is more than a pleasant feeling. It is a God-given characteristic of the Spirit-filled Christian. In the face of adversity, it provides a strength that the world does not understand. It puts a song in the heart of the godly individual—a song that is not muted by the pressures and disappointments of life.

The Hebrew word that is translated *strength* in Nehemiah 8:10 also means "a place of refuge," or "a stronghold." It is imperative that God's people experience this refuge from the rigors of life, which would otherwise weaken and destroy them.

In Nehemiah 8, we see a people prepared to experience the joy of the Lord. They were "attentive unto the book of the law" (verse 3). They respected the Word of God (verse 5). They felt undone in the presence of God, and they experienced sorrow for their sinful condition (verse 9). They were in the will of God, and they had a proper view of themselves and of God. Because they met the conditions, they were able to experience the joy of the Lord, in spite of difficult circumstances. Having this joy, they were able to move ahead with the work of God.

Bible Reading: Nehemiah 8:1-12
One Year Bible Reading Plan:
Luke 11:29-54
Ruth 1–4

Where do we stand today? Are we experiencing the joy God intended for us? If not, let us allow Him to remove whatever obstacles may exist in our lives, so that we may enjoy this refuge from the storms of life.

Samson Eicher, Grabill, IN

God's joy is more than an emotion—it is the strength of His people.

April 9

Value of Godliness

Say ye to the righteous, that it shall be well with him:
for they shall eat the fruit of their doings.
Isaiah 3:10

We live in an ungodly nation—a nation in which moral decay, broken homes, crime, and drug addiction are rampant.

In spite of all this, we can live godly lives. How? Because God has made great promises to those who live godly lives.

One such promise we find in Deuteronomy 4:40, which says that if our lives are upright, God will bless us, and it will be well with us.

There is also in Deuteronomy 4:40 a vision of what godliness can do for the next generation. When our children come up after us, following in our footsteps, they, too, will receive the Lord's blessings. Yet, the blessing does not stop there, either, for they will pass godliness on to their children, and they, in turn, will pass it on to the next generation. Future generations' lives hinge on how we live ours.

If you want to see what ungodliness has done, just look around you. There is plenty of evidence. "But godliness with contentment is great gain" (1 Timothy 6:6).

Bible Reading: 1 Timothy 4:6-11; Deuteronomy 4:39-40
One Year Bible Reading Plan:
Luke 12:1-34
1 Samuel 1–3

Timothy Miller, Crossville, TN

Our godliness is the active ingredient
that preserves the next generation's faith.

104

Is It I?

*And they were exceeding sorrowful, and began
every one of them to say unto him, Lord, is it I?*
Matthew 26:22

In these three words we see the disciples grief-stricken, quite unlike their normal finger-pointing, fault-finding, human ways.

"Lord, is it I?" The question burned and stung their consciences as each one recognized his potential for committing this awful deed.

"Lord, is it I?" Can you not almost see them, wanting to know, yet hardly daring to ask, "Lord, is it I?" Oh perish the thought! They might have stayed in their seats, pointing a judicial finger at another.

But instead of speculating about others, they looked within and left a proper example for us to do the same. Oh, that we would be like David when confronted by Nathan, and admit, "I have sinned," rather than being like Adam in the Garden, who said, "It was the woman you gave me," or like Saul, who blamed his people for his own failure.

Our tendency is to blame circumstances or others. However, we will never experience the healing balm of God's forgiveness, as long as we make excuses for our behavior. We find it only when we accept full responsibility for our sin.

Becoming accountable for our actions puts us sometimes in a lonely position, but it is the only way to personal maturity, and it will prepare us for the day when we shall stand before the Judge of all the earth. The publican of Jesus' day is a good example of this oft-neglected principle, who cried out, "God be merciful to me a sinner."

> **Bible Reading:** 2 Samuel 12:1-15
> **One Year Bible Reading Plan:**
> Luke 12:35-59
> 1 Samuel 4–6

J.Y., Auburn, KY

Boys say, "It broke."
Men say, "I broke it."

Christ's Little Shadows

Therefore if any man be in Christ, he is a new creature: old things are passed away; behold, all things are become new.
2 Corinthians 5:17

A new creature in Christ is absolutely the most beautiful creation of all! He has a redeemed soul, a changed heart, and a new life. We call this creature a Christian, or little shadow of Christ.

When Jesus told Nicodemus, "Ye must be born again," the Jewish teacher asked, "How can this be?" Jesus answered, "Except a man be born of water and of the Spirit, he cannot enter into the kingdom of God." Therefore, a new creature in Christ is one who has been born again; one who has "crucified the flesh with the affections and lusts," and has put on the Lord Jesus Christ. He presents his body "a living sacrifice, holy, acceptable unto God," and considers it the least he can do for God. He strives to please God more each day. He abstains from the works of the flesh listed in Galatians 5. He bears fruit, the fruit of the Spirit, which is love, joy, peace, longsuffering, gentleness, goodness, faith, meekness, and temperance. He "runs well the race of life," not desiring personal glory, but to glorify our Lord and Savior Jesus Christ. He does not devour others but strives to build them up in the most holy faith. He gladly trades his rags of self-righteousness for the righteousness of faith in Jesus Christ.

He is the most beautiful creature of all, growing more and more into the likeness of his great Creator.

Kevin Miller, Auburn, KY

Bible Reading: Galatians 5:13-26
One Year Bible Reading Plan:
Luke 13:1-21
1 Samuel 7-9

WARNING: New creatures are not maintenance free.

Italics portion was added by the publisher.

God's Purpose in Trials

But he knoweth the way that I take: when he
hath tried me, I shall come forth as gold.
Job 23

"For whom the Lord loveth he chasteneth, and scourgeth every son whom he receiveth" (Hebrews 12:6). Many times we face testings in life and overlook God's purpose in permitting them. We become disappointed when things don't go our way. We wonder why we have hardships. Our flesh recoils, and we may even become bitter. We miss out on blessings God has in store for us.

If we are to walk in the Spirit, we must remember the words of Paul: "My son, despise not thou the chastening of the Lord, nor faint when thou art rebuked of him" (Hebrews 12:5b). We then will have a more positive response to trials. We also will realize that our heavenly Father permits these testings to make us more aware of our need to walk closely with our Savior. It is His desire that we draw closer to Him. Remember the vineyard of Isaiah 5. "He fenced it, he gathered out the stones thereof and planted it with the choicest vine." God seeks to remove the stones from our lives to fit the soil of our hearts, that we may bring forth much fruit.

Friend, if today you face disappointments, remember your Father in heaven cares. It is His intention that you come forth as gold.

Jason Wanner, Conneautville, PA

Bible Reading: Job 23
One Year Bible Reading Plan:
Luke 13:22-35
1 Samuel 10–12

God gives us steppingstones, not stumbling blocks.

The Three Crosses

Lord, remember me.
Luke 23:42

Jesus hung on that awful cross with a thief on either side. The Scripture records a conversation spoken by those three hanging on their crosses. One thief vented his pain and frustration upon Jesus. He railed, "If thou be Christ, save thyself and us." The other thief made a humble request, "Lord, remember me when thou comest into thy kingdom." What did the second thief see in his fellow sufferer on the middle cross?

Paul called Jesus Lord when he fell down on the way to Damascus (Acts 9:6). Peter called Jesus Lord as he began sinking beneath the waves (Matthew 14:30). Thomas called Jesus Lord after he had examined His scars (John 20:28). However, this poor thief called Jesus Lord when Jesus was hanging on the cross beside him! The term Lord connotes triumph, kingliness, and authority. Although this thief did not understand all that was happening on that hill, he did sense that the One beside him was a Divine Presence. In faith he called out to Him.

Eventually, all people will acknowledge Him as Lord (Philippians 2:11). The Christian should develop the practice of asking himself in times of decision—whether great or small—"Can the Lord Jesus smile His approval upon this decision?" Call Jesus Lord now, while you have a choice. Do not wait until later, when you will have no choice? You will find that it is the path to true freedom and fulfillment.

Bible Reading: Luke 23:33-46
One Year Bible Reading Plan:
Luke 14:1-24
1 Samuel 13, 14

Jim Yoder, Leitchfield, KY

Three men were dying on crosses.
One dying in sin, one dying to sin, and one dying for sin.

Pumpkins Are Pumpkins

All unrighteousness is sin: and there is a sin not unto death.
1 John 5:17

I know a man who for many years believed that there were degrees of sin. He was of the opinion that there were big, gross sins "which thing the Lord hateth," and small, seemingly innocuous sins, at which he felt the Lord would "wink." These, he believed, would not unduly mar a person's relationship with the heavenly Father.

While he was traveling one day through a market garden region, the Lord brought home to this man that sin is sin. As he drove, he passed a field that had been planted with pumpkins. He observed that the pumpkin vines had died off, but the pumpkins themselves had not yet been harvested. He further noted that the unharvested pumpkins varied greatly in size, from the very small to the very large. At this point, a very simple thought occurred to him. Despite their obvious variations, they were all still pumpkins, regardless of size or variety. The Lord illustrated to this man that sin is sin, regardless of whether or not man considers it "large" or "small," "gross" or "innocuous."

How do we treat sin? Are we endeavoring to rename sin and attempting to soothe our consciences by labeling sins "mistakes," "errors of judgment," or "weakness"? Are we hoping the Lord will "wink" at these?

No matter what palliative we may select, in the Lord's eyes, sin is sin! It cannot and will not be forgiven until it is confessed and forsaken. Don't be deceived! God will not "wink" at sin.

2 Corinthians 13:5 instructs us, "Examine yourselves. . . ." If an open and honest self-examination finds us lacking, let us in all humility and contrition of heart confess and forsake our sins.

Oh, what peace will be ours, when He who is "faithful and just" hears our earnest prayer, forgives us, and cleanses us from all unrighteousness!

Peter McGrath, Victoria, Australia

Bible Reading: 1 John 5
One Year Bible Reading Plan:
Luke 14:25-35
1 Samuel 15, 16

Oh, the joy of sin forgiven!

109

Disobedience

And having in a readiness to revenge all disobedience.
2 Corinthians 10:6

An incident that took place during Leonardo da Vinci's painting of *The Last Supper* epitomizes the results of disobedience. While painting his masterpiece, da Vinci sought long for a model of his Christ. At last, he located a chorister in one of the churches of Rome who was lovely in life and features, a young man named Pietro Bandinelli.

Years passed, and the painting was still unfinished. All the disciples had been portrayed, save one—Judas Iscariot. Now da Vinci started out to find a man whose face was hardened and distorted by sin. And at last he found a beggar on the streets of Rome with a face so villainous that he shuddered when he looked at him. He hired the man to sit for him as he painted the face of Judas on his canvas. When he was about to dismiss the man, he said, "I have not yet found out your name."

"I am Pietro Bandinelli," the man replied. "I also sat for you as your model of Christ."

Our minds must be single, always ready to follow the Lord's commands. We must bring every thought and every part of our existence under His direction. Disobedience causes us to be unstable and double-minded. Doubt in God's Word and pride in our own strength go hand-in-hand, and make us, like Jeremiah's girdle, good for nothing.

Satan is the "father of lies," who wishes to keep us in disobedience. But God's loving chastisement can bring us back to obedience, so that we will not suffer eternally the consequences of disobedience.

Bible Reading: Jeremiah 13:1-15
One Year Bible Reading Plan:
Luke 15:1-10
1 Samuel 17, 18

Laverne Miller, Hicksville, OH

_____

Sin may open bright as the morning;
but it will close as dark as the night.
—Talmage

The Value of Meditation

This book of the law shall not depart out of thy mouth;
but thou shalt meditate therein day and night.
Joshua 1:8

To *meditate* means "to focus one's thoughts on; to reflect or ponder over." Meditating on the Scripture does the same thing for us spiritually as our digestive system does with natural food for our physical body. The digestive process breaks down our food so its nutrients can enter our blood stream and give life, strength, and growth to our bodies. We receive little or no benefit from God's Word if our minds are elsewhere while we read or hear it. But the more we think about a truth and ponder over it, the more spiritual nourishment we receive for our souls.

The quality of our character and the depth of our Christlikeness is closely connected with the amount of time we spend meditating on the Scripture. As Joshua 1:8 indicates, meditation motivates obedience. It conditions us to receive the blessing of God. So, Psalm 1 tells us that one who meditates on God's law will be like a tree planted by the rivers of water.

In our personal devotions, it is not as important how much we read as that a message gets through to us. We should look for at least one outstanding point to meditate on each morning. Address God when you awaken. Receive a message from His Word to meditate on as you go to work. Communicate with Him throughout the day. Fellowship with Him before retiring for the night. If you wake up at night, turn your thoughts to Him, "for then thou shalt make thy way prosperous, and then thou shalt have good success."

John E. Glick, Gap, PA

Bible Reading: Joshua 1:1-9
One Year Bible Reading Plan:
Luke 15:11-32
1 Samuel 19–21

To believe a thing is to see the cool crystal water sparkling in the cup.
But to meditate on it is to drink of it.
—Spurgeon

Power of the Tongue

Keep thy tongue from evil, and thy lips from speaking guile.
Psalm 34:13

The tongue can manipulate public opinion and shape social policy. Have you noticed how behavior once considered immoral is being sanitized through subtle shifts in terminology? For example, people do not commit adultery anymore, they have "affairs." People who were at one time dope addicts, now have a "chemical dependency" because of "substance abuse." Men aren't sodomites. They are pursuing an "alternate lifestyle." Women do not kill their unborn babies, they merely "terminate pregnancies." It is frightening how attitudes toward morality are being unconsciously shaped by simple shifts in terminology. Such is the power of words.

Some people would never have endured times of distress, had it not been for words of encouragement, or the words of a caring friend. "Heaviness in the heart of a man maketh it stoop: but a good word maketh it glad" (Proverbs 12:25). "Pleasant words are as an honeycomb, sweet to the soul, and health to the bones" (Proverbs 16:24).

It is also frightening to think that some people carry indelible emotional scars because of simple careless comments. Reckless words pierce like a sword (Proverbs 12:18). We must never forget that "a wholesome tongue is a tree of life: but perverseness therein is a breach in the spirit" (Proverbs 15:4).

Lloyd Swartzentruber, Montezuma, GA

Bible Reading: Psalm 34
One Year Bible Reading Plan:
Luke 16:1-18
1 Samuel 22–24

Kind words are short to speak, but their echoes are endless.

My Tributes

*Thou shalt rise up before the hoary head, and honour
the face of the old man, and fear thy God: I am the LORD.*
Leviticus 19:32

I call her Auntie, even though the only relation I can claim is through the blood of Christ. The dear, elderly sister has been battling with sickness lately. When I asked about her illness, her reply was, "I am waiting for the doctor to give me the results from a recent lung test. If the test comes back showing that something is wrong, then that is good," she said. "It is from the Lord." Then she added with a smile, "But if the test shows that nothing is wrong, then that is even better! It too is from the Lord." Such trust! Such serenity! Years of walking with her Lord have taught her that He knows best.

Then there is my grandpa. His life is about spent. He has reared eight children. They, along with their children, are serving the Lord. While only eternity will show the full effect his life has had, his wisdom is much appreciated today. When I visit him, he is always ready with a story. His life is an example of the faithfulness of God.

Our lives are greatly enriched by friendship with elderly brothers and sisters. Their wisdom coupled with youthful vigor provides the ingredients for strong teamwork in the church.

These elderly folk have been walking with the Lord for many years. They have proven that God is faithful. Through their example, we can see that the Christian life not only is possible, but also that it is the best life.

How often we fail to appreciate the elderly! So often we let their gold mine of wisdom, gained through experience, lie untapped. How sad if the real experts among us feel unneeded, as we scurry to read what the latest scholars have to say about the issues of life!

Let us praise God for the example and advice of elderly brothers and sisters. Through them, our lives have been bettered.

Michael Overholt, Belize City, Belize

Bible Reading: 1 Kings 12:1-15; Isaiah 46:3, 4
One Year Bible Reading Plan: Luke 16:19-31; 1 Samuel 25, 26

The hoary head is a crown of glory.

Faithful From Start to Finish

And let us not be weary in well doing: for in
due season we shall reap, if we faint not.
Galatians 6:9

To many people, Bezaleel and Aholiab are just some hard-to-pronounce names in the Old Testament. They are not recorded in Hebrews 11 with the heroes of faith. We can be sure, however, that even before God gave them a special assignment in Exodus 31, they had shown their faithfulness to Him.

This is a great comfort and encouragement to us. When God calls us to a special task, He will also fill us with His Spirit, "in wisdom, and in understanding, and in knowledge." When our resources come from God, there will always be enough to get the job done.

Bezaleel and Aholiab's faithfulness was rewarded with the highest tribute that can be paid: "You have finished the work that I gave you to do."

Neither of these men ever became a celebrity. Praise God that our effectiveness in His work is not measured by how many people notice what we have accomplished. Instead, it depends on our faithfulness in accepting the responsibilities given to us.

It is easy to make a verbal commitment in the excitement of a new project. But too often, we fail to carry through. Bezaleel and Aholiab were not just beginners. They were also finishers. Let us also be finishers.

Marvin H. Miller, LaGrange, IN

Bible Reading: Exodus 31:1-11; 35:30-35
One Year Bible Reading Plan: Luke 17:1-19
1 Samuel 27–29

You will never win if you never begin.

Quench Not the Spirit

But they rebelled, and vexed his holy Spirit.
Isaiah 63:10a

Have you started for glory and heaven,
Have you left this old world far behind;
In your heart is the Comforter dwelling?
Can you say, "Praise the Lord, He is mine"?
—*Mrs. S. W. Suffield*

The yoke of Satan is so heavy to bear. Contrast it with the words of Jesus, "For my yoke is easy, and my burden is light." It took me several years before I was finally at the end of myself and ready to let Jesus have my burden. I can still almost feel again that wave of relief when Jesus took over. No more were my nights horrible, waking up with nightmares of hell and missing heaven. Instead my nights were calm and peaceful with Jesus at my side. Jesus is the best of companions. When times get rough, He lifts me over the ruts and ditches, instead of pushing me into them like the devil does. In everything I do, there is no one with me who is so kind and true as my Jesus.

Will you not give in to the Spirit and enjoy the peace and joy of being God's child? You have the same opportunity as was given to King Agrippa in our reading. King Agrippa said, "Almost thou persuadest me to be a Christian." But remember—almost is still lost.

So please, do not quench the Spirit any longer. His arms are stretched out, waiting to take you to Himself. What a glorious invitation! Let us not miss it.

Bible Reading: Acts 26
One Year Bible Reading Plan:
Luke 17:20-37
1 Samuel 30, 31

Stewart Gerber, Millbank, ON

Always be ready for Christ's return, as tomorrow may never come.

One Word—Many Languages

But these are written, that ye might believe that Jesus is the Christ, the Son of God; and that believing ye might have life through his name.
John 20:31

What language do you suppose Adam and Eve spoke in paradise? No one knows the answer.

We do know that because of pride and other sins at the Tower of Babel, God "confound[ed] the language of all the earth" (Genesis 11:9). Today more than 7,000 distinct languages are spoken worldwide.

But, as always, God has provided a way of escape from our mistakes and misery. Two thousand years ago "the Word was made flesh, and dwelt among us" (John 1:14). The road back to God's favor and our peace was provided through Jesus Christ. Salvation is offered to every people, every group, and every race through this one Savior, who unites us in one faith and one hope for the future. Today, let us be thankful that God's thoughts can be expressed in any language and by anyone He has chosen to be a channel of His revelation. It is a thrill to worship with Christians from other lands and cultures, knowing that together we have the same Book and the same Spirit, from one Word. Although languages still differ, the curse of Babel has been overcome through Jesus Christ, our Savior. Portions of the Scripture have been translated into more than 2,240 languages. No other book comes close to that record. Let us believe the Gospel message and not be bashful about sharing God's great news with all the peoples of the world.

Bible Reading: Ephesians 4:11-19
One Year Bible Reading Plan:
Luke 18:1-17
2 Samuel 1–3

Ludlow Walker, Sr., Homestead, FL

Maintaining the unity of the Spirit is the challenge of the redeemed.

116

How Big Is Your God?

If it be so, our God whom we serve is able to deliver us from the burning fiery furnace, and He will deliver us out of thine hand, O king.
Daniel 3:17

Nebuchadnezzar was a proud man. He had an image nine feet wide and ninety feet high built of gold. He wanted everyone to see and to worship it.

He became very angry when three young men dared to disobey him. The king gave the three young men an ultimatum: "If ye worship not [the image], ye shall be cast the same hour into the midst of a burning fiery furnace; and who is that God that shall deliver you out of my hands?"

I like the way Nebuchadnezzar answered his own question. In verse 29, he made a decree that no one "speak any thing amiss against the God of Shadrach, Meshach, and Abednego," for, he said, "there is no other God that can deliver after this sort."

Our God, whom we serve, is the same today as He was in Daniel's time. Can we say with Shadrach, Meshach, and Abednego that "our God whom we serve is able to deliver us"? Even if He does not spare us from the fire, "we will not serve [their] gods, nor worship the golden image which [they have] set up."

"Jesus Christ the same yesterday, and to day, and for ever" (Hebrews 13:8).

William Miller, Blackville, SC

Bible Reading: Daniel 3:1-18
One Year Bible Reading Plan:
Luke 18:18-43
2 Samuel 4–6

Salvation is found only in the Rock of Ages.

Acceptable Fasting

Is not this the fast that I have chosen?
Isaiah 58:6

The Lord asks a pointed question in Isaiah 58:6. He was not pleased with the way the Jewish people fasted. Theirs was a formal fast which they did only because that certain day was a special day to fast. It was kept in much the same way as the feasts were kept. There is a wrong way and a right way to fast. The Lord says the right way to fast is to have a burden, when something is heavy on our hearts. We fast then because this burden takes priority, to the point that food takes second place. The Lord knows our attitude, and He takes note of it.

Isaiah 58:8 tells us that fasting will affect three areas in our lives. Fast will affect us mentally, helping us to think clearly; it will affect our physical health; and it will enhance our spiritual life.

It is not in vain to refrain from food for a day or two, or even more. The Lord will richly reward us for it.

> **Bible Reading:** Isaiah 58
> **One Year Bible Reading Plan:**
> Luke 19:1-28
> 2 Samuel 7–9

LaVerne Yoder, Woodburn, KY

Mean business with God—fast!

Show Us the Father

Our Father which art in heaven, Hallowed be thy name.
Matthew 6:9b

I often marvel at the results of the earthly ministry and work of the Lord Jesus. In approximately three years' time, He touched the lives of thousands of people, meeting needs that no one else could. The reason for His great success was that He knew the Father. In our Scripture passage for today, Jesus mentions His Father thirteen times. His chief objective was to bring glory to the Father.

We live in a world and time in which there is little awareness of God. People live for themselves, and for their own satisfaction. This is not supposed to be true of the child of God, but how many times during the day do we think about God and His presence with us? Do we really believe that God is always here, and sees everything we do, hears everything we say, and even knows everything we think before we speak any words?

For a little personal exercise, check yourself during any one day. Throughout the day keep count of how often you consciously think about God. Try to work up to at least ten times a day. Do this for thirty days, and you will find you are spending more and more time thinking about God, His greatness, His faithfulness, and His love for His creation.

Bible Reading: John 14:1-14
One Year Bible Reading Plan:
Luke 19:29-48
2 Samuel 10–12

As we reflect on God's greatness, it implants within us a fear and a reverence for Him, which is so sadly lacking in our society, and yet so greatly needed.

Steve Stoltzfus, Kennedyville, MD

Being God-conscious is an incentive to holy living.

Turmoil or Surrender?

For the eyes of the Lord are over the righteous,
and his ears are open unto their prayers:
but the face of the Lord is against them that do evil.
1 Peter 3:12

Recently in our neighborhood there was an accident. A young, sixteen-year-old boy ran his car off the road into a yard and hit a tree. The car was totaled. He was trying to take his own life.

As I thought about that young boy, I wondered, What caused him to despair of living? In their search for happiness and fulfillment, people who do not have Christ living in their hearts try different things—sports, jobs, possessions, or other things that please them—leaving God out of the picture. When they face disappointments and troubles, they have no one to go to for help. They turn to tobacco, parties, strong drink, or drugs to try to forget their problems. These things give them a thrill for a while, but afterwards they leave a void and empty feeling, and a longing for more.

In contrast, the Christian serving God wholeheartedly has that deep satisfaction and peace that only Christ can give. When we face trials and temptations, we have Jesus for our refuge and strength. He is waiting for us, longing to help us.

Most of us have the privileges of being part of a Bible-believing church, of having Christian parents who are concerned for our souls, and of fellowshiping with friends who encourage us and help us in our weak points. Most of all, we have the power of God available to us. Let us keep our eyes fixed on Jesus and totally surrender our lives to Him.

Bible Reading: 1 Peter 3:9-22
One Year Bible Reading Plan:
Luke 20:1-26
2 Samuel 13, 14

Marlin Stoll, Clarkson, KY

The world has nothing to offer the soul that has once known God.

Emergency Warning!

But the day of the Lord will come as a thief in the night; in the which the heavens shall pass away with a great noise.
2 Peter 3:10

The hurricane may be here by morning! The warning spread across the country. Business doubled as people began stocking supplies to last through the expected duration of Hurricane Mitch. All day the sound of hammers was heard as people boarded up their houses. All other work was set aside in the urgency of preparation. After all, what good would it do to continue in one's routine, only to see the results blown away? We had to be ready! To not have been ready could have resulted in the loss of property, or even lives.

The Lord may be here by morning! Preachers shout the proclamation across the pulpits. Christian workers spread the message, and tons of literature warning of the upcoming event are distributed freely.

But alas! The response to the warning of Christ's return is very different from the response to the hurricane warning. Very few preparations are being made. There is little sense of urgency in the work. Mr. Jones lazily flips a line into the lake on Sunday morning, while Farmer Brown finishes planting his corn. After all, next week the bass might not be biting; it might be too wet to plant corn, also. It does not occur to them that all will be lost when Christ returns.

Mr. Beiler attends church regularly, but refuses to forgive Brother Dan. Young John refuses to dedicate his life fully to the Lord, afraid of the cost. Sister Ruth puts off speaking to the neighbor lady about her need of repentance, thinking that surely tomorrow will afford an easier opportunity. All three go to church most Sundays and sing with gusto, "Be Ready When He Comes!"

What would your reaction be if you knew that eternity for you would begin tomorrow? Is your life in order? Jesus is coming!

Michael Overholt, Belize City, Belize

Bible Reading: Luke 21:25-36
One Year Bible Reading Plan:
Luke 20:27-47
2 Samuel 15, 16

The future that we study and plan for begins today.
—Fischer

Corban

*Honour thy father and thy mother, as the L*ORD *thy God hath commanded thee; that thy days may be prolonged, and that it may go well with thee, in the land which the L*ORD *thy God giveth thee.*
Deuteronomy 5:16

"But ye say, If a man shall say to his father or mother, It is Corban, that is to say, a gift, by whatsoever thou mightest be profited by me; he shall be free" (Mark 7:11). Jesus rebukes the Jews who nullify God's commandment by their tradition. *In the Corban offering, a person dedicated his property to the Lord. When he died, his possessions became the Lord's property. The offering was abused by some who neglected to care for elderly parents by saying that they had no undedicated money with which to support them.*

While studying this passage for Sunday school, Jesus' teaching became clear to me. My responsibility to my parents includes caring and providing for them in time of need. Giving regularly to other people in need is good, but that does not free me of my responsibility to my parents.

If we took this commandment of God seriously, would the nursing homes be so full? I realize there are those folks who need more care than their children can give, but let's do our best. "My little children, let us not love in word, neither in tongue; but in deed and in truth (1 John 3:18).

Bible Reading: Mark 7:1-23
One Year Bible Reading Plan:
Luke 21:1-19
2 Samuel 17, 18

Glen Helmuth, Belvidere, TN

---

*Do we honor our parents as we desire
to be honored by our children?*

Italics portion was added by the publisher.

Lot's Choice

Set your affection on things above, not on things on the earth.
Colossians 3:2

Sheep bleating, oxen bellowing, servants arguing, tempers flaring. Enough of this, Abram decided one day. Drawing his nephew Lot aside he said, "I believe it's time we separate. There's lots of room out here. You choose yourself a portion of land, and I'll take what's left."

Lot's mind started spinning. "Hmmm, I get to have first choice! Let's see. . . . The valley of Jordan has excellent grazing, water is in abundance, lots of room, and places for trade. Economy looks good. Yes, yes, I'll take this side, the valley of Jordan.

The exciting thing about the story of Lot was that he could choose his own lot in life. Now he could have wealth and social position.

But what seemed to be a wise choice, led to the ruin of a righteous man's family. Lot's terrible mistake is recorded in Genesis 13:12: "And Lot dwelled in the cities of the plain, and pitched his tent toward Sodom."

Reality struck home when Lot lost his wife and some of his children because of his own lack of spiritual vision and discernment of God's direction. Lot's descendants, the Moabites and the Ammonites, were the result of a righteous man choosing to associate himself with the world. The same results will happen today to a righteous man who does not set his affections on things above, rather than things on the earth.

Kevin Miller, Auburn, KY

Bible Reading: Genesis 3:7-13; 19:1-14
One Year Bible Reading Plan:
Luke 21:20-38
2 Samuel 19, 20

Do not err, my beloved brethren.

Lord, What Wilt Thou Have Me to Do?

. . . Arise, and go into the city . . .
Acts 9:6

"Good morning, Lord. 'What wilt thou have me to do?'" Is that the prayer of your heart this morning?

The apostle Paul learned a lesson on the road to Damascus that we all must learn—the lesson of surrendering our will to God's will. Before his conversion, Paul was a zealous, energetic man of the straitest sect of the Pharisees. He thought that he ought to do many things contrary to the name of Jesus of Nazareth. Here was a man who thought he was doing what was right; but it was not until he prayed, "Lord, what wilt thou have me to do?" that he found God's will for his life.

Why is it so hard to pray for God's direction in our lives? Why are we afraid to commit everything to Him? Are we afraid that our lives will be endangered, or that God might ask something of us that we do not want to do, or require us to go where we do not want to go? Our reaction to God's calling demonstrates our sincerity in following Him. Notice Paul's reaction when Christ spoke to him on the way to Damascus. When he suddenly realized that he was working against God, he cried, "Lord, what wilt thou have me to do?" Without reserve, Paul began at once to follow God's instructions.

Do you find it hard to trade your plans for God's plans? How hard is it to trust God's judgment over your own, as Ananias did when God told him to go find Saul and restore his sight? This seemed very dangerous to Ananias. Yet, when God told him to go, he went.

"Oh Lord, help me today to trust You with my life. I want to meet You on Your terms and pray—Lord, what wilt thou have me to do?"

Kevin Miller, Auburn, KY

Bible Reading: Acts 9:1-24
One Year Bible Reading Plan:
Luke 22:1-30
2 Samuel 21, 22

The lordship of Christ, if you take Christ seriously, will guide you around many of the temptations and decisions over which most believers agonize.
—Robert A. Cook

O Taste and See That the Lord Is Good

O magnify the LORD with me, and let us exalt his name together.
Psalm 34:3

You must be a partaker of something to know that it is truly good. This is the way it is with the celestial treasures that man can experience. If we do not actually partake of the true riches that are attainable only in Christ, we will never know how truly good they are.

It is just like eating food. You look at something that appears very tasty, and predetermine that it is good. But do you really *know* that it is good?

A child cried at having to eat a small amount of something he had decided was not good, even though he had never tasted it. After he was forced to eat it, the child burst forth in tears once again because it was so good that he wanted more.

Are you a poor, hungry soul experiencing spiritual starvation? Come and be a partaker! If you will only come and taste of the goodness of God, you will surely cry for more!

Peter Whitt, Montezuma, GA

Bible Reading: Psalm 34:1-8
One Year Bible Reading Plan:
  Luke 22:31-53
  2 Samuel 23, 24

Blessedness consists in the satisfaction of our desires;
and, in only having the right desires.
— Augustine

_____

How Do You Gauge Unbelief?

He that hath my commandments,
and keepeth them, he it is that loveth me.
John 14:21

We sometimes hear expressions such as, "That Scripture is not relevant for our day," or, "That was written years ago in a different culture."

What commandments are we to keep? Jesus said, "My comandments." We are to keep all the commandments of Christ—both those He gave personally while on earth, and those He delivered through His messengers, the apostles.

In Hebrews 3:5-19, we are warned against being guilty of the unbelief of the Israelites. If you had asked them if they believed in God, they would have said, "Yes!" and they would have objected to being called unbelievers. And yet, they doubted God's commands and failed to obey God. Of all the large multitude of people who left Egypt, only two who were older than twenty entered the promised land. The rest could not enter because of unbelief.

How may I be guilty of unbelief? "Therefore to him that knoweth to do good, and doeth it not, to him it is sin" (James 4:17).

Honestly ask the question: Am I following God's Word, or are there some things that I would rather do differently, so that I do not always keep Christ's commands? I may even justify my actions with the argument that other professing Christians don't keep this or that command, and therefore I do not see why I should have to. We must always remember, we will be judged by what Christ has said, not by what people say or do.

| **Bible Reading:** Hebrews 3:5-19 |
| **One Year Bible Reading Plan:** Luke 22:54-71 / 1 Kings 1, 2 |

Paul A. Maust, Grantsville, MD

_____

If a man love me, he will keep my words.
—John 14:23

God's Way of Pruning

Every branch in me that beareth not fruit he taketh away:
and every branch that beareth fruit, he purgeth it,
that it may bring forth more fruit.
John 15:2

This past summer we put up a greenhouse to raise tomatoes. When it was done, we planted our seeds and gave them water and fertilizer. The seeds eventually sprouted, and from then on we watched the plants as they grew and checked them daily for disease and insects.

As they grew, little shoots called "suckers" appeared on the vines. These had to be removed, or they would affect the quality and quantity of the fruit.

One day as I was "suckering," I thought of Jesus' words in John 15. I realized that God must remove the "suckers" from my life for the same reason that I must remove the suckers from my tomato vines: "that it may bring forth more fruit."

We all have "suckers" in our lives that need pruning. Perhaps a "sucker" in your life is a sin that you have struggled with and want to get rid of. I have noticed that if I leave a sucker on the plant too long, it gets more difficult to remove. So it is with sins.

Bible Reading: John 15:1-8;
  Hebrews 12:1-13
One Year Bible Reading Plan:
  Luke 23:1-26
  1 Kings 3–5

Maybe you are faced with a difficulty or obstacle that seems to overwhelm you. God is probably doing some pruning. Maybe He sees an area in your life that is not completely yielded to Him. Yield your all to Him!

Oft we shrink from the purging and pruning,
Forgetting the husbandman knows
That the deeper the cutting and paring,
The richer the cluster grows.

Robert Burkholder, Monticello, KY

We need affliction to make us fruitful.

127

The Evidence of Things Not Seen

Now faith is the substance of things hoped for,
the evidence of things not seen.
Hebrews 11:1

The odds against Mordecai were unreal. His nation, the Jews, were captives of war in a foreign country. Their rights were extremely limited. But his anguish was caused primarily by the fact that Haman, who was second only to the king in power, wanted to annihilate his nation totally. What could Mordecai do?

Mordecai put his total trust in God to rescue His people. Two statements in Esther 4 reveal his faith. In Esther 4:14, Mordecai shows that he does not doubt that God will deliver the Jews from another place if Esther fails to act. Secondly, Mordecai challenges Esther, saying that it is likely that the providence of God has placed her in such a position, purposely to intercede for her people.

Mordecai's faith was "the substance of things hoped for, the evidence of things not seen." May we exercise faith like Mordecai's when the way gets difficult, and the future is dark. Let us always be sensitive to God's providential timings and opportunities, as Esther was, for we know that there is a divine purpose for each situation. "And we know that all things work together for good to them that love God, to them who are the called according to his purpose" (Romans 8:28).

> **Bible Reading:** Esther 4
> **One Year Bible Reading Plan:**
>   Luke 23:27-38
>   1 Kings 6, 7

Michael Jantzi, Kiev, Ukraine

Faith's answer to the question "How?" is one word, "God!"

Choices

Proving what is acceptable unto the Lord.
Ephesians 5:10

Life is filled with choices. Some are minor, the results inconsequential. Others have effects that continue for years, sometimes for the duration of our life on earth.

One of the driving forces behind our choices is the desire for approval. We see it in very small children, when they do something that makes us laugh. When they see that they have gained our approval, they do it again and again, hoping to receive the same recognition. When people yield to wrong peer pressure, this desire for approval is their primary motivation. This longing for the approval of others has more influence on our choices than most of us want to admit.

Ephesians 5:10 emphasizes the need for every child of God to turn from seeking the approval of people to being assured of God's approval on his choices. God's smile of approval is our most precious treasure. We should value it so highly that we can withstand any degree of shame or ridicule man might direct at us.

There is only one way that we can be assured of God's favor.

Bible Reading: Ephesians 5:1-21
One Year Bible Reading Plan:
Luke 23:39-56
1 Kings 8, 9

Verse 8 directs us to walk as children of light. First John 1:7 also insists on this, if we are to have fellowship with Him. Let us ask ourselves this very personal question: who do I desire to please?

Elmer Smucker, Lott, TX

God gives us the freedom to make our own choices,
but not the privilege to choose the consequences of those choices.

Wake Up!

Awake thou that sleepest, and arise from the dead,
and Christ shall give thee light.
Ephesians 5:14

Ringggg. The alarm clock goes off, telling you it's time to wake up. You push the snooze, and roll over and go back to sleep. Ten minutes later, **ringggg,** it goes off again. Again you push the snooze, roll over and go on sleeping. You do this three or four times; and you have lost half an hour. Did you allow for that half hour? Will you still be on time for your appointments? You'll have to get things done and meet your appointments by being late for some and putting others off; but, life goes on. What did you lose, more than half an hour?

Ringggg goes God's alarm clock. "Wake up; set your house in order." You rouse for a second, then push the snooze. "Not today, Lord." You go on doing your own thing. **Ringggg.** God reminds you again, it's time to wake up. Again you push the snooze. "Not just yet, just a little bit longer." And you go on doing your own things. Again God reminds you. Again you make excuses. It's getting later. You are losing time. But, unlike the natural illustration, you cannot rush around in eternity and make up for lost time, or put some things off until tomorrow. Tomorrow, it will be too late.

Awake out of your sleep. Arise from dead works, and Christ's light will shine on and through you. Awake, and work for Christ!

Bible Reading: Ephesians 5:6-21
One Year Bible Reading Plan:
  Luke 24:1-35
  1 Kings 10, 11

Joe Miller, Belleville, PA

_____

Awake, Arise, and Shine.

Wisdom for All

But the wisdom that is from above is first pure, then peaceable,
gentle, and easy to be intreated, full of mercy and good fruits,
without partiality, and without hypocrisy.
James 3:17

Wisdom. What a packed word! I used to think that wisdom was something only old men had. I have learned that it is something for young men as well. Webster's says *wisdom* is "good judgment; learning; knowledge, etc." A friend gave me a definition that I like even better. He said, "Wisdom is knowing how to apply knowledge to everyday living." This wisdom is found in James 3:17—the wisdom from above.

What is the wisdom from above? It is the wisdom we receive from hearing God's Word. It will help us to make good decisions. James says that this wisdom is peaceable. As we go about our duties each day, we often find that it takes wisdom to keep things peaceful. If we choose our words with wisdom, for example, that will help us to be better witnesses for Christ.

James also says that heavenly wisdom is without hypocrisy. True wisdom will be without a false front. Seek the heavenly wisdom that will help you make the right decisions throughout your day, and throughout the rest of your life.

Dwight Stoltzfoos, Kinzer, PA

Bible Reading: Proverbs 8:1-26
One Year Bible Reading Plan:
  Luke 24:35-53
  1 Kings 12, 13

The man who gains knowledge but does not conform his life to it,
is like a farmer who plows his field but never sows seed.
—Saadi (adapted)

Caught in the Sinful Act

But God commendeth his love toward us, in that,
while we were yet sinners, Christ died for us.
Romans 5:8

One day, some religious leaders brought before Jesus a woman who had been caught in adultery. They were intent on condemning her according to the law, but Jesus Christ was interested in freeing her and saving her from her sins. After Jesus challenged anyone sinless among them to cast the first stone, her accusers dispersed. Then He said to her, "Neither do I condemn thee: go, and sin no more" (John 8:11).

God's great revelation to Paul was that God does not wait for us to come to Him. His agape love does not wait until we are lovely. Any notion we might have about meeting God halfway, or making up for something Jesus has left undone, is mistaken. It is entirely God's doing.

Salvation is God's free gift to people who are as guilty and powerless to save themselves as that adulterous woman was. If Jesus did not die for us "while we were yet sinners," we would be sinners forever. As it is, we are still sinners, but with this crucial difference: When we believe in Jesus and become followers of Him, we are sinners saved by grace. We are set free from sin's power and condemnation by the God who reached out His loving arms and caught us in the sinful act. God demonstrated His own love for us in this: "While we were yet sinners, Christ died for us."

Bible Reading: Romans 5:1-8
One Year Bible Reading Plan:
John 1:1-28
1 Kings 14, 15

Ludlow Walker, Sr., Homestead, FL

None is deserving of salvation—it is a free gift!

People Pleasers?

For do I now persuade men, or God? or do I seek to please men?
for if I yet pleased men, I should not be the servant of Christ.
Galatians 1:10

Have you ever struggled with the fear of man? If your answer is yes, you are just like most people. Teenagers call it *peer pressure.* Adults call it *the fear of man.* The modern term is *codependency.* It can be summed up in two words: *people pleasing.*

Peter struggled with pleasing people. A young maid asked him if he had been with Jesus, and he denied Christ by saying, "I know not what thou sayest" (Matthew 26:70). He was controlled by his fear of others. In the same way, Saul, when confronted by Samuel for not destroying the Amalekites, and being reminded that rebellion is like the sin of witchcraft, said, "I have transgressed the commandment of the Lord . . . because I feared the people" (1 Samuel 15:24).

Why do we fear people? Because we lack faith. It is so much easier to listen to people we can see, than to obey the One whom we can't see.

When we yield to the fear of man, we are being controlled by others. But "God has not given us the spirit of fear, but of power, and of love, and of a sound mind" (2 Timothy 1:7). When we love Christ single-heartedly, that love removes the fear of men. God does not give us any allowances for people pleasing, but we are to serve others because we love them and Him.

James Miller, Evart, MI

> **Bible Reading:** Mark 14:66-72; 1 Samuel 15:1-25
> **One Year Bible Reading Plan:**
> John 1:29-51
> 1 Kings 16–18

Please people less and love people more.

I Can Face Tomorrow

As the living Father hath sent me, and I live by the Father:
so he that eateth me, even he shall live by me.
John 6:57

I can face tomorrow—because of the empty tomb. Death has lost its sting because Jesus lives.

I can face tomorrow—with all my limitations and handicaps; for God has said that His strength is made perfect in our weakness, and that He "hath chosen the weak things of the world to confound the things which are mighty."

I can face tomorrow—face a difficult task or a new challenge that I have never faced before, because Jesus said, "Nevertheless not my will, but thine, be done."

I can face tomorrow—through lean and hard times; for this world is not my home, but I am looking "for a city which hath foundations, whose builder and maker is God."

I can face tomorrow—serving God in other lands; for God will be with me, stabilizing me with His presence.

I can face tomorrow—though my home and worldly goods be taken; for the prophet Habakkuk said, though he should lose all, "Yet I will rejoice in the LORD, I will joy in the God of my salvation" (Hab. 3:18).

I can face tomorrow—with my body in pain and near death, for the Lord faced it. Then He overcame the power of darkness and rose triumphant from the grip of death and led captivity captive. I know my life here is but a vapor, and then I shall be with the Lord in eternity, for that is His dwelling, and He has prepared a place for me.

I can face eternity—for my sins are forgiven, and God will wipe away all the tears from my eyes.

Because of all these things— I can face tomorrow.

Arnold Willey, Abbeville, SC

Bible Reading: John 6:30-40
One Year Bible Reading Plan:
John 2
1 Kings 19, 20

We endure, seeing Him who is invisible.

Five Loaves and Two Fishes

There is a lad here, which hath five barley loaves,
and two small fishes: but what are they among so many?
John 6:9

Have you ever wondered just whom God uses to accomplish His plans? Do you ever feel that your gifts are few, your talents are limited, and you wonder if God can really use you?

Consider for a moment how the disciples must have felt in John 6. After crossing the Sea of Galilee, expecting to find peace and quiet, instead they faced a great multitude of people. Later, as the day was ending, a great need became obvious. Exactly how should they feed thousands, especially in the countryside?

Andrew, one of Jesus' disciples, informed Jesus that there was a lad in the crowd with five loaves and two small fishes. The disciples thought, *How could this possibly be a solution?* However, Jesus had a lesson in mind.

Why did Jesus choose to feed a huge crowd with one willing boy's lunch? Why not call the nearest food relief agency, or send the people home?

Similar incidents occur over and over again throughout the Bible. Gideon, for example, was instructed to organize an army to fight against a great enemy. Would 32,000 trained soldiers be enough? Gideon thought so, but God had other ideas. Over 99% of Gideon's original army was sent home. Even though the task seemed ridiculously large, God accomplished His plan through Gideon's small band.

God specializes in using small things. Why? Because He then receives the greater glory! Are you willing to be used?

Mark Petersheim, Abbeville, SC

Bible Reading: John 6:1-13
One Year Bible Reading Plan:
John 3:1-21
1 Kings 21, 22

Little is much when God is in it.

Hell

In flaming fire taking vengeance on them that know not God,
and that obey not the gospel of our Lord Jesus Christ.
2 Thessalonians 1:8

Mainstream Christianity prefers to stay away from the subject of hell. It makes people uncomfortable when the preacher says that God will cast unbelievers and liars into a lake that burns with fire and brimstone (Matthew 13:41, 42 and Revelation 21:8). So instead, they have their preachers talk only about God's great love. He *is* merciful, longsuffering, and slow to anger, and, on top of that, He loves every person. If that was all that I knew about God, I wonder how highly I would value His love. I would think that He was a very nice God, but I might not be all that interested in dedicating my life to Him, either.

God's love becomes precious when a person realizes that if God had not rescued him, he would have spent eternity in hell. God did not owe that rescue to us. He simply loved us and did not want anyone to be lost eternally. God did not make hell for the punishment of people. Hell was prepared for the devil and his angels (Matthew 25:41).

The more we really understand what we are saved from, the more dedicated we become to serving God out of gratitude, rather than duty. We also have a greater burden for the lost. Let us not forget what God has saved us from, and the future that awaits those who do not know God.

Bible Reading: Luke 16:19-31
One Year Bible Reading Plan:
John 3:22-36
2 Kings 1–3

Barry Hochstetler, Hicksville, OH

Remembering the bad makes us appreciate the good.

Lord Willing

For that ye ought to say, if the Lord will,
we shall live, and do this, or that.
James 4:15

While we have a very limited knowledge of what lies ahead, our great sovereign God knows the future just as well as the past. God sees fit not to reveal the future in detail to us.

Luke 12:16-21 tells of a rich man who made grand and selfish plans for the future. He planned to lay up many treasures and then to enjoy a life of ease and pleasure. His plans never materialized, however. That very night he died, and his wealth was left for someone else. If he would have acknowledged that his increase was from God, and would have given it to the poor, he could have been blessed. The Bible promises many blessings for those who give to the poor and needy.

James 4:15 tells us that all our plans should be made in submission to the will of God. It is not wrong to make plans for the future. Many times it is practical and necessary; but we must always give God the right to change our plans, if He sees fit.

The Scriptures do not say that in every detail we must always actually say, "If the Lord will," but that we must always have that attitude. However, we do well to express that attitude verbally.

Let us submit our plans to the Lord and allow Him to give His blessing as He sees fit.

John Glick, Gap, PA

Bible Reading: Luke 12:13-31
One Year Bible Reading Plan:
John 4:1-30
2 Kings 4, 5

I know Who holds tomorrow, and I know Who holds my hand.

May 13

Are You "Just a Housewife"?

*Favour is deceitful, and beauty is vain: but a woman
that feareth the LORD, she shall be praised.*
Proverbs 31:30

Sometimes when asked about their occupation our dear wives reply, "I'm just a housewife."

A while ago I heard a story about a mother who went to hear a well-known evangelist. After the altar call was given and many responded, she told the counselor that she feels like she has done nothing for the Lord except take care of housework, sew clothes for her family, and help her husband. With tears she said she was old, and her family had all grown and married. All were Christians. Some were ministers, and some were missionaries. She felt like she had done so little compared to the minister who held meetings. Many people had been saved through His preaching the Word.

The evangelist looked at the woman and said, "Woman, you have taught your children well and have been a good example to them. They have turned out to love and serve the Lord, and yet you say you have done nothing! I would be glad to trade crowns with you when we get to heaven."

Dear godly mothers, do not think your job is unimportant. It thrills my soul to see godly mothers who love and care enough for their families to remain at home rather than seeking this world's fortune. I greatly appreciate the teaching of my godly mother.

> **Bible Reading:** Proverbs 31:10-31
> **One Year Bible Reading Plan:**
> John 4:31-54
> 2 Kings 6–8

John Hostetler, Auburn, KY

An ounce of mother is worth a ton of clergy.

Volunteer for Jesus

And David said to Saul, Let no man's heart fail because of him;
thy servant will go and fight with this Philistine.
1 Samuel 17:32

As I ponder Goliath's defiant challenge to Israel, I am inspired by David's response. Here was Goliath, over nine feet tall and a man of war from his youth. Not one of the soldiers in Saul's army was willing to fight this huge man! Yet David volunteered to go and fight with Goliath. He was confident that God, who had helped him kill the lion and the bear, would also help him kill this giant Philistine, who had defied the armies of the living God.

Volunteers for God fill the Bible's pages. Ruth threw herself whole-heartedly into supporting Naomi. Under Ezra, the elders of Israel reconstructed the temple to the honor of God and, later, Nehemiah volunteered to rebuild the walls of Jerusalem—a complicated job involving challenges from several different quarters. Isaiah responded to the Lord's "whom shall I send?" by volunteering enthusiastically, "Here am I, send me!"

The Good Samaritan's voluntary mercy shows what blessings our service may bring to others. One day we were traveling on a large highway, and we saw a man who had a flat tire. We stopped and helped him change his tire. He told us afterward that he had just had a hip replacement, and he was afraid he might have problems and not be able to get up by himself if he bent over far enough to change the tire. He was very thankful that we had stopped.

Of course, Jesus was the greatest volunteer. Take His example, and volunteer to do whatever God would have you to do.

Bible Reading: 1 Samuel 17:32-54
One Year Bible Reading Plan:
John 5:1-24
2 Kings 9–11

Joe Gingerich, Plain City, OH

Wherever there is a human need,
there is opportunity to do a kind deed.

Knocking!

But prayer was made without ceasing of the church unto God.
Acts 12:5

The night was dark. The birds were quiet. Nature was resting. The prison was shut, locked, and guarded. The soldiers inside were also resting, convinced that their prisoner could not escape.

Somewhere in a house on a small street in the slumbering city, a band of believers was knocking from the depths of their hearts on heaven's door for one of their own.

On a dirty prison floor someone was calmly sleeping, chained to Roman guards. His life was in God's hands, and this thought brought him security and peace. But down that small street in the city people continued "knocking." The men in prison slept on, unaware of the knocking.

But the knocking was heard in heaven. God heard, and He acted. In the prison a light was seen. It radiated from an angel, who woke the prisoner. The prisoner stood, while his fetters clanged to the prison floor. He put on his sandals and garment; he was led out of the jail to freedom. While the "knocking" of his friends continued, he made his way through the sleeping city, until he arrived at the house where they were.

How persistent are you in your "knocking"? Does it get heaven's attention? In the parable of the persistent widow, Jesus teaches us to persevere in prayer to our heavenly Father. He also assures us of success in prayer, saying, "And shall not God avenge his own elect, which cry day and night unto him?" (Luke 18)

Our story in Acts underscores the importance of patient persistence in prayer. The iron gate of the prison swung open of its own accord for Peter, yet he must patiently knock on the door of his friends' house to be permitted entrance.

Be steadfast and faithful! Keep knocking!

Philip Beachy, Millersburg, OH

Bible Reading: Acts 12:1-19
One Year Bible Reading Plan:
John 5:25-47
2 Kings 12–14

God's resources are always greater than man's requirements.

Ichabod or Emmanuel?

*Let us hear the conclusion of the whole matter: Fear God, and
keep his commandments: for this is the whole duty of man.*
Ecclesiastes 12:13

Her husband? Dead. Her father-in-law? Dead. Thirty-four thousand noble soldiers? Dead. The ark of the covenant? Gone. Her newborn son's name? "Ichabod" — "The glory is departed." Indeed, a sad state of affairs.

Israel not only lost the battle, they also lost their God. Why? They had neglected to maintain a healthy fear of God. What are the indicators that they no longer had a healthy fear of God? 1) The priests were sons of Belial — they knew not the Lord (1 Samuel 2:12). 2) Their high priest was passive and unrestraining (3:13). 3) The sacred ark in the tabernacle was removed from the holy of holies, which was to be entered only once a year by the high priest. 4) Israel put its trust in a religious object, rather than in God Himself. As a result of not fearing God as they ought . . . Ichabod: "The glory is departed."

In our Matthew reading, the impending birth of Christ is announced to the worried Joseph. "They shall call his name Emmanuel, which being interpreted is, 'God with us.' " Jesus embodied all the glory of the Godhead. As He is within us, we may also say, "The glory is with us." When Jesus is the sole resident of our hearts, we will fear God as we ought, and even men of "Ichabod" origin can declare, "Emmanuel!" — God is with us.

Who is the spiritual forefather of your life — Ichabod or Emmanuel? Has the glory departed, or is it present with you? Does the evidence of your life say "Ichabod," or is there sufficient evidence to proclaim "Emmanuel"?

Bible Reading: 1 Samuel 4;
Matthew 1:22-23
One Year Bible Reading Plan:
John 6:1-21
2 Kings 15–17

Ken Kauffman, Falkville, AL

*The fear of God precedes holiness,
produces trust, provides power, and preserves life.*

Beautiful Feet?

How then shall they call on him in whom they have not believed?
Romans 10:14

In China thirty thousand people come to know Jesus Christ as their Lord and Savior every day. "My," you say, "it won't take long, and that great, godless nation will be all Christian!" Think again! With a population of more than one billion, it will take over ninety-one years to reach every one of those precious souls for whom Christ died.

It is no wonder that the feet of those who preach the Gospel of peace are called "beautiful." Our Father in heaven yearns for all humanity to hear the good news of salvation, which He freely offers to all who will receive it. However, He depends on Gospel workers' feet to go into all the world (Mark 16:15) with the greatest message ever told. Those who have heard and responded to the Gospel testify to the "beautiful" feet of missionaries who brought them the salvation message.

Prime time television, the radio news, the front page of every newspaper in every nation on the face of the whole earth ought to be devoted to telling the Good News, that Jesus Christ came to redeem sinners and to call out a people for the kingdom of heaven.

But the news media is silent about the great eternal truth, being devoted to merely telling what happened yesterday, and will be forgotten tomorrow. So then, our Lord Jesus is depending on our feet to take the good news of salvation into a desperately needy world and to make disciples of all nations, until that day when He comes to gather His own unto Himself in glory. Will He tarry ninety-one years?

Bible Reading: Romans 10:11-18
One Year Bible Reading Plan:
John 6:22-44
2 Kings 18, 19

Eli Kauffman, Montezuma, GA

Freely ye have received, freely give.
—Matthew 10:8b

How Often With God?

Every day will I bless thee.
Psalm 145:2

Early morning seems to be the best time for private fellowship with the Lord in Bible reading and prayer. If we bathe our minds and souls in the Word first, before involving ourselves in the daily rounds of duty, we are better prepared to cope with whatever comes along. When the unexpected presents itself, our responses have already been made alone with God.

This reminds me of a an older brother's remark one Sunday morning. He said, "Reading the Bible is like going down to the spring for a drink of fresh water. It is so pure and so refreshing."

I remember another church-going man who remarked that he had faith strong enough, that reading the Word and going to church only on Sunday is enough to take him through the whole week. For him, needing Bible reading during the week represented a lack of faith.

I observed the lives of these two men.

The first man had five sons. Four of them were called to the ministry. Twelve or more of his grandchildren are in the ministry, too.

The second man's later years were not so pleasant. His wife rejected him, and he lived the life of a near-beggar.

We must keenly sense our need to commune daily with God and daily to receive His grace for living. We have no strength in ourselves, but God gives His power freely to those who humbly acknowledge their need and meet Him continually to accept His grace.

Let us develop a thirst for His fresh water!

Andy Miller, Leitchfield, KY

Bible Reading: Psalm 6
One Year Bible Reading Plan:
John 6:45-71
2 Kings 20–22

The Bible is like a telescope; it is not to look at, *but to look* through.

*May 19*_____

Christ Denial or Self-Denial?

*Whosoever shall deny me before men, him will I also deny
before my Father which is in heaven.*
Matthew 10:33

The line snaked ahead of me. Our family was visiting the Air and Space Museum in Washington, D.C., and I was waiting in line to buy tickets for the 2:30 event. The line moved slowly. It was almost 2:15, and I was getting impatient.

Suddenly I saw a gap in the line. A group of foreign tourists was having a discussion and momentarily failed to advance. I ducked under the barricades and stepped to the front of the line. Furtively glancing around, I congratulated myself on having pulled off this maneuver, when a loud voice spoke up from the back of the crowd.

"Hey, weren't you at the back of the line?" I turned and nodded dumbly. "That's not fair!" she said in a withering tone. "I have four children . . ." I began weakly. "We have family too!" she retorted. The whole line was watching. The ticket lady was waiting. I took my ill-gotten tickets and hurried away with a flushing face.

My first concern was for myself. I quickly lost myself in the crowds. My next concern was for my wife. If this lady saw us together, would my wife's character be called into question? I decided not to tell my wife about the situation. Next, I thought of the church. Perhaps I was the first Mennonite this lady ever saw. Maybe her opinion of all the plain people will be colored by this encounter. (I'm sorry about that.)

Walking through the crowds, the truth hit me. I had been concerned about my reputation, my wife's, and the church's. But what about God's reputation? By my actions I had denied the sweet, gentle Christ. I had dishonored the Name of God. The Lord has forgiven me, but the shame of that incident remains.

Bible Reading: Luke 22:54-62
One Year Bible Reading Plan:
John 7:1-31
2 Kings 23–25

Ken Miller, Stuarts Draft, VA

_____

In the wake of your presence, will people say, "I saw Jesus in you"?

Christ's Teenage Years

And Jesus increased in wisdom and stature,
and in favour with God and man.
Luke 2:52

Have you ever wondered about what Jesus did as a boy? I like to think of Him playing games with other children. I believe He was always fair and looked out for the good of others.

We know very little about the early years of Jesus' life. In verse 40 of our Bible reading, we see that as Jesus grew, He waxed strong in spirit. He was also filled with wisdom, and the grace of God was upon Him.

If you are a teenager, this devotional is especially for you. If you have already passed through this stage, please encourage some teenager with this challenge. How did Jesus spend His teen years? Look, teenager, at verse 52.

Jesus increased in wisdom: not human wisdom, but wisdom from God. The fear of the Lord is the beginning of wisdom. Teenager, fear the Lord. Follow the example of Jesus and increase in wisdom.

Jesus increased in stature. It is a normal part of life to grow taller, older, and more mature. Jesus also faced these changes and challenges in His life. You do not need to rebel against these changes in your life even if you do know some grumpy adults. God's wisdom will enable you to accept and respond in a Christ-like manner to the changes that come during your teenage years.

Jesus increased in favor with God and man. Jesus did not sow wild oats. He was careful to please God with His life. He filled His teenage years with deeds that gave Him favor with God. Notice, too, that Jesus increased in favor with man—He must have been always a blessing to His parents, as He sought to please them.

Ask God to help you grow in godly wisdom. As you grow older, follow God's plan for your life, and you will experience God's blessings.

Bible Reading: Luke 2:40-52
One Year Bible Reading Plan:
John 7:32-53
1 Chronicles 1, 2

Mark Webb, Hicksville, OH

Am I increasing in wisdom and in favor with God and man?

May 21

Service and Worship

They that worship him must worship him in spirit and in truth.
John 4:24

The Samaritans insisted that Mount Gerizim was the proper place to worship God. The Jews insisted that He could only be approached in the Temple at Jerusalem. But Jesus told the woman at the well that the time was at hand when a totally new worship experience would become the standard. All men would worship God in spirit and in truth.

God is a Spirit. Man is spirit in the inmost part of his being. This inner being cries out to God. Within man's spirit, faith reaches out to God and makes contact with Him. This faith, however, must affect our daily life and work, our goals, our jobs, and all our home and community life. It produces a commitment to God in service, and a Christ-like love and compassion toward our fellowman. It creates within us a desire to serve God.

The Samaritan woman experienced this desire to serve Jesus. She left her water pot and immediately went into her home community, telling of her experience at Jacob's well. She had great news to share, which delighted many people.

We cannot separate worship and service. They go hand in hand. Our Sunday morning worship service should be a special time to celebrate our week of problems, trials, victories, and service; rejoicing in the overcoming life in Christ Jesus!

Bible Reading: John 4:19-26, 39-42
One Year Bible Reading Plan: John 8:1-20
1 Chronicles 3–5

Ben Coblentz, Millersburg, OH

Worship the Lord in the beauty of holiness.

A Beautiful House or a Christian Home?

*Except the L*ORD *build the house, they labour in vain that build it:*
*except the L*ORD *keep the city, the watchman waketh but in vain.*
Psalm 127:1

Have you ever watched a house go through the stages of construction? The foundation is poured and then the walls are framed. The house is plumbed and wired and, later, fixtures, cabinets, and floor coverings are put in place. The result? A beautiful house. But, it is only a beautiful house.

A beautiful, Christian home is different. Its foundation is Jesus Christ. Its blueprint is His commands. Daddy is foreman, and Mamma the assistant foreman. The materials for building are not loads of lumber, but the fruit of the Holy Spirit: love, joy, peace, long-suffering, gentleness, goodness, faith, meekness, and temperance.

While the family builds, Satan sits on a nearby hill, waiting for an opportunity to slip in some faulty materials: adultery, uncleanness, idolatry, hatred, variance, strife, envy, and other similar rotten materials. If the builders allow any of the enemy's stuff to go into the building, they will have to do some remodeling on that wing. Evil walls have to be torn down, and bad wood replaced with God's good timbers. If the rooms are abandoned, but never properly remodeled, Satan will find them empty and occupy them. He'll bring with him other tramps, who will make the place worse than it was before!

But enough on the enemy! Think of the beauty of a spiritual home built on Christ. If Dad and Mom follow His blueprints, and build with strong, biblical timbers, they will have a beautiful home indeed. And it will be able to withstand the enemy's attacks. It's walls will be filled with love—yes, love in every room. I like to watch that kind of home being built!

Andrew M. Troyer, Conneautville, PA

Bible Reading: Revelation
3:11-22; Matthew 12:43-45
One Year Bible Reading Plan:
John 8:21-36
1 Chronicles 6, 7

I'd rather live in a cardboard shack that houses a Christian
home, than in a mansion that is only a beautiful house.

Exposing the Enemy

(For the weapons of our warfare are not carnal, but mighty through God to the pulling down of strong holds;) Casting down imaginations, and every high thing that exalteth itself against the knowledge of God, and bringing into captivity every thought to the obedience of Christ.
2 Corinthians 10:4, 5

Included in the effective armory of a Christian is a clear conscience. The lack of it gives the enemy an opportunity to gain the advantage and build an enemy fortress in your life. Once established there, he will wreak the havoc of retreat and defeat in your life.

Those who humble themselves by confessing and forsaking sin receive God's grace and the power of a clear conscience. They pull down strongholds stone by stone. Deceptions from false conclusions are replaced with a godly perspective and spiritual discernment.

Turn deaf ears to the rationalizing thought that God does not quite mean what He says. Bring your thoughts under the control, the liberation, and the unction of the Holy Spirit. As our thoughts become coordinated under His supreme command, they become lethal in counter attack against an identified, exposed, and real enemy, the arch-deceiver, Satan!

Bible Reading: Ephesians 6:10-18
One Year Bible Reading Plan:
John 8:37-59
1 Chronicles 8–10

Frederick Helmuth, Piedmont, OH

If you have no conflict—be alarmed!
When there is conflict, identify the real enemy.

Guiding Lights

. . . Speak the same thing . . . be perfectly
joined together in the same mind.
1 Corinthians 1:10

Between mainland Australia and the island state of Tasmania lies Bass Strait, a wild and turbulent body of water. In the days of sailing ships, many a vessel came to grief along the coasts of this region. Bass Strait contains a number of islands, whose shores are littered with wrecks. Flinders Island, at the eastern edge of Bass Strait, is said to have almost two shipwrecks for every mile of the entire length of its 200 mile coast line. This is hardly surprising, given the storm tossed ocean and driving winds which prevail in the strait. But it is suspected that the elements are not solely to blame for this. It is thought by many that the wild strait men who lived on Flinders Island in the 1800's lured many a ship aground by the use of false signals, so they could plunder the wrecks. They kept the lights along the shore, in order to deceive and lead innocent people to destruction.

The port of Warrnambool lies on the north of Bass Strait. Situated high on a hill above the harbor is a beacon. A vessel attempting to enter the harbor needs to have the beacon and two other lower lights in alignment. When all three are in alignment, the weary traveler knows that it is safe to proceed. If there is no alignment, there is danger!

God has given us His Word as a sure beacon. And there are two lower lights, which we must keep aligned with that beacon: our relationship with our brothers in Christ and our own conformity to God's Word.

Are _you_ in alignment with the _Word_ and your _brethren_, showing a safe channel for others to enter? If we are out of alignment, chances are we may be like those wild strait men, confusing others and leading them to destruction. Oh, how terrible!

Bible Reading: Ephesians 4:1-16
One Year Bible Reading Plan:
John 9:1-23
1 Chronicles 11–13

Peter McGrath, Victoria, Australia

Arise, shine; for thy light is come, and the
glory of the Lord is risen upon thee.
—Isaiah 60:1

From a Finger to the Head

Rejoice with them that do rejoice, and weep with them that weep.
Romans 12:15

Recently at work, I accidentally shot a nail through my finger. Not only did the finger suffer, but the whole body suffered also. Because the finger is attached to the body, its suffering hindered the productiveness of the rest of the members. The body began to sympathize with this invaded and penetrated member, so that healing could take place.

When we endeavor to meet the needs of suffering members, the whole body receives strength. A restored member, in turn, helps to increase the productivity of the rest of the body, and health and growth result. If the legs try to run faster than the feet can carry the body, the body will stumble. This is the message of Romans 12:4, 5. No matter how small the member, its importance is equal to that of the most prominent member.

Wounds must be purified and kept clean in order to heal properly. If a wound is exposed to the filth of the world, it may become deeply infected, and eventually have to be severed from the body. Let us work together, endeavoring to build up the kingdom rather than letting the filth of the world infect disunified members, tearing the body down. When the body is edified, encouragement takes place. An encouraged, healthy, active, ministering body is powerful in the kingdom of God, to the glory of Christ, the Head.

Bible Reading: 1 Corinthians 12:12-31
One Year Bible Reading Plan:
John 9:24-41
1 Chronicles 14–16

Brad Lester, Montezuma, GA

Through a schism the body may tear,
may we other's burdens bear.

Is Your Tongue Nonresistant?

*. . . Love your enemies, bless them that curse you, do good
to them that hate you, and pray for them. . .*
Matthew 5:44

We live in a society geared for self-defense. What message about self-defense are we sending to the world?

We say that nonresistance is the measuring stick of the spiritual stature of a body of believers, but often, when we think of nonresistance, we think of abstaining from military service. What about the tongue? How easy it is, when we are treated wrongfully or falsely accused, to lash back with sharp words of defense!

James tells us, in his epistle, "If any man offend not in word, the same is a perfect man, and able also to bridle the whole body" (James 3:2).

No one is able to control his tongue. We must allow the Prince of Peace to have full control of our lives. He not only gives us the power to control our tongue, but also helps us to love those who have wronged us. He was our perfect example of nonresistance. At the time of His betrayal, He could have called more than twelve legions of angels to His relief, but He offered absolutely no resistance. He promised to give us the wisdom from above, which is peaceable and easily entreated. With it comes God's control over the self-defensive tongue.

Bible Reading: Matthew 5:38-48; Romans 12:17-21
One Year Bible Reading Plan:
John 10:1-21
1 Chronicles 17–19

If Christ endured such intense suffering for us, should we not be willing to suffer patiently for His sake?

Delmar Miller, Loogootee, IN

*The first law of nature is to defend yourself.
The first law of grace is to deny yourself.*

Crept in Unawares

*Beloved, . . . I . . . exhort you that ye should earnestly contend
for the faith which was once delivered unto the saints.*
Jude 3

Jude paints a vivid picture of a people dominated by their passions and lusts, reveling in rebellion (verse 8), boasting in confusion and error (verse 16), and running greedily after reward (verse 11). An ugly picture, with which no Christian wants to be identified.

But note verse four, which says these people had "crept in unawares." They had entered stealthily and secretly by a side door. Jesus said, "He that entereth not by the door into the sheepfold, but climbeth up some other way, the same is a thief and a robber" (John 10:1). They had not entered by the Door, but neither had they come in boldly, introducing themselves as false teachers, blatantly promoting their errors. Rather, they identified themselves as "Christians," and, as wolves in sheep's clothing, they took up fellowship with the body of believers.

Such "filthy dreamers" still exist. They still love to be called "Christians" and "brothers in the Lord" while disregarding the Biblical call to holiness. They say: "Grace is freedom! We can do as we please and God's grace will cover it." They deny Christ's power to overcome sin, using His grace as a license for the lusts of the flesh.

We cannot endorse a large part of what the world calls "Christian" today. Let us beware, lest it affect us and dim our vision of God's high standard of purity and holiness for His people.

Bible Reading: Jude
One Year Bible Reading Plan:
John 10:22-42
1 Chronicles 20–22

"Wherefore by their fruits ye shall know them" (Matthew 7:20).

Nathan Kreider, Grandview, TX

One great security against sin lies in being shocked at it.

Who Pierced Your Ear?

*For ye are bought with a price: therefore glorify God
in your body, and in your spirit, which are God's.*
1 Corinthians 6:20

Who pierced your ear? Whose doorpost bears the imprint? Who bore the awl? The fascinating account of voluntary servanthood found in Exodus 21 has implications for us today. If personalized, it conducts us into the uninhibited freedom found in serving Christ. I cannot serve self, sin, and pleasure, and remain Christ's bondslave.

Slave. We don't like the word. It sounds so restrictive, but it's a reality. You are serving someone. You are not really your own boss. Someone is controlling what you do.

Serving self is so confining. Serving sin is so condemning. Serving Satan is so exhausting. But serving the Savior is so liberating.

Real freedom is to be liberated to serve the Liberator. Freedom is serving the One you love. Love is the decisive factor. If you love your master, you are free. You see, slavery is binding only if you don't like your master; it is freedom if you love Him.

This is your year of freedom—your year of jubilee. Declare your love and allegiance for the Master. Come before the judges—the congregation of the holy. Lay your head upon the bloodstained doorpost of Grace. Let the Master of Love pierce your ear with the awl of sanctification. You have been set apart as a bondslave—free to serve whom you love. The pierced ear reminds you of your commitment. It serves as a witness to others of the dignity of your position—a bondslave.

Bible Reading: Exodus 21:1-6;
Romans 8:1-14
One Year Bible Reading Plan:
John 11:1-16
1 Chronicles 23–25

Ken Kauffman, Falkville, AL

Fully surrendered, Lord divine; I will be true to thee.
C. H. Morris (1913)

Something Wrong?

*Up, sanctify the people, and say, Sanctify yourselves against
tomorrow: for thus saith the* LORD *God of Israel,
There is an accursed thing in the midst of thee, O Israel.*
Joshua 7:13

Have you been feeling defeated lately? Do you feel like everything is getting on top of you in your Christian life? Israel was defeated at Ai because there was sin in the camp. Only one man had taken of the accursed things, but that is all it took. They were being defeated by the Amorites.

God will never tolerate sin. Like the children of Israel, we cannot be victorious until we get the unclean areas in our lives taken care of.

Thank the Lord that there is forgiveness today, and that we do not need to be destroyed as were Achan, his family, and all his possessions. Christ's blood will cleanse you, if you but ask Him.

Why not do some earnest heart-searching? Is anything hindering your relationship with God? Up, and sanctify yourself!

Bible Reading: Joshua 7:10-26
One Year Bible Reading Plan:
John 11:17-46
1 Chronicles 26, 27

Michael Gerber, Millbank, ON

"Create in me a clean heart, O God!"
—Psalm 51:10

Leave the Treetops

And forgive us our debts, as we forgive our debtors.
Matthew 6:12

In my trade—managing and marketing other landowners' timber—I sometimes have to deal with less-than-appreciative neighbors.

One incident involved a sixty-five-year-old lady. Several treetops and some brush went over the property line onto her side. It was an accident on the part of our timber-cutter. The landowner who had engaged my services talked with the lady about it, and seemed to think that as long as we did not tear up any property corners, she could live with it. I left it at that and did not bother cleaning it up, because the landowner accepted full responsibility for the damage.

It came as a great surprise to me one day to find that this lady was very upset with me. Being the one in charge, I saw it as my duty to make amends for the damage. I went to speak with her.

The first thing she said was, "I'm so upset that I don't know if I'll ever get over it!"

I told her I was there to do whatever it took to restore peace. I mentioned money, clean-up, and building a new fence. She said there was nothing we could do to make it right. She said to leave everything as it was, so she could go up there and remind herself again and stew over it some more.

Sometimes, I have held onto the treetops of an unforgiving attitude. Sometimes, I have stewed over hurts, enjoying being the offended one. Jesus instructs us to clear the treetops away.

Bible Reading: Matthew
18:21-35
One Year Bible Reading Plan:
John 11:47-57
1 Chronicles 28, 29

I am so thankful for the complete peace and joy He gives when I allow Him to clean up the mess I have made and restore me to His fellowship.

David Lee Yoder, Russellville, KY

One pardons to the degree one loves.

Honesty

Let us walk honestly, as in the day; not in rioting and drunkenness,
not in chambering and wantonness, not in strife and envying.
Romans 13:13

Honesty is a must for every child of God. If you stick to the truth, you will always feel free. A dishonest man often talks himself into a trap, and he has to tell more lies to try to get out of it. A truthful person does not say one thing today and something different tomorrow. He is always free to say the same thing. Remember, it is possible to fool man part of the time, but you can never fool God; he even knows your thoughts and the intentions of your heart.

I think back to when I was a child. I remember that my father was so honest that it was embarrassing to me at times. But now I thank God for my father's honest example. Total honesty may be unhandy to this body of flesh, but it is well worth the cost. There is nothing more blessed than a guilt-free conscience.

If you make a habit of being honest in everything, honesty will become so much a part of your life, that it will even show on your face. All heaven will rejoice with you—the angels and God Himself will rejoice. Honesty will help you fight against the evil one, too. And think what a joy it will be for those who come in contact with you in everyday life! Let us walk in honesty, like children of the day!

Abner Overholt, Auburn, KY

Bible Reading: Romans 13
One Year Bible Reading Plan:
  John 12:1-19
  2 Chronicles 1–3

What your conscience says is more important
than what your neighbors say.

Gossiping Christians—Right or Wrong?

He that covereth a transgression seeketh love;
but he that repeateth a matter separateth very friends.
Proverbs 17:9

It seems like gossip has always been a problem in the church. Is it right or is it wrong?

After reading today's verses, I can only conclude that it is sin; and we need to call it sin. We need to recognize that gossip can destroy our souls and the reputations of those about whom we gossip.

Is that too strong? No! You will not think it is too strong when you realize the power of gossip; that it sends souls to hell, destroys churches, and wreaks havoc among Christian people. Consider the young people whose lives have been ruined because they became the subject of a church's gossip chain. Our Lord tells us in Mark 9:42, "And whosoever shall offend one of these little ones that believe in me, it is better for him that a millstone were hanged about his neck, and he were cast into the sea."

Let us realize the seriousness of gossip and think twice before we speak, and then, speak only if it will build up our brothers and sisters. Let us remember to be steppingstones and not stumblingblocks in each other's lives. If we would spend as much time praying for our brothers and sisters as we do talking about them, we would have a lot less to talk about.

Let us search our lives and ask God to forgive us where we have gossiped in the past. Let us purpose in our hearts to be builders and not destroyers in the kingdom!

May God bless!

David L. Mullet, Columbiana, OH

Bible Reading: Proverbs 16:3, 23-28
One Year Bible Reading Plan:
John 12:20-50
2 Chronicles 4–6

Gossip is a breeze stirred up by a few windbags.

*June 2*_____

For Whom Do You Work?

And whatsoever ye do, do it heartily,
as to the Lord, and not unto men.
Colossians 3:23

Do you like your job? Be careful who you ask this question. Some people will answer with a long list of complaints about their work. They are not appreciated. They don't receive enough wages and benefits. Their employer is taking advantage of them. A housewife may feel sometimes as though her life consists of an endless routine of dishes, cleaning, cooking, and washing, over and over.

We can see work either as a blessing or a curse. We must realize, however, that it is God's plan that we work to provide for our own needs, and also for others in need. This realization helps us do our work for the Lord, which tremendously boosts our attitude. Sure, your employer may take advantage of you. As a housewife, you may not be thanked regularly for your daily tasks. But you can be satisfied to know that you have done your best for the Lord. For whom do you work?

In Nehemiah 3, the names of those who rebuilt the wall of Jerusalem are recorded. Verse 5 says certain nobles did not put their "necks" to the work. We still have people today who refuse to work. In contrast to these lazy nobles, verse 20 says Baruch, son of Zabbai, tackled his job with real zeal. Baruch not only repaired his section of the wall, but he "earnestly" repaired it. He went beyond his duty and, apparently, repaired a large section of the wall. The Jews were able to build the wall in only fifty-two days, because some people had a mind to work. They were doing what God wanted them to do. They were not merely working for Nehemiah, they were working for the Lord. "Whatsoever thy hand findeth to do, do it with thy might." God has said that we must work. And He wants us to work for Him. We do not go to our jobs only to satisfy our employer or the customer, but the Lord. For whom do I work?

Mark Webb, Birmingham, AL

Bible Reading: Nehemiah 3:17-22; 4:1-6
One Year Bible Reading Plan: John 13:1-17
2 Chronicles 7–9

_____

Too many people stop looking for work when they get a job.

Giving Thanks for God's Love

For God so loved the world, that he gave his only begotten Son, that whosoever believeth in him should not perish, but have everlasting life.
John 3:16

I am thankful for the abundant life I have as a follower of Jesus Christ. The Christian life is not always easy, but it does give life incredible meaning and purpose. In Christ Jesus we find the only true reason for living, and we are called to serve Him. Loving Him places a burden in our hearts to love our fellow human beings, to extend the kingdom of God, and to disciple those around us (Matthew 28:19-20).

Have you spoken to any unbelievers lately? Usually, they want to know what we believers think about God. There is little to be gained by examining what philosophers and others think about God. This approach begins at the wrong point. Focus instead on God's viewpoint. What does God think of us? What does God see when He looks at me? The answer is found in John 3:17.

The words of Jesus in our reading for today give us a whole new perspective. Jesus says that God looks at us with great love, in the midst of His dislike for our sins. God regards His creatures with compassion and love in spite of their unworthiness. Through His mercy He has created a way of salvation by giving His most precious gift—His Son—at a cost of immeasurable pain and suffering.

> **Bible Reading:** John 3:16-21
> **One Year Bible Reading Plan:**
> John 13:18-38
> 2 Chronicles 10–12

Let us again give thanks to God for His marvelous love for all the world, and for His willingness to send His Son for us. Amazing grace!

Ludlow Walker, Homestead, FL

The love of God exceeds all human understanding.

June 4

Sand Burrs and Future Generations

*I went by the field of the slothful, and by the vineyard of the
man void of understanding; and, lo, it was all grown over
with thorns, and nettles had covered the face thereof,
and the stone wall thereof was broken down.*
Proverbs 24:30, 31

Our plot of land is small, but it is amazing how many weeds can grow there. While none of the weeds are desirable, most of them do not bother me too much except when they invade the garden. There they need to be removed. Elsewhere, they can be mowed, with one notable exception. The nettles and sand burrs must be pulled and destroyed; otherwise, the thorns will still be there for little feet to step into.

After considerable effort during the summer to eradicate this year's crop of nettles and sand burrs, I asked myself why I was going to so much trouble to get rid of the nasty things. After all, the children are not as little as they once were. It is not as though they are unable to help themselves if they step into something unpleasant. They might get a rude surprise, but they would still be able to pretty much take care of themselves if they picked up a few burrs.

Then this thought came to me: *if the Lord tarries, there will be oncoming generations.* We must make every effort to keep the weeds, thorns, and thistles under control. We need to make every effort to maintain a safe environment for our children's children, and all who will come after us until the Lord returns. Of course, we need to be concerned about more than just our land. We must also keep our homes, churches, and communities safe for future generations. God's people have a responsibility to those who will follow us.

Joe Schmucker, Haven, KS

Bible Reading: Genesis 3:1-19
One Year Bible Reading Plan:
John 14
2 Chronicles 13–16

---

*For the LORD is good; his mercy is everlasting;
and his truth endureth to all generations.*
—Psalm 100:5

Hope in Death

*Precious in the sight of the L*ORD* is the death of his saints.*
Psalm 116:15

Some years ago tragedy struck the home of our next-door neighbors (a family in our church), when their young daughter, who had just learned how to walk, was run over by the gas truck and killed.

The next morning after chores, I went to see if I could do something to help with the work. Upon arriving, our other neighbor (a non-Christian) also arrived to borrow a piece of machinery. I asked him if he had heard what had happened. He said he had not. So I told him. Immediately he went into a rage—cursing, swearing, screaming, and throwing his hat on the ground.

Meanwhile, I prayed for words to say to this man, and after what seemed like a long time, he finally calmed down. I assured him that all is well and the child is safe in the arms of Jesus and is free from all earthly cares.

He said that he realized that we are very religious, and that we can handle this better than he can, but, he said, "You know, sometimes I really wonder if there is a God, when things like this happen to people like you!"

Whenever one of our loved ones is taken from us, it causes pain and sorrow, because wherever love is, the parting is painful and hard. We can shed tears of joy, though, when we have the confidence that one more saint has arrived safely.

> **Bible Reading:** 2 Corinthians
> 5:1-10; 1 Corinthians 15:51-58
> **One Year Bible Reading Plan:**
> John 15
> 2 Chronicles 17–19

Let us look beyond the grave to heaven, where we shall part no more.

Delbert Farmwald, Monticello, KY

Sorrow not, even as others which have no hope.
1 Thessalonians 4:13

Christ's Burden

For he is our peace, who hath made both one.
Ephesians 2:14

Christ entreated the Father on behalf of all believers, praying, "Neither pray I for these alone, but for them also which shall believe on me through their word; that they all may be one; as thou, Father, art in me, and I in thee, that they also may be one in us" (John 17:20, 21).

See now the burden of His prayer—that we all abide in absolute unity, as the Father and the Son are one. What a great sin a person commits when he divides the unity and peace of the body of Christ. For Christ knew that dissension cannot come into the kingdom of God.

How do we react when our own personal ideas are contrary to the standards of the body of believers of which we are a member? Does the way we react promote peace and unity in the spirit?

Bible Reading: Ephesians 2:11-22
One Year Bible Reading Plan:
John 16:1-15
2 Chronicles 20–22

Lloyd Swartzentruber, Montezuma, GA

The preeminence of the church . . .
is in its oneness.
—Clement of Alexandria

Hope, the Anchor of the Soul

Which hope we have as an anchor of the soul.
Hebrews 6:19

You surely have noticed all the hopelessness in today's society. The son of the president of our state college committed suicide at the age of twenty-six. We wonder why so many take this route. The answer is simple: hopelessness.

Man's life is like a ship in the sea. During life's storms, we desperately need a good anchor to keep us from being blown away and wrecked. Discouragement makes our ship drift, and calls for putting down our anchor. We can see neither the anchor, nor the cable fastened to it, but by faith we know it is there, because it holds the ship steady. How wonderful that we can sink our anchor into the great rock of Jesus. The cable is passed from His heart to ours, and we can survive the worst of Satan's storms.

Why look for hope in prestige, money, or education? Real hope comes only through a surrendered life, humility, and a good education in God's Word. True hope is a desire fueled by confident expectation. It inspires us to live a pure and holy life.

Bible Reading: Hebrews 6:9-20
One Year Bible Reading Plan:
John 16:16-33
2 Chronicles 23–25

Keep on sailing with Jesus until you reach that heavenly shore and there drop your anchor for the last time.

Sam Nisly, Cullman, AL

May hope ever be a bright part of your life's equipment.
—Crowell

More Than I Can Count

Unto me . . . is this grace given, that I should preach
among the Gentiles the unsearchable riches of Christ.
Ephesians 3:8

An extremely wealthy man was being interviewed for a magazine article. The interviewer asked him several questions about the extent of his vast holdings in industry and commerce. Finally, the writer asked, "We'd be interested in knowing, just what is your net worth?"

The interviewer expressed surprise when the man responded, "I have no idea. I just know it's more than I can count."

I thought about that. That is a problem I know I'll never have. Imagine having more money than you can count! Then I thought, as a believer in Jesus Christ that does apply to me, spiritually.

Writing to the believers in Ephesus, Paul spoke of "the unsearchable riches of Christ." Our spiritual wealth is so vast that it cannot be measured. The word "unsearchable" literally means that which cannot be tracked. It appears one other time in the New Testament to describe God's judgments, which are far beyond our comprehension. Read Romans 11:33.

Feeling poor and helpless? Does it seem that everyone else is doing better than you? Then read Ephesians 3:8 again. You are wealthy! You have access to the unfathomable, inexhaustible, eternal riches of God. You can say about your spiritual riches in Christ, "I have more than I can count!"

We need a keen awareness that God wants to share with us the priceless treasures found in Jesus—we are rich beyond comparison!

Bible Reading: Ephesians 3:1-13
One Year Bible Reading Plan:
John 17
2 Chronicles 26–28

William Miller, Middlebury, IN

A man is rich according to what he is,
not according to what he has.
—Henry Ward Beecher

Seeking the Heart of God

But David encouraged himself in the LORD *his God.*
1 Samuel 30:6

David could have been terribly discouraged. Saul had sought his life, forcing him to flee to the land of the Philistines. Now in the land of the enemy, David went to battle against his own nation. He is sent home before the battle because the Philistines do not trust him. Returning home after three days of travel, he discovers his house and the houses of his loyal followers have been burned by the Amalekites. Their families have been carried away. Two of David's wives are among the captives. The final letdown comes when his followers begin to speak of stoning him.

David was a man after God's own heart, because he continually sought the heart of God. Instead of challenging God by asking, "Where are you?" he encouraged himself in the Lord his God. His daily desire toward God enabled him to endure very stressful experiences without doubting God. Many years before, he had trusted God to help him protect his sheep from the claws of the bear and lion. Later, when he had heard the roar of the giant, his response was the same: "The Lord will deliver." And now, as he leads a flock of people, he asks, "God, what shall I do?" When God instructs him to pursue, he pursues, and overcomes the Amalekite army. He carries home the spoil, not for himself, but for those communities of Judah among which he had found shelter when Saul was pursuing him. *David had been prepared, through years of seeking the heart of God, to be used by God even in the most difficult circumstances.* God can use best those who have practiced seeking the heart of God.

Bible Reading: 1 Samuel 30
One Year Bible Reading Plan:
John 18:1-23
2 Chronicles 29–31

Merle Beachy, Free Union, VA

God tests us to make us better, not bitter.

Italics portion was added by the publisher.

Victory for Temptations

*There hath no temptation taken you but such as is common to man:
but God is faithful, who will not suffer you to be tempted
above that ye are able; but will with the temptation also
make a way to escape, that ye may be able to bear it.*
I Corinthians 10:13

Have you ever wondered why Eve listened to and gave in to Satan's allurement? Can we learn anything from her mistake? Yes we can, and that is to say, "No," right away. Many people trifle with temptation, rather than immediately responding "no!" while they are at their strongest. Eve lingered by the tree. Let us not linger at the spot of temptation, but flee, as Joseph did. Joseph has been a real inspiration to me in this regard. He said, "No," and meant it. Then he ran from the source of temptation. This is also our secret to victory.

Jesus is our prime example in responding to temptation. He immediately quoted Scripture, and was always victorious. Hebrews 2:18 tells us that He understands our temptations and knows how to help and comfort us. His Spirit always immediately warns us when temptation arises, prompting us to say "no!" If we will follow His leading immediately, and remove ourselves from temptation's way, grace will flow into our lives in abundance.

Satan tells us that our temptation is different from other people's and that there is no way out. God tells us that all temptation is similar, and He always makes a way to escape.

We are in a battlefield between righteousness and sin. Idle minds are the devil's workshop, so let us fill them with God's Word, and we will have better reflexes to quickly say "no!" to Satan's lies.

Bible Reading: Matthew 4:1-11
One Year Bible Reading Plan:
John 18:24-40
2 Chronicles 32, 33

Samuel Nisly, Hartselle, AL

_____

Flee also youthful lusts: but follow righteousness.
—2 Timothy 2:22

Restoration

When we were enemies, we were reconciled
to God by the death of his Son.
Romans 5:10

Some years ago I was involved in some restoration work. We were restoring old houses to their original condition. The goal was never to remodel, but to restore. We were not to improve them with modern improvements, but to make them as near to the original as possible. Genuine, authentic, real, and original were the key words. We scrounged around a lot, looking for authentic yet usable materials to work with.

In our Scripture reading for today, we see Israel in a sorry, depraved state. But God promises to restore her to her earlier glory and honor.

Man originally was created in the image of God. Every day he experienced peace, beauty, love, and perfect communion with God. Because of sin, man fell into guilt, ugliness, hatred, and alienation from God. But God sent His Son, Jesus, to make a way for us to trade our guilt for peace, our ugliness for beauty, our hate for love, our estrangement from God for fellowship with Him and His people.

Is there guilt from sin in your life, discouraging circumstances or busyness blocking out the memory of God's goodness? Let us pray with David, "Restore unto me the joy of thy salvation" (Psalm 51:12). Praise God for restoration!

Bible Reading: Jeremiah 30:4-22
One Year Bible Reading Plan:
John 19:1-22
2 Chronicles 34–36

Roger Byers, Free Union, VA

Man can remodel, but only God can restore.

Jesus, Master

And they lifted up their voices, and said,
Jesus, Master, have mercy on us.
Luke 17:13

The simple phrase, "Jesus, Master," speaks volumes about the way in which a person views our Lord. There is a great difference between calling our Savior "Jesus" and calling Him "Master." Calling Him "Jesus" simply acknowledges His existence, but the name "Master" implies much more.

Many people know Jesus by name. They want to be called Christians. They desire the blessings of God and covet the privilege of being seen as "God's man." But it seems that they know Jesus by name only, for they retain command over their own lives.

Calling Him Master says that we are His servants. It declares that we have given Jesus the lordship of our lives. We have utterly given up our will, our self-motivation, and our identity for the cause of Christ. His purpose has become our purpose, His will has become our delight, and His kingdom has become our all-consuming passion.

Our own agenda must be traded for kingdom-building. Our life of ease must be traded for the life of the cross. Our house slippers must be traded for work shoes.

As servants, we must never seek to be noticed, never seek praise, and never receive the credit that man so desperately covets.

Are you willing to call Jesus "Master"? Call Him "Jesus" as your friend; "Master" as His devoted servant.

Michael Overholt, Isabella Bank, Belize

Bible Reading: Matthew 10:24-42
One Year Bible Reading Plan:
John 19:23-42
Ezra 1, 2

Service can never become slavery to one who loves.

I Don't Have Time

Redeeming the time, because the days are evil.
Ephesians 5:16

Imagine the ruler with the sick daughter earnestly imploring Jesus to come and heal her before she dies, and Jesus saying, "Oh, I don't have time. Can't you see that I am busy? Look at all the people thronging around me who also need help."

"Oh, I don't have time." How often have we used those words when someone asks us to do something? Can you imagine Jesus using them?

We move along in our somewhat self-centered lives and all of a sudden an unexpected funeral of a close friend or relative comes up, right in the midst of our busy schedule. Do we postpone our own things so that we can attend because we want to, or because it would reflect dishonorably on us if we didn't? It takes time to write that overdue letter or visit the sick or needy and the elderly. It takes time to live the Christian life and to study the Word. It takes time to raise a Christian family. God is grieved when we do not take time to love and serve Him.

Too often our excuses border on neglect, but we accomplish what we consider really important. Let us not come to the day of Christ with deep regret over the things we left undone, which we would have done, if we would have considered what was really important. The rewards of sacrifice for the benefit of others are manifold.

Bible Reading: Ecclesiastes 3:1-15
One Year Bible Reading Plan:
John 20
Ezra 3–5

Wilmer Beachy, Liberty, KY

A time to be born and a time to die . . .
but there is an interval between these of infinite importance.
—Richmond

What a Price to Pay!

He that covereth his sins shall not prosper: but whoso
confesseth and forsaketh them shall have mercy.
Proverbs 28:13

The mighty fortress of Jericho was now a pile of smoldering ashes, and the children of Israel were ready to move on. Since the next town was a small one and the road was mostly uphill, only a small group of men was sent to take Ai. Unfortunately, the Israelites suffered a crushing defeat, which quite unnerved them. As a result of this battle, "the hearts of the people melted, and became as water."

Joshua cried out to the Lord, asking for wisdom in this hour of crisis. He received an unexpected answer: there was sin in the camp! "Israel hath sinned . . . therefore the children of Israel could not stand before their enemies."

This Old Testament story illustrates a principle that is still true today. Sin must be dealt with before God's blessing can rest on our lives. Unconfessed sin brings disaster and defeat. It is not unusual for Christians to have blind spots in areas related to unconfessed sins of the past. These sins have far-reaching consequences, and warped thinking patterns are among the side effects. The Scriptures plainly tell us that deception will be rampant in the last times. The enemy of our souls is apparently permitted access to our thinking patterns in areas where we have not completely cleaned house.

It is worth the effort to ask our heavenly Father if there is a forgotten and unconfessed sin in some defeated area of my life. We must then be faithful to do what needs to be done so that our eyes may be opened to more. Deception is a terrible consequence of unconfessed sin.

Bible Reading: Joshua 7:1-12
One Year Bible Reading Plan:
John 21
Ezra 6–8

J. Samuel Nisly, Partridge, KS

_____

Calvary's blood cannot cover what we fail to uncover.

Daddy, Where Are You Going?

_But thou, O man of God, flee these things; and follow after
righteousness, godliness, faith, love, patience, meekness._
1 Timothy 6:11

As we were traveling the long distance home, the ride became
a bit trying for our six-year-old son. His uneasiness grew as the sun
set behind us. Finally, from the back seat came a few questions:
"Dad, how long till we get home? Is this the same road that we
came on? Is this road going to get us home? Daddy, are you sure
you have enough gas?"

I assured him that there was enough fuel, that it would not be
long before we got home, and that we had a map along to show us
the way home. His fears were calmed, and soon he was fast asleep,
after having put his trust in his father.

Meditating on this conversation with my son, I became aware
in a new way of the responsibility that I have to my children. Do I
take seriously enough my responsibility to teach my children? Am
I portraying to my children the image of their heavenly Father?
What a responsibility and privilege!

As fathers, we need continually to pattern our lives after the
heavenly Father, putting our trust in Him. We must get into the
Bible (the map) and spend time there until we know the way home.

Our children know where our interests are. They can see which
book or magazine we spend the most time with. We cannot con-
vince them that they are precious to us if we are gone evening after
evening pursuing business. If our hobbies come before helping in a
church work night, will they believe that we are interested in building the church of Jesus Christ?

Paul's instructions to Timothy (1 Timothy 6:11-21) contain good
directions for the difficult jour-
ney we are making. Let us take
our responsibility and calling seriously, and carefully refer to the
map.

Bible Reading: 1 Timothy 6
One Year Bible Reading Plan:
  Acts 1
  Ezra 9, 10

Dennis Eash, Free Union, VA

_Oh, for a closer walk with God, A calm and heavenly frame,
A light to shine upon the road that leads me to the Lamb!_
—William Cowper

Broken Pitchers

I can do all things through Christ which strengtheneth me.
Philippians 4:13

The story in Judges 7 is exciting! And yet looking at it from Gideon's viewpoint, it must have been scary. God asked him to fight with only 300 men against a great host of trained men! The odds were against Gideon. He did not stand a chance to win.

How very much like the Christian today! The pressures of life come in swift and strong, needing attention. Wickedness becomes more and more open and accepted. And what can we do about it?

In our own strength we can do nothing. But wait, there is hope! There is a way by which we can have the victory Gideon had! How? Notice verse 20. Gideon's men blew their trumpets; they broke their pitchers; they held up their lamps; and they shouted!

Let us proclaim the goodness of God far and wide! Let us break our pitchers of selfishness, fleshly desires, and pride. God can use us only after we are broken.

The pitchers that Gideon's men held hid their lights. They had to be broken. If our pitchers of self-will and pride are still in one piece, they will hide our light. Only as we are broken, can we hold up the Light of lights, Jesus our Savior. He is the only One who can light my candle and make it shine!

Then, and only then, can we have the victory! Praise His name!

Bible Reading: Judges 7:9-21
One Year Bible Reading Plan:
Acts 2:1-13
Nehemiah 1–3

Stephen Beachy, Huntland, TN

I asked a man what made his life so radiant. He answered,
"Looking. Looking always toward the Light."
—Anonymous

Wrestling With God

But without faith it is impossible to please him:
for he that cometh to God must believe that he is,
and that he is a rewarder of them that diligently seek him.
Hebrews 11:6

"Man's greatest wrestling match is not with the devil, but with God." In this morning's text Jacob wrestled with God. When he began, he was Jacob, a deceiver: one who catches another by the heel. When he had finished, he was Israel, a prince of God.

Have you ever wrestled with God? God has a high calling for us. He wants us to be holy. But often, God's sanctification requires us to do exactly what we do not want to do. As God works on us where we need it most, sanctification becomes a battle within us. Are we going to submit to God, or not? That is life's greatest battle. Once we submit to God, we are able to serve Him with strength— as Jacob did after Bethel.

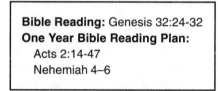

Bible Reading: Genesis 32:24-32
One Year Bible Reading Plan:
Acts 2:14-47
Nehemiah 4–6

If God is in control, we have power to overcome the evil one and grace to do what Christ asks of us. Praise be to God! May we, like Jacob, when we find ourselves wrestling with God, come away different men.

Lawrence Overholt, Russellville, KY

Our natural powers can be used mightily by God,
but only when we think nothing of them.
—Knight

June 18

The Measure of Success

*. . . that thou mayest observe to do according to all that is
written therein: for then thou shalt make thy way
prosperous, and then thou shalt have good success.*
Joshua 1:8b

The minister of a large American church was visiting overseas and was invited to speak to a small Christian group. In the course of his remarks, he boasted about the size of his church in America. "We have a church of two thousand members," he boasted. "Why, we even have two hundred people in prayer meeting every week."

When the speaker finished, a man stood up and said, "I suggest we have a season of prayer for our brother and his church. They have eighteen hundred members who do not go to prayer meeting."

What seems like a success to us may not be successful to God. God measures success by a different yardstick than we do. We are impressed by numbers; God is impressed by the measure of faith. We are impressed by size; God is impressed by our trust. We are impressed by appearance; God is impressed by how much we love others. Our willingness to reach out to one person in need may be more important to God than the ability to sway multitudes. Too often, we define success in worldly terms: prominent position, large income, social standing. But as Jesus pointed out many times, these must never be our goals.

The cross was hardly the greatest success story of the first century. Measured in terms of worldly success, it was a failure. Measured in terms of God's plan, it is the greatest success story of all time.

Bible Reading: 2 Corinthians
10:12-18
One Year Bible Reading Plan:
Acts 3
Nehemiah 7, 8

Mervin Graber, Auburn, KY

---

*What the world measured failure,
the resurrection measured success.*

174

Sin Lieth at the Door

If thou doest well, shalt thou not be accepted?
and if thou doest not well, sin lieth at the door.
Genesis 4:7

In my growing up years at home there were times when everyone seemed wrong, and nothing went my way. I would walk around, grouchy and angry at the world. Then my mother would quote Genesis 4:7 to me.

Here is a quick self-inspection verse. It tells me that when I am upset and angry at the world, the problem is always with me. Anger is always a decision. We choose to get angry or not to get angry. We are not forced into anger. Every situation that we face is a test of our character. Cain was angry at Abel. Cain's problem was not Abel; Cain's problem was Cain. In today's world, Cain would have found a support group in which to vent his feelings of rejection and sibling rivalry. Ultimately, he would have found someone to affirm his actions and outburst of anger.

We must recognize that it is sin that builds walls between us and other people. Pride, jealousy, self-pity, fear, mistrust, lust, anger, and wrath are sin. We need to acknowledge that we have a sin problem, confess it, repent, and go on in the joy of the Lord. Real happiness and joy do not consist in having the perfect surroundings, but in responding in a Christ-like way to the difficulties with which we are faced.

Bible Reading: Genesis 4:1-8
One Year Bible Reading Plan:
Acts 4:1-22
Nehemiah 9–11

Paul H. Miller, Nappanee, IN

Be your brother's keeper.

175

I Will Not Do This Thing

. . . and as thy soul liveth, I will not do this thing.
2 Samuel 11:11

Such convictions! Such character! Such courage! A vicious war was on. The king had offered Uriah a reprieve from his valiant fighting, in an effort to disguise the consequences of his own sinful actions. But Uriah refused the offer, not because he suspected the truth, but because he was a valiant man of war. He could not conscientiously live in pleasure while his brothers' lives were being snuffed out. He could not sleep in his own comfortable bed in safety, while his brothers slept on the ground in mortal danger every minute. He would not follow the king's cowardly example of living in ease, while his men were fighting. Uriah made a noble choice. He went against the king's commandment. "I will not do this thing." It cost him his life.

A spiritual warfare is raging. Our brothers are in the heat of battle. Many are suffering persecution, especially in Muslim-dominated countries. More Christians died for their faith in the twentieth century than in all the previous centuries combined. Can we dare to live in pleasure, while our brothers are suffering in the battle? Life in North America offers us pleasure, comfort, and reprieve from the battle. Will you accept the offer? Or will you cast your lot with your brothers in the battle? Uriah made the right choice. "I will not do this thing." Will you?

Bible Reading: 2 Samuel 11:1-17
One Year Bible Reading Plan:
Acts 4:23-37
Nehemiah 12, 13

Ken Kauffman, Falkville, AL

Woe to them that are at ease in Zion.
—Amos 6:1

Spiritual Production and Reproduction

_I beseech you therefore, brethren, by the mercies of God,
that ye present your bodies a living sacrifice, holy,
acceptable unto God, which is your reasonable service._
Romans 12:1

Have you ever wondered why Jesus turned aside the request of the Gadarene man, when he asked to go with Jesus after he was healed? Jesus did not say, "Come and follow me," but He said, "Go home to thy friends, and tell them how great things the Lord hath done for thee."

He went back and gave his testimony to a village full of people, who moments before had begged Jesus to depart out of their coasts.

It is most certainly a marvelous thing how effectively God can use a changed man—born again, washed, and cleansed in the blood of Jesus—and bring about spiritual production and reproduction as He did through this man. The Bible says the former demoniac began to proclaim throughout the region of Decapolis what Christ had done for him. In Mark 7 Jesus returned to Decapolis, and multitudes received Him. Jesus then fed the four thousand, all because one man took to heart the words of Jesus.

Today, perhaps you too may be given an opportunity to testify and to tell someone the great things Jesus has done for you.

Bible Reading: Mark 5:1-20
One Year Bible Reading Plan:
Acts 5:1-16
Esther 1–3

Production and reproduction are truly the work of God, but today He may be looking to you to be the vessel.

Lee Stoltzfus, Gap, PA

_It is not the possession of extraordinary gifts that makes
extraordinary usefulness, but the dedication of
what we have to the service of God._
—Robertson

A Second Chance

Honour thy father and thy mother: that thy days may be long
upon the land which the LORD thy God giveth thee.
Exodus 20:12

My mother is eighty-seven years old and lives with my youngest sister. Over the years she has become increasingly confused and childlike. It is difficult to deal with the changes associated with her aging, especially when I remember her earlier years. We occasionally bring Mother home with us to give my sister a break. Mother is often not happy anywhere but at home, and sometimes not even there. She frequently cries to go home and does not understand why she cannot stay by herself. She is convinced someone is trying to get her things. She often hides things, then blames others when she cannot find them. Her inability to hear well, even with two hearing aids, does not make things easier. It can be trying to care for someone like this, especially if she is your mother. I consider it a blessing, although a bittersweet one at times, to be able to give back to her some of what she has given to her children over the years.

We often hear that we have only one chance with our children. I am convinced God has given us another chance. As our children watch our interaction with their grandmother, we have a second opportunity to teach them respect for their elders: patience, kindness, and forbearance. As they observe how we respond to her needs, we have another chance to teach them their responsibility to family. We are being given another opportunity to demonstrate grace, unselfishness, and the importance of fulfilling Scriptural injunctions to care for our parents. They can see if we do it gracefully and out of love, or whether it is a burden to us.

Bible Reading: 1 Timothy 5:4-8; Matthew 15:4-6
One Year Bible Reading Plan: Acts 5:17–42
Esther 4–6

Joe Schmucker, Haven, KS

. . . despise not thy mother when she is old.
—Proverbs 23:22

Let Us Be Honest

Recompense to no man evil for evil.
Provide things honest in the sight of all men.
Romans 12:17

A stranger was riding through the countryside when he saw a most unusual sight. At various levels on the side of an old barn, he saw several targets, and in the center of every target—right in the bull's eye—there was an arrow. The stranger stopped to ask who was such an expert marksman. The farmer replied that no one around there was an expert marksman as far as he knew.

"But what about those arrows in the bull's eyes?" asked the stranger.

"Oh," said the farmer. "There is a man from the village who does that. He comes out here and shoots arrows into the side of my barn, and then he paints targets around them."

Romans 12:6 tells us that by God's grace every Christian is given a gift or ability to do something well. The verses that follow name these gifts and give instructions on how to exercise them. Then, in verse 9, we are challenged to love without dissimulation—or hypocrisy. This must be true in the exercising of our gifts. What is our aim in exercising our gifts? Are there ulterior motives? Or do we seek to edify the body and glorify Christ?

When we use our gifts to attract attention to ourselves, we become guilty of hyprocrisy. Only as we choose as our targets to glorify God and build up others will we be able to exercise our gifts effectively.

Bible Reading: Romans 12
One Year Bible Reading Plan:
Acts 6
Esther 7–10

Mervin Graber, Auburn, KY

Choose honesty by first choosing the right target.

Who Are My Brethren?

Now therefore ye are no more strangers and foreigners,
but fellow citizens with the saints, and of the household of God.
Ephesians 2:19

Our family reunion is coming up in just a few weeks. Most plain people look forward to their family reunions. Having large families reuniting occasionally can be a great blessing, especially if those family members have kept the faith once delivered to the saints.

We don't have a godly background, and, unfortunately, our family reunions are not very happy occasions for us. The majority of our family members are unsaved, living their lives for themselves, without Christ. There are many divorces and remarriages, alcohol, and much drug abuse among my cousins. Some give lip service to our Lord, but their actions denote otherwise.

Jesus made it quite clear that His real family members were those who did His Father's will. As we strive to serve the Lord and keep His commandments, we meet many we can call "brethren."

Jesus said in John 3:6, "That which is born of the flesh is flesh; and that which is born of the Spirit is spirit." Our fleshly brethren may break our hearts, but our spiritual brethren are a great blessing to our lives. My family is thrilled to live among and be a part of our spiritual family.

I'm looking forward to the day when we can attend our spiritual family reunion in heaven. There we will know who our brethren really are. Which reunion are you looking forward to?

> **Bible Reading:** Matthew 12:46-50
> **One Year Bible Reading Plan:**
> Acts 7:1-19
> Job 1–3

Terry A. Lester, Montezuma, GA

I'll see you at heaven's jubilee.

Another Religion?

Give diligence to make your calling and election sure.
2 Peter 1:10

One of the fondest memories of my later teen years is spending one afternoon each month with the youth group, going to one of the many villages in our area. We first gathered around for prayer, after which we were each given a handful of tracts. We passed them out to whomever we met. Very seldom did anyone refuse the tracts.

One time, I offered a tract to a middle-aged woman. Turning slowly, she said in utter disgust, "What is this? Another religion?" By her cold reception, she spoke the thoughts of many who are confused by the various professions of religion in our day. This generation needs to take heed to Jesus' warning in Matthew 7:21, "Not every one that saith unto me, Lord, Lord, shall enter into the kingdom of heaven; but he that doeth the will of my Father which is in heaven."

"Pure religion and undefiled before God and the Father is this, To visit the fatherless and widows in their affliction, and to keep himself unspotted from the world" (James 1:27).

We need a true love for our fellowmen and a true love for God, expressed in daily living and practice. This is the life, separated from the world and conformed to the image of Jesus Christ, which can address our society's confusion about religion.

Roger Rangai, Lott, TX

Bible Reading: 2 Timothy 3
One Year Bible Reading Plan:
Acts 7:20-43
Job 4–6

I'll live for Him who died for me.
—R. E. Hudson

Saved By the Blood

But if we walk in the light, as he is in the light,
we have fellowship one with another, and the blood of
Jesus Christ his Son cleanseth us from all sin.
1 John 1:7

When the children of Israel were delivered from bondage in the land of Egypt, the Lord instituted the Passover. They were to take a year-old male lamb—one without blemish—kill it in the evening, and with the blood paint the side posts and upper lintels of their doors. And the Lord said, "I will pass through the land . . . and smite the firstborn . . . and when I see the blood, I will pass over you."

This points to our redemption under the new covenant. Jesus is the perfect Lamb—not one spot or sin stain is in Him. There was no one else in the whole world, and no angel in heaven, who could be the perfect Lamb for us. We would have been lost forever, had He not had pity on us.

He shed His blood on the cross at Calvary, and we need to apply it by faith to the door of our hearts. And it will save us, not from natural death, but from a much greater calamity, eternal death!

"Forasmuch as ye know that ye were not redeemed with corruptible things, as silver and gold, from your vain conversation received by tradition from your fathers; but with the precious blood of Christ, as of a lamb without blemish and without spot" (1 Peter 1:18-19).

Bible Reading: Exodus 12:1-13
One Year Bible Reading Plan:
Acts 7:44-60
Job 7–9

Joe Kurtz, Belleville, PA

God does not see sin if it is covered by the blood.

How Long to Get Rid of Sin?

*Therefore if any man be in Christ, he is a new creature: old things
are passed away; behold, all things are become new.*
2 Corinthians 5:17

Do we accept what this verse says, or are we still dabbling around in our besetting sins?

A few weeks ago I talked with a man who was an alcoholic. He said that his life had become a mess. His wife and children were ready to leave him, and he was losing his job and their house. But he came to the end of himself; he went to his bedroom and fell on his knees in prayer. He totally gave everything over to the Lord. Because he meant business with God, he came out of the bedroom happy and free. He said he has had no more desire for liquor since that night.

He has a radiant smile on his face and always has a good word for the Lord. He is like the woman caught in the act of adultery, whom Jesus told, "Neither do I condemn thee: go, and sin no more."

How is it with us? Do we expect some time for excuses, or say that Satan's temptations are just too powerful, and it is too hard to quit?

Let us claim the promise of 2 Corinthians 5:17, and the power of Jesus. Let us allow Him to work in us, so that we can overcome our shortcomings and failures.

John Hostetler, Auburn, KY

Bible Reading: John 8:1-12
One Year Bible Reading Plan:
Acts 8:1-25
Job 10–12

Sin and hell are married, unless repentance proclaims the divorce.
—Spurgeon

June 28

Building the Church

*From whom the whole body fitly joined together and
compacted by that which every joint supplieth,
according to the effectual working in the measure of every part,
maketh increase of the body unto the edifying of itself in love.*
Ephesians 4:16

The past several days I have been working on a new building. As we were putting up the rafters and purlins and bolting them together, I was reminded of our key verse. As we put this building together piece by piece, everything fit together. Every angle was just right, and all the bolt holes were just right. (Though some of the bolts needed a little persuading!) It was designed to fit together, and it needed all its parts.

So God designed the church. We need each other, and everyone has a place to fill. Verses 4 and 5 in our Bible reading for today tell us that there are different gifts and administrations. Verse 17 says, "If the whole body were an eye, where were the hearing? If the whole were hearing, where were the smelling?" We might say, "If all were preachers, where were the listeners?" Or, "If all were teachers, where were the students?" God has given each one a position in the church. It is up to us to fill our position.

Verse 22 says that the members which seem to be more feeble are necessary. Consider the steel building again. The rafters are held together by comparatively small bolts. Looking at the structure, you would hardly notice the bolts; but if you started taking them out, the building would not stand very long. In the church, if it were not for the prayers that sometimes go unnoticed, the church could not stand against the evil forces around us. We put the most bolts at the joints, the weakest places, and they are made strong. Let us direct our prayers to areas where we see weaknesses, and God can make them strong.

Bible Reading: 1 Corinthians 12
One Year Bible Reading Plan:
Acts 8:26-40
Job 13–15

Freeman Miller, Auburn, KY

---

*There is nothing that makes us love a man
so much as praying for him.*
—William Law

Tug of War

Knowing that Christ being raised from the dead dieth no more;
death hath no more dominion over him.
Romans 6:9

When I was in school, we liked to play "tug of war." We had two teams, and they pulled against each other with a strong rope. We pulled with all our might, trying to get the best possible grip in the dirt, leaning, grunting, and groaning, until finally one side pulled the other across the line. There was always a winner, one side or the other.

Life is a tug of war: death on the one side and life on the other. Death will always win. Sooner or later death will win. Death will pull each life across the line. You may be saved from an accident, but sooner or later death will visit your doorstep.

Yet Jesus fought another tug of war with death. And Jesus defeated death, yanked it right over the line and trampled it.

Christians do not need to fear death, nor do they need to fight it. Since Jesus defeated death, it has become for us the door into eternal life, where death has no power. We die as a result of being Adam's sons; but we live forever as a result of becoming God's sons.

Bible Reading: Romans 5:13-21
One Year Bible Reading Plan:
Acts 9:1-22
Job 16–18

Paul H. Miller, Nappanee, IN

Death to the believer is the door to life.

When Christ Knocks

Behold, I stand at the door, and knock . . .
Revelation 3:20

The other night in the early morning hours, I was awakened by what I thought was a knock at the door. I checked the doors, but no one was there. As I lay down again, the verse came to mind, "Behold, I stand at the door, and knock: if any man hear my voice, and open the door, I will come in to him, and will sup with him, and he with me" (Revelation 3:20). Would I have been ready to open the door if Christ had been knocking?

Or are there things in my home that I would be ashamed to have Christ see? It is a challenging thought—are our homes in such a condition that we could have Christ as a guest?

Is my spiritual house pure and free from sin and unrighteousness? Am I sanctified and meet for the Master's use (2 Timothy 2:21)? Am I ready and waiting to open immediately when He comes and knocks to take His bride home with Him (Luke 12:36)? Blessed are we, if He finds us watching. He will sit us down to meat and serve us (verse 37).

We also need to be dressed with our lamps burning (Luke 12:35), when He knocks to call us to new a responsibility. Let us be useful right where we are.

Bible Reading: Luke 12:34-48
One Year Bible Reading Plan:
 Acts 9:23-43
 Job 19, 20

Steve Hershberger, Monticello, KY

Let us be ready at all times to open our hearts when He knocks.

Weep for What?

Oh that my head were waters, and mine eyes
a fountain of tears, that I might weep day and night
for the slain of the daughter of my people!
Jeremiah 9:1

When did you last cry out to God in weeping for lost souls around you? Do you have a clear understanding of hell? When was the last time you mourned for your sins?

When we think of mourning and weeping, we usually think of funerals. But that is not the only time Christians weep. The key verse records a time when Jeremiah wept for his people. Likewise, Jesus wept over Jerusalem because of the wickedness that was there. He knew what their end would be. Jesus' tears give us a good example to follow today. We ought to weep for sinners, knowing how terrible hell is.

As Jesus was being led to Calvary, some women followed Him, weeping. He turned and said to them, "Weep not for me, but weep for yourselves, and for your children" (Luke 23:28).

Jesus is still saying that to us today. We must also mourn for our own sins. When we stop mourning for our sins, we tend to forget what God has done for us.

We have a wonderful promise in Revelation 7:17, which says that in heaven God shall wipe away all tears from our eyes. What a joy that will be!

Kevin Graber, Odon, IN

Bible Reading: Matthew
  13:36-43
One Year Bible Reading Plan:
  Acts 10:1-23
  Job 21, 22

Blessed are they that mourn: for they shall be comforted.
—Matthew 5:4

Two Fellows, Same Ship—Fellowship

I am the good shepherd, and know my sheep,
and am known of mine.
John 10:14

The company a person keeps has a great deal to do with the character he develops. In the New Testament, the social pronouns— we, they, and us—are found often.

God intends that a fellowship of believers should worship and work together. It is still true, however, that each of us must meet God personally and begin our walk of faith, just as each child is born separately from the rest, but is still born into a family. After birth, he becomes a part of the family.

The church is the family of God, and it is an ideal place to grow in faith. Just as children do not grow up to be normal adults if forced to live alone, so also do those suffer who withdraw from the fellowship of other Christians. They become warped and one-dimensional. It is not good to get too much of oneself and not enough of others.

God has made us social beings. From our brothers we can learn how to do things, and sometimes how not to do things. The preacher or father who hears only himself will soon accept his ideas as the most excellent ones and not realize that he has become an "island."

God's people are like sheep, who live in flocks. When one loses sight of the Shepherd, he can go to the flock to find Him. The Shepherd always stays with His flock.

> **Bible Reading:** Psalm 84
> **One Year Bible Reading Plan:**
> Acts 10:24-48
> Job 23–25

Andrew Miller, Jr., Plain City, OH

No man is an island. No man stands alone.
—John Donne

A Beautiful Life

But he knoweth the way that I take: when he
hath tried me, I shall come forth as gold.
Job 23:10

Some sunsets are breathtaking! Recently many of us at church saw one such sunset, and everyone remarked how beautiful it was!

What makes some sunsets more glorious than others? There are several things that affect their beauty, but by far the clouds are most important. Now, most people do not like clouds. They hide the sun. So people grumble and complain on rainy days! But which is more important—the sun, or the clouds that bring rain? We need the right amount of both. And, with the right amount of both, sunsets are made more beautiful.

Life has its clouds—trials, hardships, sickness, and grief. Most people think they are bad, but the Scriptures tell us otherwise. James 1:3 says, "The trying of your faith worketh patience." With the right amount of trials, we become stronger, deeper, and more beautiful in God's eyes. We need clouds in our lives to make us beautiful. Consider the times in your life that you grew closer to God and found Him more precious. Were they not times when your skies were cloudy? Remember, clouds make sunsets more beautiful!

Bible Reading: 1 Peter 1:1-9
One Year Bible Reading Plan:
Acts 11
Job 26–28

Jeffery D. Bigger, Reading, PA

As clouds beautify a sunset, so God uses trials to beautify our lives.

July 4 _____

I Sacrificed My Son for You!

Forasmuch as ye know that ye were not redeemed with corruptible things . . . But with the precious blood of Christ . . .
1 Peter 1:18, 19

A young man had great dreams for his son. One day he decided to take the young lad to work with him.

His job was operating a railroad bridge. At noon they went to the observation deck to eat. At once, he heard the sound of a train whistle and knew it would be at the bridge in a few short minutes. So the father gave some very calm instructions to his young son to stay. Leaving the son on the deck, he hurried down the ladder to the control room, unaware of the son's attempt to follow him.

Making a final check before pulling the lever to lower the bridge, he saw his son had fallen from the ladder onto the massive gears that moved the bridge. His son was hurt, but conscious.

In that instant, he realized he must make a decision. Either his son, or the four hundred people riding the train would perish! What would he do? What must he do? Burying his face under his arm, he pulled the lever seconds before the train came rushing over the bridge. As the train passed by, he observed people eating and drinking, sleeping or displaying a carefree attitude. As they passed, he called out in anguish, "Don't you realize? Don't you care? Don't you know I've sacrificed my son for you?" But no one responded nor even looked his way. The train passengers were completely unaware that the boy had died so they could remain safe.

This is but a faint glimpse of what God the Father has done for us in sacrificing His Son that we might have life everlasting. Jesus' death, unlike the boy's, was not an accident. He gave His life willingly for you and me.

Ben Weaver, Auburn, KY

> **Bible Reading:** 1 Peter 1:13-25
> **One Year Bible Reading Plan:**
> Acts 12
> Job 29, 30

_____

When we think of the atonement, we are apt to think only of what man gains. We must remember what it cost God.
—Fitt

190

Pure Bread of God

For to me to live is Christ, and to die is gain.
Philippians 1:21

"I would rather die for Christ than rule the world. It is glorious to go down in the world in order to go up unto God." These are the words of Ignatius, a great early church leader and writer.

Ignatius besought the Romans: "Leave me to the beasts that I may by them be made partaker of God. I am a grain of wheat of God, and I would be ground by the teeth of the wild beast that I may be found pure bread of God. Pray the Lord for me that through these instruments I may be found a sacrifice to God."

Ignatius got his wish. A short while later, he was taken to Rome and there thrown to lions in the Coliseum. Ignatius had given up his will totally for service to His master, Jesus Christ.

Today, we call it a sacrifice to have to do something a little inconvenient. Why do we think we should have it so nice? Christ has not promised us a life of ease. He did not even tell us we would be comfortable in this life.

God calls us to voluntary, sacrificial servanthood. We will do whatever He asks, not sparing the flesh. If it should please Him, we will even die for our God.

Bible Reading: 2 Timothy 2:1-15
One Year Bible Reading Plan:
Acts 13:1-24
Job 31, 32

Gerald D. Wagler, Washington, IN

You cannot win without sacrifice.
—Buxton

Leaning on Jesus

Being confident of this very thing, that he which hath begun a good work in you will perform it until the day of Jesus Christ.
Philippians 1:6

We are on the sea of life, often severely tossed about by difficulties and trials. The winds are contrary, just as they were for the disciples in their small boat in the middle of the night. I can imagine how it was. The boat was riding up and down on the waves and filling up with water; the wind was blowing in their faces. They were about ready to give up on reaching the other side.

But look—who is coming? Jesus comes, walking across the water. Christ is always on time. He speaks comforting words: "Be of good cheer; it is I; be not afraid." He will help us through. Our Lord is always on time, and He is always ready to lend a helping hand.

In this account, Peter was again the bold one, and said, "Lord, if it be thou, bid me come unto thee on the water." Peter had a little faith that Jesus could help him do this, but when he saw the waters, he lost his faith and started sinking. How often do we do the same thing when trials come into our lives? The wind seems contrary, we feel overwhelmed, and we begin to sink. If we cry, "Lord, save [me]!" as Peter did, Jesus immediately comes to our aid. He stretches forth His hand, lifts us up, and carries us through all our temptations and trials.

As soon as Jesus stepped into the boat, the wind ceased, and all was calm in a split second. That is how it is, no matter what comes into our lives. When we give it all over to Him, and give up ourselves to His will, He gives us His peace.

Bible Reading: Matthew 14:22-33
One Year Bible Reading Plan: Acts 13:25-52
Job 33, 34

Jason Slabaugh, Sugarcreek, OH

Depend on Jesus: He will help you through all the way!

Teaching Children's Children

Children's children are the crown of old men;
and the glory of children are their fathers.
Proverbs 17:6

Johnny's toy wagon had a broken hitch. When Mother went to Grandpa's place, Johnny took his wagon along and asked Grandpa if he would fix it. Grandpas can usually fix anything. Sure enough, Grandpa fixed the broken hitch. Johnny told Grandpa to give him a bill. This is what it said, " 'Children obey your parents in all things; for this is well pleasing unto the Lord' (Colossians 3:20). Johnny, you do this, and your bill is paid in full—Grandpa."

Grandfathers, you can have much influence in the lives of your grandchildren, as you direct and encourage them to honor and obey their parents in the Lord. Your encouragement will help your grandchildren become "olive plants round about thy table" (Psalm 128:3b). The olive plant—a source of oil—refers to "illumination" or "the light of Jesus" flowing through those who fear the Lord and walk in His ways. They are a light and witness to those who are living in sin and darkness, in need of the salvation of Jesus.

Obedience is so very important to godly character. It must be taught in the home. If children learn obedience at home, they will also be obedient to God, in the church, and to the laws of our land.

Bible Reading: Psalm 128;
Proverbs 6:20-24
One Year Bible Reading Plan:
Acts 14
Job 35–37

Thank you, Lord, for grandpas and grandmas who encourage their children's children to obey God's Word.

Ben S. Stoltzfus, Parkesburg, PA

A good man leaveth an inheritance to his children's children.

God Is Still Searching!

And I sought for a man among them.
Ezekiel 22:30a

God wants to impress upon our minds the urgent need of the hour, as He did to Ezekiel many years ago. Many times God spoke to Ezekiel, the "son of man," about the children of Israel's rebellion against Him. The leaders as well as the people were worshiping statues made of wood, stone, and clay. They had taken dishonest gain, used deceit, and profaned His name. And God searched for a man among them that would stand in the gap before Him for the nation, but He found none. None! So here He is, telling Ezekiel, a prisoner of the Chaldeans: "Their own way have I recompensed upon their heads."

Oh, faithful few! Today many religious leaders have brought much reproach to the name of God. Sin within the church is not dealt with. Many have gone so far as to place their stamp of approval upon divorce and remarriage, which is adultery, and say that God has sanctioned it. Many Christians place greater importance on the dollar than on God's kingdom, and have been caught up into the world's system.

In the days of Ezekiel, these same sins separated Israel from God, and in our day they still blight the church.

God is looking for faithful men who will build again the walls of righteousness that guard the land. He is looking for men who will stand in the gap and pray that God would be merciful, and stay His hand of judgment.

Bible Reading: Ezekiel 22:17-31
One Year Bible Reading Plan:
Acts 15:1-21
Job 38, 39

Kevin Miller, Auburn, KY

Ye are the salt of the earth: but if the salt have lost his savour, wherewith shall it be salted?
—Matthew 5:13

Now, Father?

But of that day and hour knoweth no man, no,
not the angels of heaven, but my Father only.
Matthew 24:36

Many times as a family we plan some special activity for a certain day in the near future. How often do our smaller children who have not mastered the concept of time come to us and say, "Now, Daddy? Are we going today?" We have to explain to them that it is not yet time; we are waiting for a certain time or a certain day.

Now, let us lift our eyes from earth to heaven. God is sitting on the throne, Jesus is on His right hand surrounded by thousands of angels and saints. The scene is glorious. There is singing, rejoicing, and adoration. Yet something is lacking. The saints are not all home yet. Jesus looks forward to gathering all His followers to Him. He looks to the Father and asks, "Now, Father? May we go today?"

The Father replies, "Not today. Perhaps there are still others that will come. Wait a little longer."

Bible Reading: 2 Peter 3:1-18
One Year Bible Reading Plan:
Acts 15:22-41
Job 40–42

The Lord "is longsuffering to us-ward, not willing that any should perish, but that all should come to repentance."

Is He waiting on you?

Alvino Miller, Crossville, TN

God asks no man whether he will accept life. That is not the choice.
You must take it. The only choice is how.
—Henry W. Beecher

NaCl
(Sodium Chloride)

Have salt in yourselves, and have peace one with another.
Mark 9:50

Jesus used the statement, "Ye are the salt of the earth," to tell His followers how useful and necessary His people can be on earth. This is possible only if they do not lose their saltiness.

Salt, as we know it, has around 1,400 different uses. Salt is used for seasoning food, melting ice, preserving food and meats, softening water, and as an antiseptic in medicine. These are just the most familiar of the multiple uses of salt.

How salty am I? Do I contain enough "salt" to melt the icy hearts of those who oppose the Gospel? Am I salty enough to soften my neighbor so that he desires to discuss God's Word? Do I have enough salt to preserve my life from destruction and also effectively pass on the faith to my children and others? Am I salty enough to cleanse out that evil infection that Satan tries to implant in my life? How salty am I?

One of the most important areas in which we ought to be salty is found in Colossians 4:6, which says, "Let your speech be alway with grace, seasoned with salt, that ye may know how ye ought to answer every man." Using the right amount of salt in our speech makes it more acceptable to others.

"Ye are the salt of the earth." This is an enormous challenge. Let us look to the One who gives us a fresh supply of salt. Only then will we be able to have a satisfactory effect on those around us.

Mark Webb, Hicksville, OH

> **Bible Reading:** Matthew 5:1-13
> **One Year Bible Reading Plan:**
> Acts 16:1-15
> Psalms 1–3

Do not let your life lose its saltiness!

"Someday" May Never Come

Now it is high time to awaken out of sleep.
Romans 13:11

Recently, I talked with a man who did not hesitate to tell me that he does not serve the Lord.

My heart went out to this man, and I soon found out that he was quite open and willing to talk. I asked him if he knows where he will spend eternity if he keeps living the way he is living. He said, "Yes, I do." He told me he wants to enjoy life the way he is living now. But someday, he wants to change and live for the Lord.

How is it with us? Do we put things off? Do we wait till the eleventh hour and think we will then make things right? Or do we keep our lives free from sin and our hearts unburdened before God, so that whatever hour Jesus may come, He will find us ready and waiting for His return?

Bible Reading: Romans 13:8-14
One Year Bible Reading Plan:
Acts 16:16-40
Psalms 4–6

"The night is far spent, the day is at hand: let us therefore cast off the works of darkness, and let us put on the armour of light" (Romans 13:12).

Galen Wagler, Monticello, KY

Let me live as though Jesus had died for me yesterday,
rose this morning, and is coming tomorrow.

Submissive or Stubborn

*The sacrifices of God are a broken spirit: a broken
and a contrite heart, O God, thou wilt not despise.*
Psalm 51:17

Donkeys are stubborn by nature. They are self-willed and contrary. In Honduras a couple of boys were seen trying to lead their donkey. They pushed, they pulled, and finally, they beat him with a stick; but the donkey would not cooperate.

In Matthew 21 we read that Jesus rode the colt of an ass on which never a man had sat. But when Jesus made contact with this young donkey, the donkey lost his self-willed, stubborn nature, and became submissive, obedient, and docile, even to the point of being willing to walk over the branches and clothes that people had strewn in the way.

Besides that, the commotion that the people made by crying, "Hosanna to the Son of David: Blessed is he that cometh in the name of the Lord; Hosanna in the highest," would have been enough to scare any animal; but the little donkey calmly kept on going. Such was the effect that Jesus had on this young donkey.

Man is by nature stubborn, selfish, uncooperative, and a little contrary—like a donkey. But when Jesus and man make heart contact, that "donkey" nature within us is transformed into a submissive, willing, cooperative spirit. The individual is changed! When testings and trials are strewn in his way, he will calmly step over the obstacles and trust God to help him overcome.

Has your contact with Jesus made you submissive, willing, obedient and cooperative? Or do you still have some of the donkey nature left in you? We lose our self-will at the foot of the cross.

Bible Reading: Matthew 21:1-16
One Year Bible Reading Plan:
Acts 17:1-15
Psalms 7–9

Samuel Hochstetler, Worthington, IN

Self needs to be shattered like the glass of a broken window.

The Making of a Name

And I will bless thee, and make thy name great;
and thou shalt be a blessing.
Genesis 12:2

The tower of Babel has long symbolized the folly of human ambition and pride. The builders of this magnificent edifice wanted to "make . . . a name" (Genesis 11: 4). Their ambition was to build a monument to human genius, but God effectively thwarted their vain plans, and this half-built tower stands in history as a monument to human folly. These foolish builders got themselves "a name," but not the name they anticipated. God had the last word. But then, does He not always?

Many years later, in the same region, a man loaded all his belongings onto camels and donkeys. In obedience to God's call, he moved from his idol-worshiping neighborhood toward an unknown land that God would show him. It never occurred to this humble man to stop and build monuments to himself. He remembered God's promise: "I will. . . make thy name great." What was his driving ambition? It was simple obedience. He let God do with his name what He wanted. God had the last word. Today Abraham's name is among the greatest in Bible history.

Let us evaluate ourselves. Why do we do what we do? How many towers of Babel are under construction? Are we more concerned with serving ourselves, or obeying God? His criteria for greatness are not written in familiar human terms. It is ironic that people too humble to seek a great name are the very ones that receive one. It goes to show us that God will have the last word about great names. Abandon the Babel project and strike out for the unknown land of promise and blessing.

Bible Reading: Genesis 11:1-9; 12:1-9
One Year Bible Reading Plan:
Acts 17:16-34
Psalms 10–12

Ken Kauffman, Falkville, AL

If you are too big for a little place,
you are too little for a big place.

Love—A Bond of Strength

This is my commandment, That ye love
one another, as I have loved you.
John 15:12

Have you ever watched a bricklayer build a wall? He uses his trowel to spread the mortar and skillfully lays each brick in place. After the wall is completed, its strength provides protection.

I like to think of the individual believer as a brick. When many individuals bond together, it has a strengthening affect. Together, they can withstand the storms of life.

How can we do this? It takes the mortar of love. If believers have no love for each other, it will not take much to knock their wall down. Love builds the wall. It unites the individuals to each other, making them one strong whole.

Because of love, God cares for us. It was His love that held Jesus on the cross—not the nails. We deserved to be punished forever, but because God loved us, He used Jesus' death and resurrection to save us.

To love others, we must love God, and to love God we must love one another. God forgave us, and we need to forgive others also. God gives us strength and grace for our trials. In the same way, we need to give encouragement to each other. When someone is doing something wrong, it takes love to show him his error. If we want truly to love God and each other more, we need to spend more time with God in prayer.

Stop, and think about how much God loves you. This should make you eager to practice God's love on those around you.

Kristen Miller, Honey Grove, PA

Bible Reading: 1 John 4:7-21
One Year Bible Reading Plan:
Acts 18
Psalms 13–16

Walk in love, as Christ also hath loved us.
—Ephesians 5:2

Nonresistance Is for All Believers

But I say unto you, That ye resist not evil: but whosoever shall smite thee on thy right cheek, turn to him the other also.
Matthew 5:39

A clear message to cease from self-defense and strife arises from Jesus' instruction to believers in the Sermon on the Mount. His words are for all those who are persecuted with Jesus for the sake of the Gospel, and for the poor who are condemned, sometimes abused, and murdered by the rich. Jesus' counsel to all believers is to not retaliate. Christians should not return evil for evil. Jesus commanded over and over that we must not seek vengeance.

We are members of the army of the Lord. He does not suggest that we turn the other cheek, He commands it (Matthew 5:39). Remember what happened when Jesus was finally brought to trial. When they hurled their insults at Him, He did not retaliate. When He suffered, He made no threats. Instead, He entrusted Himself to Him who judges justly (1 Peter 2:23).

Though Christians do not retaliate, they are by no means defenseless. The injustices they experience cry out to the Lord for vengeance (James 5:4-6). God certainly is watching, and the Lord will exact justice for all believers who practice and teach Christian nonresistance.

Bible Reading: Luke 6:20-36
One Year Bible Reading Plan:
Acts 19:1-20
Psalms 17, 18

Ludlow Walker, Sr., Homestead, FL

God is faithful to right all wrongs.

Do We Have Time to Spare?

Behold, now is the accepted time;
behold, now is the day of salvation.
2 Corinthians 6:2

What is time? It cannot be seen. Although it is measured in minutes, hours, and days, it cannot be controlled by man. We can see the hand on the clock move, but we cannot make time move faster or slow it down. It is as God ordained it in the beginning. God alone is in control of time. That is why time is so important. Do we use our time here for God's benefit, or do we use it for our own interests?

There are so many needs in the world today—both physical and spiritual—that we have no time to squander. "See then that ye walk circumspectly, not as fools, but as wise, redeeming the time, because the days are evil" (Ephesians 5:15, 16). Let us be active in the Lord's work and look for opportunities to do good. An opportunity lost cannot be recalled, for time is like sand; it slips through our fingers, and we cannot hold on to it!

Let us not be idle, but let us be actively engaged in the Lord's work. Our labors will not be in vain. Our daily communion with the Lord is a most important time, for in Jesus is our ultimate salvation. When Jesus comes, time will be no more.

"And the angel which I saw stand upon the sea and upon the earth lifted up his hand to heaven, and sware by him that liveth for ever and ever, who created heaven, and the things that therein are, and the earth, and the things that therein are, and the sea, and the things which are therein, that there should be time no longer" (Revelation 10:5-6).

Bible Reading: 2 Corinthians 6
One Year Bible Reading Plan:
   Acts 19:21-41
   Psalms 19–21

Amos Garber, Rosebush, MI

_____

Are we ready to be ushered into eternity?

God's Mark of Ownership

. . . for when I am weak, then am I strong.
2 Corinthians 12:10

Paul wrote much of the New Testament. His epistles were encouraging and bold. We regard him as a spiritual giant. However, in today's reading we learn that Paul faced many problems. He was beaten, stoned, shipwrecked; he faced hunger and thirst, and experienced pain, among other things. At one point, Paul asked the Lord to take away a thorn in his flesh. Notice God's answer: "My grace is sufficient for thee" (2 Corinthians 12:9a).

How many times have you asked the Lord to remove an obstacle from your path? Pain, or sickness, or circumstances? Many people would have us believe that if God does not remove these obstacles, it is a sign of a life without the Spirit. Was Paul's life without the Spirit? All the twelve apostles except John died martyrs' deaths. Were their lives without the Spirit? In the Garden of Gethsemane Jesus prayed, "If it be possible, let this cup pass from me" (Matthew 26:39). The Father did not take away the cup. God's power was made perfect in Jesus' human weakness.

Just as God's grace was sufficient for Christ and Paul, and for all the apostles and true Christians throughout the ages, so it is sufficient for you and me! Should I ask God to take away my infirmity, when it might be the very thing that makes God's strength perfect in my life? Our infirmities are often God's mark of ownership on our lives—testimonies of His perfect strength.

Bible Reading: 2 Corinthians 11:25–12:10
One Year Bible Reading Plan:
Acts 20:1-16
Psalms 22–24

Terry Lester, Montezuma, GA

Troubles are the tools by which God fashions us for better things.
—Henry Ward Beecher

203

True Science

He stretcheth out the north over the empty place,
and hangeth the earth upon nothing.
Job 26:7

Many people wonder, *How can I know the Bible is true?* There are several ways we can know, especially as we observe the accuracy of its contents, and consider the great time span over which it was written.

While the Bible is not a science book, it is scientifically accurate. In Christopher Columbus' day, people thought the earth was flat, like a plate. They were afraid to sail too far out on the ocean for fear of falling over the edge. Ferdinand Magellan (1480-1521) proved this fear to be false by sailing around the earth. In recent years, man sent satellites and spaceships with people into outer space, and, from space, took pictures that show the earth is a sphere.

God had already revealed this fact long ago in His Word. To Isaiah He said, "It is he that sitteth upon the circle of the earth," revealing that the earth is round. Not only did God reveal to Isaiah that the earth is round, but many, many years before, He told Job, who lived about as far north as San Antonio, Texas, that in the north is an empty place, and that the earth hangs on nothing.

We know that Job and Isaiah did not have sophisticated instruments like we have today. Though they lived several thousand years ago, they had more than an instrument—they had God, the all-knowing God, the Creator of heaven and earth. These Scriptures' agreement with scientific fact is one source of assurance that the Bible is true.

Bible Reading: Isaiah 40:12-21
One Year Bible Reading Plan:
  Acts 20:17-38
  Psalms 25–27

Laverne Yoder, Auburn, KY

Often man's word and thinking is theory;
but God's Word, when searched out, remains true fact.

Gulls, God, and Grace

But the men marvelled, saying, what manner of man
is this, that even the winds and the sea obey him!
Matthew 8:27

Recently we went on a deep sea fishing trip with our youth group. We were looking forward to a great catch of fish. As the boat headed for open water, the waves became pretty rough. We were tossed to and fro, and many of us on the boat became seasick. In the midst of all this, I noticed the sea gulls. The wind, waves, and rain were making our day uncomfortable, but the gulls were virtually unaffected by these circumstances. They flew gracefully against the wind and rain, and dove effortlessly into the waves to eat the bait we threw to them. As I watched these marvelous creatures of God, the word "grace" came to my mind time and again.

I was reminded of God's grace in our lives. The gulls were able to battle the elements of the sea with ease, while we, who were on the boat, struggled. Likewise, God's grace enables us to face the storms of life, just as the sea gulls were able to fly through the rough weather.

Luke 8:24 shows Jesus rebuking the wind and the waves; immediately there was a calm. God's grace can bring such calm into our lives when a storm rages. Then people will notice the grace in our lives, just as I noticed the grace of the sea gull's flight.

Bible Reading: Mark 6:45-51; Titus 2:11-14
One Year Bible Reading Plan: Acts 21:1-14
Psalms 28–30

Terry Lester, Montezuma, GA

Amazing grace, how sweet the sound!
—John Newton

205

God Is Able

*Again I say unto you, That if two of you shall agree
on earth as touching any thing that they shall ask,
it shall be done for them of my Father which is in heaven.*
Matthew 18:19

The phone rang. It was the neighbor, asking for someone to baby-sit her children that day, as her regular baby-sitter was sick.

The little baby girl loved to be rocked and cuddled. As the mother who was baby-sitting looked into the sweet angelic little face with the blue eyes and blond hair, her mother's heart was moved with compassion. What chance did this child have to find salvation? Her mother worked, leaving her with various baby-sitters. Her father was an alcoholic and very abusive. As the godly mother rocked, she prayed, "Dear Father, please make a way for this soul to be with You in heaven some day."

The daughter of the home and a friend who lived there also took turns with the mother to rock the baby. All three silently prayed the same prayer that day but never mentioned it to anyone.

Two years passed. One day the mother was reading the weekly newspaper. All at once, an article caught her attention: "Two-Year-Old Daughter Dies From Crib Death." It was the sweet little baby she had cuddled and prayed for, and now her soul was safe in heaven. Her heart rejoiced, and she praised God for honoring her request. Later that day, she told her daughter and her friend about the article. It was then she found out that the other two had prayed the same prayer that day.

> **Bible Reading:** James 5:16-20;
> Ephesians 3:14-21
> **One Year Bible Reading Plan:**
> Acts 21:15-40
> Psalms 31–33

Sam Hostetler, Linn, MO

---

*In prayer it is better to have a heart without words,
than words without a heart.*
—Bunyan

Can You Sleep Through a Storm?

When thou liest down, thou shalt not be afraid:
yea, thou shalt lie down, and thy sleep shall be sweet.
Proverbs 3:24

A teenage boy looking for work saw an ad that read "Boy Wanted." He applied for the job, and when the manager asked him what his qualifications were, he said, "I can sleep through a storm."

"What do you mean, you can sleep through a storm?" the manager asked.

"Well, sir," the boy replied, "I grew up on a farm where we always had lots of chores to do, such as milking cows, feeding pigs and chickens, cultivating corn, etc. I've always been careful to put the tools away when I'm finished using them, and when I come through the pastures, I close the gates behind me. When I come in at night, I close the chicken house door. Then in the night, if I hear the wind rising and the rain coming down, I know the doors are shut and the hen and chicks are dry in their coop, and I can turn over and go back to sleep."

The manager thought that was the kind of person he needed, and the boy got the job.

In our Bible reading today, we see that Paul also could rest in peace in the midst of a storm. When those around him were ready to give up the ship, he knew that his affairs were in order, and he could safely trust his life into the hands of the God to whom he belonged and whom he served. He was able to cheer his fellow travelers.

How is it with you when adversities come, and you face the storms of life? Can you say that you have been faithful in those things that have been entrusted to you, or is there someone out there who is hurting because you have withheld forgiveness or failed to give an encouraging word? Let us be true to the Lord, whose servants we are.

Bible Reading: Acts 27:6-25
One Year Bible Reading Plan:
Acts 22
Psalms 34, 35

Abner Overholt, Auburn, KY

The sleep of a labouring man is sweet.
—Ecclesiastes 5:12

Do Good to All Men

As we have therefore opportunity, let us do good unto all men,
especially unto them who are of the household of faith.
Galatians 6:10

It is three o'clock in the afternoon in Jerusalem. Time for evening prayers at the temple. Peter and John, along with many others, make their way to the main gate. Just before they go in, they hear a voice say, "A pence for a poor, lame man, please." Turning to the speaker, recognition registers on their faces. They have seen this beggar many times. He is a man just over forty years old and severely crippled. Since he cannot move without help, someone brings him daily to the temple to beg. He was born crippled, so he has become a common sight at the temple gate.

Here is a picture of someone in need. When we are faced with situations like this one, we can come up with some "good" excuses for not helping. Opportunities to help come at inopportune times. We are already late for work when we pass someone whose car has broken down. Peter and John were on the way to the temple for prayer. They could have said, "We do not have time to help this man!" But if we wait until we have time, we will probably never help anyone.

Another excuse we use is that we are not able to give the person the help they need. However, Peter and John did not have any money to give to the lame man, but they did not use that as an excuse for not stopping to help him. We may not be able to meet the apparent need, but we may be able to help in another way. We may not be able to fix their car, but we can take the opportunity to witness, and give the person a lift.

The ending of the story is a good example of how God uses us when we are willing to help those in need. Not only was the lame man healed, but many others also came to know the Lord as their Savior.

Bible Reading: Acts 3:1-10
One Year Bible Reading Plan:
Acts 23:1-11
Psalms 36, 37

Paul Beiler, Free Union, VA

Use a need to plant a seed.

Beautiful Christian Maturity

*I have fought a good fight, I have finished my course, I have kept the
faith: henceforth there is laid up for me a crown of righteousness,
which the Lord, the righteous judge, shall give me at that day:
and not to me only, but unto all them also that love his appearing.*
2 Timothy 4:7, 8

The temperature one Sunday morning was -20° F. A north wind with blowing snow made us anxious about the trip to the church house. As we drove up to the sidewalks, we noticed that the snow had all been neatly swept to the side. The lights were on in the building, and the furnace was well on its way to giving each cold newcomer a warm reception.

Who would have been brave enough to venture out so early on a blustery morning like this? Who were the ones who were willing to sacrifice their own comfort to make sure others were comfortable? They had gone beyond the call of duty to show their love and devotion to their fellowmen!

As we entered the church house, we were warmly greeted by the oldest couples in the community! I should have guessed. We can always depend on their faithfulness.

I have learned to appreciate the friendship and Christian maturity of our older brothers and sisters. They have a whole lifetime of experience there for our benefit. Deep is the wisdom beneath their gray hair.

Our older people have obtained their loving Christian character as a result of a lifetime of victorious Christian living. Their lives were not lives of ease and comfort. Some of our most virtuous older people have had the most trying times in their younger years. Many were their trials and sorrows, but they were victorious. Now, today, we can reap the benefits of the hoary head that is a crown of glory because it is found in righteousness (see Proverbs 16:31).

Stephen Miller, Loyal, WI

Bible Reading: 1 Timothy 5:1-3
One Year Bible Reading Plan:
Acts 23:12-35
Psalms 38–40

---

*The aged Christian, with the snow of time upon his head, reminds
us that the whitest points on earth are those that are nearest to heaven.*
—Chapin

Working in Unity

Except the LORD build the house, they labour in vain that build it.
Psalm 127:1

We are in the process of building a church house both physically and spiritually. Different times as we have worked together as a community, people have stopped to watch and satisfy their curiosity. Someone made a remark about getting a lot done with a group of people working together.

In our church, we have people from several different trades, yet all worked together for one cause. Different times, questions arose about how a particular thing should be done. The question was relayed to the building committee, who sometimes needed to take it to the brethren.

The question came to me, "Are we putting forth just as much effort in working together spiritually?" We all have different personalities, and no two people see every issue exactly alike; but can we yield when something is decided against our opinion, when one idea is just as good as the other? May we like Aaron and Hur hold up our leader's hands until the going down of the sun (see Exodus 17:12).

Bible Reading: 1 Corinthians 1:3-12; Isaiah 41:6, 7
One Year Bible Reading Plan:
Acts 24
Psalms 41–43

Allen Byler, Alpha, KY

He who is not actively building is a hindrance.

Called to Be Saints

To all that be in Rome, beloved of God, called to be saints.
Romans 1:7

Paul declares that believers are called to be saints. Can you imagine that? If you are a Christian, you are called to be a saint. But I fear that many "Christians" want to settle for a whole lot less than becoming saints. We are called to be saints. What if one does not measure up to this calling of God to be a saint? What is God's attitude toward those who live a "so-so" kind of Christian life? The five foolish virgins in Matthew 25:1-12 did not take too seriously the call of God upon their lives. Remember, they were barred from heaven's door when they wanted to be admitted.

Saintliness is not proved by walking around with an imaginary halo over one's head; nor is holiness procured by joining a particular denomination. Sainthood is proved when believers present their bodies a living sacrifice, holy, acceptable unto God, which is their reasonable service (see Romans 12:1-2). Saintliness (or holiness) should be evidenced early in a Christian's life by his sincere desire to please God in everything he does.

Does this sound restrictive? It is not! God created man for His pleasure (Revelation 4:11). Therefore, man finds his greatest fulfillment in life by living to please God. That is what the call of God is all about—living to please Him. When we do that, we fulfill our calling to be saints.

Bible Reading: Romans 1:1-8
One Year Bible Reading Plan:
Acts 25
Psalms 44–46

Eli Kauffman, Montezuma, GA

Do good to thy friend to keep him; to thy enemy to gain him.
—Benjamin Franklin

"Where Is Your Faith?"

Then he arose, and rebuked the wind and the raging
of the water: and they ceased, and there was a calm.
Luke 8:24

On a certain day when the disciples were in a ship on the lake, they encountered a storm. They were in jeopardy, because of the wind and water. Jesus was in the boat, asleep. They awoke Him, saying, "Master, master, we perish." He rebuked the wind and raging waters, and there was calm.

The disciples struggled against the elements of nature. We find ourselves in a similar situation today. We struggle, not against nature, but against spiritual darkness and wickedness. We need to maintain a close walk with God, so that when the storms of life assail us, we can remain firm in faith and not give way to despair.

The disciples became afraid. Jesus said unto them, "Where is your faith?" As we sail on the sea of life, we will meet up with many trials and adversities. We need not cry, "Master, master, we perish." If Jesus is near, we will experience great calm.

Amos Garber, Rosebush, MI

Bible Reading: Luke 8:22-36
One Year Bible Reading Plan:
Acts 26
Psalms 47–49

If we are filled with God's cheer,
We will be free from Satan's fear.

Danger Ahead!

So the people of Nineveh believed God.
Jonah 3:5a

For the 705 survivors who lived to see the sun rise on this memorable day 87 years ago, it must have been a bittersweet experience! How sobering to realize that 1,519 friends and family members had entered eternity in the frigid Atlantic waters only days after leaving England on the Titanic's maiden voyage. The demise of this lavish vessel with accommodations adapted for millionaires might not have been so unusual, were it not for the captain's boast about her grandeur: "Even God Himself cannot sink her."

Pride and arrogance were the hallmark of the Titanic from her design to her defeat, according to survivor testimonials. The 882 foot ship slowly sank to its dark, watery grave after being cracked open by an iceberg. The captain had repeatedly disregarded urgent warnings from nearby vessels of a dangerous ice field.

We do not typically enjoy giving warnings. We flinch as we consider being rejected or scorned. Jonah was commanded to warn a city of more than 120,000 people that their wickedness would bring God's impending judgment upon them. Though Jonah resisted at first, at last he obeyed, and the city was spared because they believed.

What is our responsibility to the "ships" around us that are facing imminent danger? The easiest response is to look the other way and hope someone else will sound the warning bell. But we must speak the truth in love to those who are headed to perdition. And let us also be encouraged as we think of the joy that awaits us on the other side, if we are faithful to our Captain — Jesus Christ.

Bible Reading: Jonah 3
One Year Bible Reading Plan:
Acts 27:1-26
Psalms 50–52

Phil Hershberger, Abbeville, SC

The vocation of every man and woman is to serve other people.
—Leo Tolstoy

Consider Jesus

Wherefore, holy brethren, partakers of the heavenly calling, consider the Apostle and High Priest of our profession, Christ Jesus.
Hebrews 3:1

When we face disappointments, struggles and trials, temptations, pain, and suffering, and when we get weary and footsore with the circumstances and hum-drum of life, there is nothing more inspiring than to consider Jesus.

No doubt you have considered Him as Creator, the Savior of mankind, the only Son of God, the King of Kings and Lord of Lords, and the First and the Last. But have you ever considered Him as a man? In this there is a tender sweetness and a balm of encouragement found in no other consideration of Jesus.

"For we have not an high priest which cannot be touched with the feeling of our infirmities; but was in all points tempted like as we are, yet without sin" (Hebrews 4:15).

"He took not on him the nature of angels" (Hebrews 2:16) . . . but "took upon him the form of a servant, and was made in the likeness of men" (Philippians 2:7).

Hebrews 2:16–18 gives us three points of strong encouragement: 1) Jesus is merciful. He is touched with your suffering. 2) Jesus is faithful. He will not forsake you. 3) Jesus is able to help you. He Himself suffered, was tempted, and is able to help them that are tempted.

Jesus is both our apostle and our high priest. An apostle's work is from God to man. The high priest's work is from man to God. In Christ we can both hear from God and speak to Him.

Glory hallelujah! As I face today, I have a friend to whom I may turn! He knows and understands me. He feels for me. He has all power, and is able to do exceeding abundantly above all that I ask or think.

Willard Hochstetler, Woodburn, IN

Bible Reading: Hebrews 2:16-18; 4:14-16
One Year Bible Reading Plan:
Acts 27:27–44
Psalms 53–55

When we consider Jesus, we have what we need for each day.

Heaven

And I saw a new heaven . . .
Revelation 21:1a

We often wonder what heaven will be like. We have friends and relatives who have passed on, and we wonder what experiences they enjoy. God, in His sovereignty, has not told us exactly what it will be like, but in Revelation 21 we get a glimpse of heaven and the life beyond.

Can you imagine not having the sun, moon, or stars to give light? On this earth, there would be total darkness, but on the new earth, the glory of God shines throughout, and there is no need for any other light. There, we will not face the hardships that we see here every day. There will be no pain, no crying or sorrow, and no more death. . . . These former things will all pass away. God will wipe away all tears, and we will never have to part with close friends or family members, as we have on earth.

Can you imagine a city of pure gold, or walking down those glittering streets? Can you imagine the glory of that place? And it is promised to us! The nations of those who are saved shall walk in it. The gates will never close, and there will never be any evil entering that wonderful place. Only those whose names are written in the Lamb's book of life will be allowed to enter. The day of Jesus' return is coming soon, so let us make sure we are ready. Then we can go to see God's glorious place with our own eyes, and put our imaginations to rest! ". . . So shall we ever be with the Lord" (1 Thessalonians. 4:17).

Bible Reading: Revelation 21
One Year Bible Reading Plan:
Acts 28:1-15
Psalms 56–58

Michael Coblentz, Hicksville, OH

Heaven is a prepared place for a prepared people.

Can I Do This in Christ's Name?

And whatsoever ye do in word or deed, do all in the name
of the Lord Jesus, giving thanks to God and the Father by him.
Colossians 3:17

Colossians 3:17 could be called "sanctification in a nutshell." "Whatever you do or say," says Paul, "let it be representative of the Lord Jesus."

Life constantly confronts us with big and little problems. Sticky situations arise, pressing upon us choices, in which it is hard to see the difference between self-interest and the right thing to do. We do not have a ready-made answer book for every situation.

The Pharisees tried to make a rule for every circumstance, and they were a sorry sight to behold, as Jesus pointed out time and again (Matthew 23:13-28; Mark 7:1-3). Instead of having a little rule book that we carry around for every dilemma, we need a standard, "Can I do this in Christ's name?"

When the Scriptures say we should do things in the name of the Lord Jesus, they are talking about our motives. Will this or that thing I am planning to do honor Jesus Christ? Will it promote His name and the cause for which He stands? Or, will it merely please me? One means of checking our motives is mentioned in our key verse, which says we are to do all giving thanks to God. Obviously, if I am doing something sinful or selfish, I cannot give the Father thanks for it. In this way, we have an automatic check on our motives, a practical way to evaluate what we have been doing, and what we plan to do.

Bible Reading: Colossians 3:1-17
One Year Bible Reading Plan:
Acts 28:16-31
Psalms 59–61

Eugene Schlabach, Free Union, VA

Whether therefore ye eat, or drink, or whatsoever ye do,
do all to the glory of God.
—1 Corinthians 10:31

Occupy Till I Come

*So that ye come behind in no gift; waiting for the
coming of our Lord Jesus Christ.*
1 Corinthians 1:7

Jesus has now returned to the Father. We are responsible to take on the work of our Lord. How thankful we can be that we were not left without direction. Jesus left His last will and testament for our road map.

How are we occupying the time God has allotted to us? Are we profitable to His kingdom, or are we preoccupied with our own pursuits and interests? As we rise each morning, do our thoughts go to God and what we might do for Him, or are we lost in our own thoughts and endeavors? "Here am I; send me," should be our motto each day. If we plan to go to town, do we tell God we are open to helping someone there with a spiritual need or question? Are we looking for opportunities to occupy in the Lord's work?

Someday our Nobleman will return to see what we have done with our pounds. We all have an equal opportunity. We will all have to give account. God will demand our profits and audit our books. When He weighs us in the balance, will we be found wanting? Life is brief—only what we do for Christ will last. Let us be occupied in the Lord's work till He comes.

Bible Reading: Luke 19:12-27
One Year Bible Reading Plan:
  Romans 1
  Psalms 62–64

Dale Troyer, Purdin, MO

---

*Let men laugh if they will, when you sacrifice desire for duty.
You have time and eternity to rejoice in.*
—Parker

_____

God Knows Us By Name

He calleth his own sheep by name, and leadeth them out.
John 10:3

The sound of our own name is usually pleasant to our ears. When people address us by name, it tells us that they know us and recognize us as individuals.

I am a farmer with a small dairy. Each of my cows has a name and number. I have a record for each of them as individuals. I am acquainted with each cow's habits, temperament, and producing ability.

Our all-knowing God also knows each of us as an individual. His books are large enough to hold the lifetime record of each of the billions of people that populate the earth. He knows each by name, and loves each one.

During Jesus' earthly ministry, He had time for individuals. One disciple, Nathaniel, was amazed that Jesus had noticed him and knew about his life. And imagine Zaccheus' surprise, perched in a tree to catch a glimpse of the Lord in the passing crowd, when Jesus looked up at him, called his name, and told him that he planned to visit in his house.

Our Savior knows us and cares about our individual needs. While it is true that in many ways we function collectively with others, yet our relationship with our Lord is also very much a personal, individual experience. Let us cultivate an intimate relationship with our loving Father.

Bible Reading: Psalm 139:1-18
One Year Bible Reading Plan:
   Romans 2
   Psalms 65–67

John Glick, Gap, PA

_____

God knows us better than we know ourselves.

218

Time Is Short, Eternity Sure

Where there is no vision, the people perish.
Proverbs 29:18

What are we doing to warn lost souls headed for eternity in hell? In hell the lost will burn forever. They will find no relief from pain, and no water to quench their thirst. Hell is total darkness, a bottomless pit, with no escape, and no hope; where the worm dieth not and the fire is not quenched.

How can we sit back in ease when souls are going to a place like that? "Let your light so shine before men, that they may see your good works, and glorify your Father which is in heaven." Let us be good examples in the way we act, talk, and dress. Pass out tracts, put up a Gospel sign out by the road, or a Gospel message plate on your vehicle, or conduct street meetings with your youth.

Renew my vision, Lord. Impress upon me the urgency of the hour, and the reality of danger, and love for men's souls. Fill me with Your love—the kind that sees beyond this present easy moment to fast approaching eternity. Give me that love which sees not just another figure, but an individual person with human thoughts, feelings, goals, and trials, whom You created and love and who is headed for one of two places —either heaven or hell.

Bible Reading: Ezekiel 33:8-9; Mark 1:14-22
One Year Bible Reading Plan: Romans 3; Psalms 68, 69

Ernest Stoll, Odon, IN

Time is running out. Today is the day of salvation.

Fellowship With Each Other

*A new commandment I give unto you, That ye love one another; as I
have loved you, that ye also love one another. By this shall all men
know that ye are my disciples, if ye have love one to another . . .*
John 13:34, 35

The word *fellowship* in the New Testament means "communion" or "intimate communication."

The kind of fellowship we have with each other in the local
congregation is a result of our fellowship with God. Many times we
act shamefully toward each other and still claim to have true fellowship with God. This is a lie, for we are clearly taught in the
Word that if we do not have love for our brethren, the love of God
is not in us, and we abide in death (see 1 John 3:14).

In order to have fellowship with and love for, each other, we
must have fellowship with the Word of Life (Jesus Christ). We must
be careful that we do not have a pretense of fellowship with each
other. When we have God's Spirit within us, we love each other
because we love the same God, and then we also share a common
ground. We share and commune with each other, which creates a
partnership between brothers.

When there is true fellowship, we do not judge one another.
We cannot bite and devour one another, nor provoke, envy, speak
evil of, or grumble about one another.

True fellowship builds up. We receive one another in a kind
and tender way. We forgive and
forbear. We practice hospitality
one to another. We are also free
to admonish, instruct, submit to,
and comfort one another. This is
true fellowship, which brings
warmth to the heart and soul.

> **Bible Reading:** 1 John 1
> **One Year Bible Reading Plan:**
> Romans 4
> Psalms 70–72

Mervin Lantz, Lott, TX

There is a world to be won; it will be won, as we are one.

What Is Your Load Limit?

There hath no temptation taken you but such as is common to man:
but God is faithful, who will not suffer you to be tempted
above that ye are able; but will with the temptation
also make a way to escape, that ye may be able to bear it.
1 Corinthians 10:13

We have all seen load limit signs on highways, bridges, or elevators. Knowing that too much strain can cause severe damage or complete collapse, engineers determine the exact amount of stress that various materials can safely bear. Posted warnings tell us not to exceed the maximum load.

Human beings also have their load limits, which vary from person to person. Some people can bear the pressure of trials and temptations better than others, yet each one has a breaking point and can take only so much.

At times, circumstances and people seem to be pushing us beyond what we can bear, but the Lord knows our limitations and never allows any difficulties to enter our lives that exceed our strength and ability to endure. This is especially true when we are enticed by sin. Our key verse tells us that our faithful God will not allow us to be tempted above that which we are able to endure. When trials and temptations press down on you, take courage! Remember, your heavenly Father knows the limits of your ability to stand up under life's pressure. Lean upon His strength and no temptation will ever be greater than you can take with God's help.

Bible Reading: 1 Corinthians 10:1-13
One Year Bible Reading Plan:
Romans 5
Psalms 73, 74

Paul Stoltzfus, Morgantown, PA

If you give in to God, you will not cave in to sin.

I Believe in God

For the invisible things of him from the creation of the world
are clearly seen, being understood by the things that are made.
Romans 1:20

Recently I made the acquaintance of a man from Spain and spent some time talking with him about religion and witnessing of the greatness of our God and the blessings of being a Christian. In the course of our conversation, it became evident that he was a humanist who believes that man is the supreme being and in himself is basically good. He spoke very much of taking care of the environment, but would not acknowledge the One who created it.

Meditating later, the question came to me, "On what do we base our faith in an all-wise, all-powerful God? Why do we believe in a Supreme Being who created the universe?" Is it not the very Creation itself, the beauty and order which we contemplate every day, that points us toward our God?

Our faith is not blind. It is based on facts, and on visible signs which we see with our natural eyes. Step outside tonight and consider the stars. Take time to admire the creation around you. Study what man has been able to learn about the laws that govern the earth. Then honor and glorify the Maker of all this.

Never let modern humanistic reasoning shake your simple faith in our Creator, the Lord of Lords and King of kings, our Savior. May we not be afraid to testify that having experienced the work of grace in our hearts, we know that our Redeemer lives.

Bible Reading: Romans 1:18-25
One Year Bible Reading Plan:
Romans 6
Psalms 75–77

Joel Showalter, Guaracacal, Honduras

That which I have seen teaches me to
believe in that which I have not seen.

God Keeps His Promises

There failed not ought of any good thing which the LORD
had spoken unto the house of Israel; all came to pass.
Joshua 21:45

God keeps His promises! He also keeps His warnings! Joshua testified that not one of the good promises God had made to Israel failed; they all came to pass. This is comforting and reassuring.

After he testified of God's faithfulness to all His promises, Joshua then pled with Israel to be careful to observe all the commandments God had given through Moses. He admonished them to be "very courageous to keep and to do all that is written in the book of the law of Moses." *Keep* means "to take care of, to attend carefully, to guard from loss, to watch over." In addition to this guarding the commandments, they were to practice them.

Then, Joshua warned Israel. If they ceased to love God and to keep and practice His commands, He would no longer drive out the enemy nations before them. These nations would become a snare and a trap to them.

God keeps His promises! Just as He keeps the promises of His blessing, so He keeps the promise of removing His blessing. "When ye have transgressed . . . ye shall perish quickly from off the good land" (Joshua 23:16). According to biblical history, God kept His pledge that Israel would lose the land if she did not follow Him fully.

The Bible is a book of promises—promises of everlasting life and sins forgiven through Jesus Christ; promises of peace and joy the world cannot give; and promises of the reward of heaven for eternity. To the faithful who sow to the Spirit, God keeps His promises. However, to the unfaithful, who sow to the flesh, the promise of reaping corruption holds true as it did for Israel.

Bible Reading: Galatians 6:6-19
One Year Bible Reading Plan:
Romans 7
Psalms 78

Reaping the good promises comes from faithful doing and keeping. Therefore, be faithful. Your labor in the Lord is not in vain.

Simon Schrock, Fairfax, VA

God promised a harvest from the seed you sow!

Rooted or Uprooted?

And he shall be like a tree planted by the rivers of water,
that bringeth forth his fruit in his season.
Psalm 1:3

Recently we were clearing some brush and were reminded that certain trees are rooted more firmly than others. Some have very shallow roots, which accounts for a tree being easily pushed over. Others have roots that reach out far and go deep.

How is it in your spiritual life? Are your roots only close to the surface? If so, when the storms of life come, you will be pushed over easily. Be like a tree whose roots reach out far and deep! Such roots come only through a close walk with God, by daily meditating on His Word and communicating with God in prayer. Then when adversities or trials come your way, you will be able to stand and point others to Christ.

The fruit of the Spirit—love, joy, peace, long-suffering, gentleness, goodness, faith, meekness, and temperance—is the product of a spiritual life with roots that go far and deep.

May we put our roots down deep by studying and following God's Word. Then will He be praised and others will be drawn to Him.

Bible Reading: Colossians 2:6-12
One Year Bible Reading Plan:
Romans 8:1-18
Psalms 79–81

Joseph Yoder, Falkville, AL

The lighthouse sounds no drums, it beats no gong,
yet, far over the waters its friendly light is seen.
—Culyer

Are You a Beggar?

*But God hath chosen the foolish things of the world to
confound the wise; and God hath chosen the weak
things of the world to confound the things which are mighty.*
1 Corinthians 1:27

The Gospels record many accounts of healing by the power of God through faith in Jesus Christ. Notice the type of people who were healed. Some were blind, some lame, some deaf, or dumb. Others were leprous or filled with evil spirits, and a few were already dead. They were "beggars." They recognized a need in their life and pled for help. With that attitude and faith, they could receive healing. Jesus, who was criticized for eating with publicans and sinners, said, "They that are whole need not a physician; but they that are sick."

Do we think we need to be great in the eyes of men, to be useful to God?

Joseph was young, despised by his brothers, sold to the Ishmaelites, falsely accused by Potiphar's wife, and thrown into prison. Joseph became governor of Egypt and recognized God's hand in it, to save many people's lives (Genesis 50:20).

Someone once said to Dr. Hudson Taylor, "You must often be conscious of the wonderful way God has prospered you in the China Inland Mission. I doubt if any man living has had a greater honor." He replied, "I do not look at it in that way. I sometimes think that God must have been looking for someone small enough and weak enough for Him to use so that all the glory might be His, and that He found me."

Bible Reading: 1 Corinthians 1:18-31
One Year Bible Reading Plan:
Romans 8:19-39
Psalms 82–84

Glen Helmuth, Belvidere, TN

Humble yourselves in the sight of the Lord, and he shall lift you up.
—James 4:10

Are You Successful?

*I have fought a good fight, I have finished
my course, I have kept the faith.*
2 Timothy 4:7

To say we live in a "success" oriented society is an understatement. Much time and effort is put into accumulating wealth and possessions and having "good" times.

In 2 Timothy 4 Paul, the aged apostle, gives a farewell charge to Timothy and includes a reminder that all men shall be judged by Jesus Christ. As he reviewed his life, Paul stated three things he had done: "I have fought a good fight. I have finished my course. I have kept the faith." Courage, endurance, and faithfulness. No mention is made of wealth or property, but wouldn't we all agree that Paul was a "success"?

How well are we doing in the good fight of faith? Successful Christian living involves conflict with evil; especially the evil that is inherent in our human nature. Although you may become weary of conflict, take courage, there will be a reward for fighting a good fight.

The course God gave you to run may be rocky, or lead through valleys with deep waters. To finish the course requires endurance. Even as a runner in a relay is disqualified if he takes a short cut or violates the rules, so we will not be rewarded unless we run with patience and endurance.

Have you kept the faith? Probably the best way to keep it is to share it with others, especially your children, neighbors, and business associates. Faithfulness in this area will certainly result in success.

Your "success" is assured as you keep the charge given to you: to fight the good fight, to endure in the course, and to keep the faith.

Ivan R. Beachy, Free Union, VA

Bible Reading: 2 Timothy 4:1-8
One Year Bible Reading Plan:
Romans 9
Psalms 85–87

---

*Success depends not on opportunity,
but on motivation and commitment.*

Help to the Finish Line

*Wherefore, seeing we also are compassed about with so great
a cloud of witnesses, let us lay aside every weight, and
the sin which doth so easily beset us, and let us run with
patience the race that is set before us.*
Hebrews 12:1

Life is like a marathon, anyone who enters may finish and be a winner. The speed of one runner may make him more noticed, but even the last one to stagger over the finish line wins. Hebrews 12:1-3 gives us several keys to help us win.

We are compassed about with many witnesses. While the praise of men should not be our desire, yet we can take courage from others who have finished the race, and witness by their lives that God does reward those who diligently seek Him (Hebrews 11:6).

We will be better able to run if we lay aside every weight. No runner carries excess baggage through a race! He sheds every hindrance to reaching his goal.

We must lay aside the sin that so easily besets us. For all of us the tendency to sin is a daily possibility. To cross the finish line, we must recognize and discard all sin.

Look to Jesus as the example. He finished His work, even though it was not easy. He endured the agony of the cross, despising the shame of that horrible death. Today, from His vantage point at the right hand of God, He remembers the suffering and the pain. His Word to us rings clear, "Consider him that endured such contradiction of sinners against himself lest ye be wearied and faint in your minds." Following Christ, you too can finish your life in triumph.

Merle Beachy, Free Union, VA

Bible Reading: Hebrews 12:1-16
One Year Bible Reading Plan:
Romans 10
Psalms 88, 89

Sprinters are everywhere, but finishers are few.

August 11

True Repentance

Therefore also now, saith the LORD, turn ye even to me with all your heart, and with fasting, and with weeping, and with mourning.
Joel 2:12

Mike considered himself a good Christian man. He did not drink or take drugs. He worked hard and always tried to be honest, and he remained faithful to his wife. He felt quite pleased with himself.

One day Mike was diagnosed with a serious illness. He was totally devastated. Fear gripped his heart each time he recalled the doctor's somber expression when he uttered that dreaded word—"cancer." Where was God, anyway? Why would He allow such a terrible thing to happen to him? Mike just could not understand.

Then Mike thought of his neighbor down the road. Farmer Ben was one man he trusted completely. His faith was genuine. Surely he would be able to help.

At the sight of his neighbor, Ben slowed the tractor engine to an idle, climbed off, and offered a welcoming hand. That was all Mike needed. He began to pour out his feelings of doubt and fear, while also calling attention to his own moral virtues. Ben listened carefully and then proceeded to testify how Jesus came to deliver us from the power of sin and the fear of death.

Mike suddenly became uneasy and was soon bidding farewell. You see, Mike had a problem. He was addicted to tobacco and was not willing to give it up. Besides, he insisted, his other good qualities would more than offset this one little sin.

Mike is typical of many professing Christians—proud, inconsistent, worldly, and weak. Their problem stems from an unsurrendered heart—one that has never fully repented.

True biblical repentance calls for mourning and weeping and restitution as much as is possible. Only thus we can grow to be individuals of character, conviction, and holiness. Search me, O God!

Bible Reading: Joel 2
One Year Bible Reading Plan:
Romans 11:1-21
Psalms 90–92

Allen Beiler, Stuarts Draft, VA

Christianity that costs nothing is also worth nothing.

228

The Fear of God

But I will forewarn you whom ye shall fear: Fear him, which after he hath killed hath power to cast into hell; yea, I say unto you, Fear him.
Luke 12:5

In Genesis 20 we read of the time Abraham and Sarah sojourned in Gerar. Abraham did not tell Abimelech the full truth about Sarah, saying, "She is my sister," because he was afraid for his life. When Abimelech reproved Abraham for saying, "She is my sister," Abraham said, "Surely the fear of God is not in this place" (Genesis 20:11). He knew that people who do not have the fear of God cannot be trusted, and it is still so today.

The fear of the Lord is sadly lacking in our society today. Yes, it is true that God is a God of love, and we are commanded: "love the Lord thy God with all thy heart, and with all thy soul, and with all thy mind, and with all thy strength" (Mark 12:30). However, we are also to have a godly fear, which, I believe, means to be afraid to do anything that is not according to God's will. To understand the balance between godly love and godly fear, we can think of how we love and respect our parents. We fear them in that we are afraid to do anything that is wrong or that they have commanded us not to do.

The fear of God is greatly needed in our day, and also needs to be taught to the oncoming generation (see Deuteronomy 31:12-13).

> **Bible Reading:** Deuteronomy 5:22-33
> **One Year Bible Reading Plan:**
> Romans 11:22-36
> Psalms 93–95

Joe Kurtz, Belleville, PA

Let us hear the conclusion of the whole matter: Fear God, and keep his commandments: for this is the whole duty of man.
—Ecclesiastes 12:13

August 13

God Sees and Cares

. . . Thou God seest me.
Genesis 16:13

It was time to quit, but I wanted to finish moving some dirt with the skid loader. Suddenly, above the hum of the motor, I heard the frantic cries of a killdeer nearby. Immediately, I shut off the machine and searched the area for the nest. No doubt I had destroyed it.

I pondered. If God's eyes were like mine, and His ears like my ears, I too could be trampled on. But thanks be to God, He sees me. He will not suffer me to be tempted above that which I am able to bear. He will never leave me, nor forsake me. He cares for me. Like Hagar, I can say, "Thou God seest me."

Of all earth's six billion people, not one person escapes His eye. His ear is open to every cry.

When Joseph was sold into Egypt and unjustly put into prison, God saw! His purposes were ripening fast.

When the prophet Elijah was fleeing from Jezebel, he may well have wondered if God saw what he was facing. God did see! He directed Elijah back to the work to which He had called him.

David knew the darkness of caves and seclusion. In agony, he voiced his questions in Psalm 10:1: "Why standest thou afar off, O Lord? Why hidest thou thyself in times of trouble?" After meditating on God's ways and His judgments, David mounts on faith's solid rock in verse 16, saying, "The Lord is King for ever and ever." Let us pray his prayer: "Lord, thou hast heard the desire of the humble: thou wilt prepare their heart, thou wilt cause thine ear to hear" (Psalm 10:17).

Clayton Weaver, Linneus, MO

Bible Reading: Genesis 21:9-21
One Year Bible Reading Plan:
Romans 12
Psalms 96–98

He whose eye is on the sparrow is also watching you.

An Incorruptible Crown

*Blessed is the man that endureth temptation, for
when he is tried he shall receive the crown of life.*
James 1:12a

Sometime ago a man in our community was rewarded for outstanding faithfulness to his job. He had worked for fifteen years without missing a single day; and in those fifteen years he had never once been late to work. This took real dedication and was worthy of recognition.

Many people are very diligent and put forth much effort for that which will soon pass away. Certainly, we need to be faithful in our daily jobs, but as Christians we have an even higher calling, to strive for an incorruptible crown. May the dedication of this man to his earthly job challenge us to strive for that crown of glory that fadeth not away (1 Peter 5:4). The apostle Paul said, "I press toward the mark for the prize of the high calling of God in Christ Jesus" (Philippians 3:14).

> **Bible Reading:** 1 Corinthians
> 9:19-27
> **One Year Bible Reading Plan:**
> Romans 13
> Psalms 99–102

Ed Hochstetler, Hicksville, OH

Be thou faithful unto death, and I will give thee a crown of life.
—Revelation 2:10

August 15

Have Faith in God

Faithful is he that calleth you, who also will do it.
1 Thessalonians 5:24

Things are going well; we are experiencing the "the joy of the LORD" within our hearts. Suddenly, an unexpected obstacle blocks our intended path. We cannot understand the purpose of it. How do we respond?

Satan will tempt us to question God or to wallow in self-pity and discouragement. But these responses are wrong and will produce sour fruit.

As Christians, we can rest in the fact that God has a purpose for allowing trials to come into our lives. As we respond properly to these situations and maintain our faith in God, what now seem like stumbling blocks will become steppingstones for us. They will enhance our Christian character and increase our faith in God.

Consider the circumstances that confronted Joseph, Moses, Elisha, and Daniel. It was not possible for them to understand fully their situations, but God was faithful! He forever will be faithful!

When you face trying situations in life, remember, "Faithful is he that calleth you, who also will do it."

John Dale Yoder, Belvidere, TN

> **Bible Reading:** Exodus 14:10-31
> **One Year Bible Reading Plan:**
>   Romans 14
>   Psalms 103, 104

---

*Man's greatest strength is often shown
in his ability to stand still and trust.*

Meats for the Belly

All things are lawful unto me, but all things are not expedient:
all things are lawful for me, but I will not be brought
under the power of any. Meats for the belly, and the belly
for meats: but God shall destroy both it and them.
1 Corinthians 6:12-13

It has often been said that the way to a man's heart is through his stomach. It was through the appetite that man fell in the garden and sin entered the human race. Down through the millennia, man has repeatedly fallen into sin because of his cravings for food. Even Noah, a man who walked with God, fell into this trap. "And Noah . . . planted a vineyard: and he drank of the wine, and was drunken; and he was uncovered within his tent" (Genesis 9:20-21). The sad story of God's people in the wilderness also reveals a failure along this line. Gluttony was the downfall of Eli, when God asked, "Wherefore kick ye at my sacrifice and at mine offering, which I have commanded in my habitation; and honourest thy sons above me, to make yourselves fat with the chiefest of all the offerings of Israel my people?" (1 Samuel 2:29).

Jesus said that "eating and drinking" would characterize the days prior to His return, just as they had in the time of Noah. This describes more than the necessary eating and drinking to sustain life; it describes the indulgence and drunkenness we see around us today: smorgasbords and buffets are commonplace, seven course meals are the Sunday norm, and diet books top the best seller lists.

The first Adam failed to control his appetite, the last Adam was victorious over his appetite. After a forty-day fast in the wilderness at the beginning of His ministry, Jesus kept His body in subjection and did not yield to its demands. By this, He set the example that few have been able to follow. He has shown us that the body is to be our servant, not our master.

Bible Reading: Luke 12:42-46; 21:34-36
One Year Bible Reading Plan:
Romans 15:1-21
Psalms 105, 106

Phil Haines, Perdmontemps, Grenada

Do we eat to live or live to eat?

And the Door Was Shut!

And while they went to buy, the bridegroom came; and they that were ready went in with him to the marriage: and the door was shut.
Matthew 25:10

Locked out! That is just what happened to me one cold, wintry afternoon. How frustrating! Finding no one at home when I came home from work, I put my lunch pail and keys on the counter and headed for the mailbox. As I shut the door behind me, I realized I had just locked myself out of the house. I got the mail and checked all the doors. I was locked out! Resignedly, I huddled in a corner of the front porch, put on my gloves, and read the daily paper, awaiting my family's return, and my rescue.

As I waited, I realized that my foolishness had brought me only temporary consequences. I recalled incidents in which people were shut out with eternal consequences. Think of the fate of those for whom it was too late to enter the ark with Noah. Think of the five foolish virgins, who appeared to be ready but found the door shut.

In today's Scripture, we find two groups of people meeting the bridegroom: the prepared and the unprepared.

Keeping our lamps trimmed and burning is the work of the Holy Spirit who directs our lives from within. He directs our thoughts and actions. His work of grace in our lives keeps our lamps from going out. We can be prepared to meet our Bridegroom, only as we listen to, and obey, the Holy Spirit's guidance. We all need our own personal walk with God. We can encourage another in his walk with the Lord, but we cannot borrow another's personal experience for our own.

Your walk with God should be preparing you for eternity with the Bridegroom.

Wayne Mishler, Goshen, IN

Bible Reading: Matthew 25:1-13
One Year Bible Reading Plan:
Romans 15:22-33
Psalms 107, 108

Now is the time to invest in eternity!

Clean Water

Wherefore come out from among them, and be ye separate, saith
the Lord, and touch not the unclean thing; and I will receive you.
2 Corinthians 6:17

If you fill two glasses—one with clean water and the other with dirty water—there will be a notable difference. If you pour off some of the dirty water into the clean glass, the dirty water will not become clean. The only way to make the dirty glass drinkable is to pour the dirty water out, wash out the glass, and fill it with new, clean water.

Life is like a glass of water. If we allow "dirty water" in our lives, it will simply make our lives dirty. One of our ministers recently attended a funeral, and a woman was behind the pulpit preaching the message. The message she gave was a Gospel message, and the songs were familiar Gospel hymns. This situation probably did not seem strange to a lot of people at the funeral. But our minister said it just did not seem right. "Know ye not that a little leaven leaveneth the whole lump?" (1 Corinthians 5:6). A child of God recognizes behavior that is out of God's order, and contrary to the teachings of Scripture.

Many churches today are being deceived and led astray by false prophets. Though these shepherds may be highly esteemed by men, they are nothing more than glasses of dirty water posing as glasses of clean water. To maintain clean lives we must stay true to the Scriptures and only "desire the sincere milk of the word" (1 Peter 2:2).

Bible Reading: 2 Corinthians 11:1-15
One Year Bible Reading Plan:
Romans 16
Psalms 109–111

Terry Lester, Montezuma, GA

Christ makes all the difference.

_____

Miserable "Supposes"

*Trust in the L*ORD*, and do good; so shalt thou dwell*
in the land, and verily thou shalt be fed.
Psalm 37:3

As I meditate on Psalm 37:3, I think of an account I read recently by a person who met a poor Christian woman who earned a precarious living by daily labor. This poor woman was a joyous and triumphant Christian. "Oh, Nancy," said a gloomy Christian lady to the poor woman one day, "it is well enough to be happy now; but I should think the thoughts of your future would sober you. Only suppose for instance, you should have a spell of sickness, and be unable to work; or, suppose your present employer should move away, and no one else should give you anything to do; or, suppose . . ."

"Stop!" cried Nancy, "I never suppose. The Lord is my Shepherd, and I know I shall not want. It's all the supposes that are making you so miserable. You had better give them all up and just trust the Lord."

How true! We sometimes suppose all the things that could go wrong, and we forget that God is in control. He takes care of all those things that we cannot see in the future.

At the start of this new day, put your full trust in Him who is able to take care of all the problems in life.

Mark Byler, Mill Creek, PA

Bible Reading: Psalm 37:1-10
One Year Bible Reading Plan:
  1 Corinthians 1
  Psalms 112–115

_____

The eagle that soars in the upper air does not
worry itself about crossing the rivers.

Woe

Woe unto them that are wise in their own eyes,
and prudent in their own sight!
Isaiah 5:21

As we read our Bibles, often we see the word *woe*. As the Old Testament prophets proclaimed God's message to His people, they often gave warnings of *woe* if God's will was not followed. *Woe* meant there would be judgment, sorrow, and affliction to those who sinned. Many woes were pronounced by the prophets upon many generations, from Isaiah to Zechariah. In the Gospels, Jesus often used the word *woe*. In Revelation, three successive woes are given to announce God's final judgment on unrighteousness (Revelation 8:13). No disobedience will be tolerated by our holy God. We must repent of all sin.

In our Bible reading today, woe is pronounced on those who call evil good and good evil; who call darkness light, and light darkness; who call bitter sweet, and sweet bitter. God has given man His Word, His truth, and His will. As we believe God and obey His Word, we are able to discern what is good and what is evil. We have the Ten Commandments and the Sermon on the Mount, very basic teachings in right and wrong. However, we are living in a time when many call evil good, and good evil. They justify adultery, killing the unborn, and lying. They are wise in their own eyes, but God says, "Woe unto them that draw iniquity with cords of vanity" (Isaiah 5:18).

In Acts 17, as the truth was proclaimed, the apostles were accused of turning the world upside down (Acts 17:6). Their accusers did not understand that the whole world lies in wickedness. The morals of sinful man have been turned the wrong way, and Paul and Silas were trying to proclaim the truth that would turn the world right side up.

Bible Reading: Isaiah 5:20-25
One Year Bible Reading Plan:
1 Corinthians 2
Psalms 116–118

Follow the truth, the light that has been given to us by God, and do not be among those who are wise in their own eyes. Does my life have God's blessing, or is He saying to me, *woe*?

Ed Hochstetler, Hicksville, OH

Blessing or woe—which will it be?

Our Great God

And we know that all things work together for good to them that love God, to them who are the called according to his purpose.
Romans 8:28

Have you ever been in a situation that caused you to question whether "all things work together for good to them that love God"? God brings us to those places so that He can glorify Himself, but we must commit everything to Him.

In our Scripture reading, we find Paul and Silas being faithful to their calling by teaching, preaching, and casting out evil spirits. Next, they end up in the inner prison, with their feet fast in the stocks. Paul and Silas might have questioned whether "all things work together for good to them that love God." But Paul and Silas did not dwell in self-pity. Instead, they prayed and sang praises to God. Then things began to happen! There was a great earthquake. The foundation of the prison was shaken, doors were opened, and everyone's bands were loosed. Then the jailer asked, "Sirs, what must I do to be saved?" They told him what he must do. The jailer was not the only one baptized, but "he and all his."

Is it not amazing what God can do when His people are faithful in doing their part? We certainly serve an awesome God. May we be challenged to be faithful in loving Him and doing that which He gives us to do.

Harry Bender, Hicksville, OH

Bible Reading: Acts 16:16-34
One Year Bible Reading Plan:
1 Corinthians 3
Psalm 119:1-48

Every step toward Christ kills a doubt.
—Theodore Culyer

Time to Care

*But whoso hath this world's good, and seeth his brother
have need, and shutteth up his bowels of compassion from him,
how dwelleth the love of God in him?*
1 John 3:17

One summer day, my wife and daughter were working in the yard, while our two youngest children played nearby. Suddenly, the sound of a siren reached them from a nearby highway. Immediately, our two-year-old son dropped everything and raced for the house. My wife asked him where he was going so fast. "Quick, quick," he gasped breathlessly. "I have to pray!" With that, he raced to the couch to pray in childish faith for those in distress.

Later, we chuckled as my wife shared this incident at the supper table. Along with the humor, though, the Lord used this little incident to point out some spiritual truths.

Compassion involves action. Matthew 9:36 tells us that Jesus was moved with compassion for the multitude. Kind words are often not enough. When the situation calls for action, we must be willing to respond.

Compassion involves sacrifice. Today's Scripture shows Jesus using seven loaves and a few little fish to feed a great multitude. Christ used someone's small sacrifice to meet a great need.

True compassion involves God. Without the blessings of Christ, seven loaves and a few fish would have made a pathetic little pile in comparison to the needs of the multitude. It was only as the sacrifice was placed into the hands of the Master that the need could be met. May God give us discernment to see and respond to the needs around us in a Christ-like way!

Samson Eicher, Grabill, IN

Bible Reading: Matthew 15:21-39
One Year Bible Reading Plan:
1 Corinthians 4
Psalm 119:49-104

God uses submitted, compassionate hearts to do His work.

_____

Let Us Sing

Rejoice in the LORD, *O ye righteous:*
for praise is comely for the upright.
Psalm 33:1

Singing has always played a vital role in the worship of God. Psalms were sung in the Temple. Jesus and his disciples sang a hymn after He had instituted the Lord's Supper. Paul encouraged believers to address one another with psalms and hymns and spiritual songs (Ephesians 5:19). Why should God's people sing? We sing because it is an effective way to express our adoration, our supplication, or our testimony. Through song, we praise our God and edify one another.

The writer of Psalm 33 called on the Israelites to sing praises to God for His powerful Word, His unfailing counsels, and His continual concern for His people. Even when we feel down, we should still sing to God.

If you truly love the Lord, join enthusiastically with others in praising Him through song. When you are all alone, and your heart is full: sing! Do not worry about how it sounds. The Lord is pleased with any melody of praise that comes from the heart.

Bible Reading: Psalm 33:1-11
One Year Bible Reading Plan:
1 Corinthans 5
Psalm 119:105-176

Paul Stoltzfus, Morgantown, PA

_____

When your heart is full of Christ, you will want to sing.
—Spurgeon

The Paradoxes of Faith

And every one that hath forsaken houses, or brethren, or sisters, or father, or mother, or wife, or children, or lands, for my name's sake, shall receive an hundredfold, and shall inherit everlasting life.
Matthew 19:29

Scripture teaches us many paradoxes. We need to remind ourselves of these from time to time. Jesus said in Matthew 19:21, "If thou wilt be perfect, go and sell that thou hast, and give to the poor, and thou shalt have treasure in heaven." Surrender of earthly treasure secures for us a spiritual treasure.

"And he [Jesus] sat down, and called the twelve, and saith unto them, If any man desire to be first, the same shall be last of all, and servant of all" (Mark 9:35). Humility leads to exaltation. Servanthood leads to becoming kings and priests in God's kingdom.

"Verily, verily, I say unto you, Except a corn of wheat fall into the ground and die, it abideth alone: but if it die, it bringeth forth much fruit" (John 12:24). Life comes out of death. As we lose our identity in giving up our will, much fruit results. "For whosoever will save his life shall lose it; but whosoever shall lose his life for my sake and the gospel's, the same shall save it" (Mark 8:35).

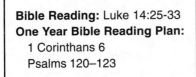

Bible Reading: Luke 14:25-33
One Year Bible Reading Plan:
1 Corinthians 6
Psalms 120–123

We seek security. We shall find it as we accept the character and will of God.

Reuben Miller, Belvidere, TN

But God hath chosen the foolish things of the world to confound the wise. . . . That no flesh should glory in his presence.
—1 Corinthians 1:27, 29

_____

A Solid Foundation

For other foundation can no man lay than
that is laid, which is Jesus Christ.
1 Corinthians 3:11

A terrific storm was sweeping over the northeast coast. The people of a certain city said to one another, "The lighthouse has gone down." Three days later, the keeper of the lighthouse was seen upon the streets of the city, and one of his friends said to him, "We heard that the lighthouse went down in the storm." The old keeper looked at him in amazement and replied, "Gone down?! It is true the storm was the fiercest I have ever known, but in all that time, she never shook."

This is also true of our foundation. Storms of temptation and trial may beset us, but the foundation stands sure. I like the way Samuel Rutherford put it: "Believe God's love and power more than you believe your own feelings and experiences."

This is what the apostle Paul had in mind when he penned the words of 2 Timothy 1:12: "Nevertheless I am not ashamed: for I know whom I have believed, and am persuaded that He is able to keep that which I have committed unto Him against that day."

This assurance is safer than any man's good record. The story goes of an old slave who had been serving the Lord for fifty years. "Well, Uncle," someone asked him, "after keeping the faith for so long, you must feel pretty confident of holding out to the end."

"Oh, no," he replied, "it's only a question of whether de Lord can hold on, and I reckon I can trust Him."

Rudy Overholt, Russelville, KY

| Bible Reading: Matthew 7:24-27; 1 Corinthians 3:5-17 |
| One Year Bible Reading Plan: 1 Corinthians 7:1-24 Psalms 124–127 |

_____

Your Rock is Christ, and it is not the Rock
which ebbs and flows, but your sea.

An Agreement With Death

Remember now thy Creator in the days of thy youth,
while the evil days come not.
Ecclesiastes 12:1

According to an old fable, a man made an unusual agreement with Death. He told the grim reaper that he would willingly accompany him when it was time to die, on one condition. Death would send a messenger well in advance to warn him.

Weeks winged away into months, and months into years. One winter evening, as the man sat thinking about all his possessions, Death suddenly entered the room and tapped him on the shoulder. Startled, the man cried out, "You're here so soon, and without warning! I thought we had an agreement."

Death replied, "I've more than kept my part. I've sent you many messengers. Look in the mirror and you'll see some of them." Death whispered, "Look at your hair! Once it was full and black; now it is thin and white. Look at the way you cock your head to listen because you can't hear very well. Observe how close to the mirror you stand to see yourself clearly. Yes, I've sent many messengers through the years. I'm sorry you're not ready. You must leave; the time has come."

All around us we see signs of Death's rapid approach. Do not be blind to the signs! Prepare today for your appointment with Death!

> **Bible Reading:** Ecclesiastes
> 12:1-7
> **One Year Bible Reading Plan:**
> 1 Corinthians 7:25-40
> Psalms 128–131

Paul Stoltzfus, Morgantown, PA

It is never too early to receive Christ,
but at any moment it could be too late.

God Is on the Throne

Submit yourselves therefore to God.
Resist the devil, and he will flee from you.
James 4:7

Several years ago I was laying up a brick fireplace face for a friend, Junior Yoder. He had built a chimney on the outside of his house, with a thimble sticking through the wall for a freestanding stove. His young son, Stanley, was sitting there watching me work. I had laid up several rows, using a string, and it looked real easy so far, but as I was nearing the thimble, Stanley looked up at me and said, "Say, how are you going to brick around that thing?"

"Well," I replied, "when things get tough, you have to get tougher!" That made him grin. Sure enough, in a matter of time, the job was finished, and he could see that what I'd told him was true.

That's the way it is in our Christian life, too. When we feel at times like there is no way out, that's when faith starts to work. We read in Philippians 4:13, "I can do all things through Christ which strengtheneth me." The beautiful thing about walking by faith is that we don't have to worry about tomorrow. We know who holds the future.

Many people think that the Christian life is a very dull way to live, no fun and no thrills at all; but it's just the opposite. A child of God has a full, happy life. He knows that God knows his every need, and He'll be there to see him through any problems that may come his way. God loves us so very much that He provided a way for us to be with Him in heaven when His will has been fulfilled for us here in this life. Trust in Him today.

Bible Reading: James 4:1-10
One Year Bible Reading Plan:
1 Corinthians 8
Psalms 132–135

Abner Overholt, Auburn, KY

If you are walking with the world, you are walking alone.

God's Way Brings Results

For as the heavens are higher than the earth, so are my ways
higher than your ways, and my thoughts than your thoughts.
Isaiah 55:9

Children sometimes hesitate to obey because they do not understand why they need to do what you have told them. In their minds it just does not make sense. They need to learn to obey those over them, even if they do not understand. There is a time to explain to them why they need to do a particular thing, but from my own experience, there are some things you cannot understand fully until you are older and more mature. Being obedient is God's way, and it will bring blessings to your life.

Learning to obey our parents helps us to obey God. We need to follow God's Word and will for our lives even when it does not make sense to us. Later, we will perhaps better understand what God was doing. But for now, when God speaks, we must listen. Remember, God is always working for our welfare.

In our Bible reading, Jesus performed a miracle in response to the disciples' obedience. The disciples had simply obeyed, not expecting the miracle that took place. Think about some of the other miracles Jesus performed. The ten lepers Jesus told to go and show themselves to the priests could have asked for healing first, but they were cleansed as they obeyed in faith. There are many such examples in the Bible. Jesus has abundant blessings in store for us as we obey Him. God's way brings outstanding results.

Mark Webb, Hicksville, OH

Bible Reading: John 21:1-7
One Year Bible Reading Plan:
1 Corinthians 9
Psalms 136–138

True obedience neither procrastinates nor questions.
—Francis Quarles

August 29

The Glory of God

The heavens declare the glory of God;
and the firmament sheweth his handiwork.
Psalm 19:1

Are there ever times in your life when things seem rather dark, or maybe you are distressed? When this happens in my life, it does me good to observe nature and see God in it. I go on a walk or a drive, see the beautiful sunrise or sunset and hear the birds singing so sweetly, and I see the glory of God in these things.

Have you ever wondered what spring and summer would be like without birds? What is more cheering than being out in the morning and hearing the birds chirping and singing praises to their Maker? We wonder, "Why do they want to sing?" We might think that it is their nature, which it is, but it is more than just their nature. God gave them that nature, and I believe God has created them to direct our thoughts toward Him.

There are birds that sing even when it is raining. How are we? Do we have a cheerful attitude even when things do not look quite so bright? Seeing the glory of God in everything will inspire a cheerful attitude in us.

When we are cheerful, we can be an encouragement to those who are discouraged. Do we have time for the glory of God during the day, or are we too busy about our business?

Norman Farmwald, Monticello, KY

Bible Reading: Psalm 148
One Year Bible Reading Plan:
1 Corinthians 10:1-13
Psalms 139–140

Earth with her thousand voices praises God.
—Coleridge

246

Peace

Thou wilt keep him in perfect peace, whose mind is stayed on thee.
Isaiah 26:3

You dreamed of a quiet, tranquil, relaxing vacation. You planned a special excursion that you were very confident would be exactly what you needed to quiet and calm your anxious, weary heart. You invested many hours of preparation in the venture, even though time was scarce. Schedules have been tight, and you have been working at a frenzied pace to allow time for your peaceful "get-away."

Now you have finally arrived. You have unpacked your suitcase. You have three whole days to relax and experience peace before you will be forced to face the daily grind again. Soon, a realization settles over you like a black cloud: this is not peace at all!

We do not find peace by seeking personal pursuits. The peace that passes all understanding is a result of experiencing Jesus Christ in our personal lives and seeking first the Kingdom of God. We read in Ephesians 2:14, "For he is our peace who hath made both one, and hath broken down the middle wall of partition between us." Too often we find ourselves anxious, weary, perplexed, and fearful, because we are focusing on the storm rather than on the Master. "Quiet contentment" can be yours as you trust in the Lord with all your heart.

Bible Reading: Hebrews 4
One Year Bible Reading Plan:
1 Corinthians 10:14-33
Psalms 141–143

Merl Beiler, Abbeville, SC

Perfect peace is a reality to the trusting and faithful heart.

Our Great God

What is man, that thou art mindful of him?
and the son of man, that thou visitest him?
Psalm 8:4

Have you considered the mighty works of God? Take a few moments to look at nature if you want a glimpse of the awesomeness of God.

One of the first things I notice in nature is that God is a God of order. Have you ever seen a pear growing on an apple tree, or a grape on a tomato vine? Of course not! Have you ever seen the sun come up in the west, veer across the sky and set in the north? No! Why? God has set things in order and keeps them in order. What about the universe? Each planet is in its place, orbiting the sun, but not colliding with the others.

Another characteristic of God that I see in nature is His great power. Just think about the effects of earthquakes, hurricanes, or tornadoes. Are these not proof enough of the power of God?

Some things in nature will probably always remain a mystery to man. How does a peanut grow without being attached to the outer shell? Why does a cantaloupe always have ten stripes and never nine or eleven?

I am amazed when I think of the many different ways we can see God in nature. But I am very thankful that, as our key verse says, even though God is great and powerful, He visits His children. He cares for you and me. Praise His name!

Matthew Hochstetler, Woodburn, IN

Bible Reading: Psalm 8;
  Psalm 19:1-6
One Year Bible Reading Plan:
  1 Corinthians 11:1-16
  Psalms 144, 145

Let the Redeemer's name be sung
Through ev'ry land, by ev'ry tongue.
—Isaac Watts

Losing Control?

That the God of our Lord Jesus Christ, the Father of glory, may give
unto you the spirit of wisdom and revelation in the knowledge of him.
Ephesians 1:17

Today is a new day. We do not know what may happen. Someone in our family may be in an accident, or we may meet someone who is hurting emotionally or is angry. Only God knows what is going to happen, but how are we going to respond?

Life consists of divinely-ordered circumstances. We do not control the circumstances that God allows in our lives. They may be painful, and they may be tough. Even when we desperately want to be in control of them, God asks us to accept the unknown, and not to lose control of ourselves (1 Peter 2:20-23).

God also has called us to move into those unknown circumstances. How do we do that? By "the spirit of wisdom and revelation" (Ephesians 1:17). We may not always know what to say or how to respond, but if we open the door for the Lord's Spirit to move into our lives, He will show us what we should do in each situation we face.

There is another key phrase in verse 17 that goes along with accepting the unknowns: "in the knowledge of him." God knows how frail we are and how quickly we tend to forget. He uses circumstances to draw our hearts to Him, that we might acknowledge Him. Who benefits from them? We do.

When God took the children of Israel through the wilderness for forty years, it was for their personal good. He said, "Remember that I led you in the wilderness, 1) to humble you, 2) to prove you, 3) to know what is in your heart, and 4) to see if you would keep my commandments." God loves us so much that He will test our motives to purify them. We need to trust Him and ask Him to cleanse our hearts today.

Bible Reading: Ephesians 1:3-23
One Year Bible Reading Plan:
1 Corinthians 11:17-34
Psalms 146, 147

Galen Miller, Auburn, KY

We need affliction to teach us submission.

September 2

Every Christian a Servant

With good will doing service, as to the Lord, and not to men.
Ephesians 6:7

When I say every Christian is a servant, I am speaking not only of service that requires leaving home. If we have a strong desire to serve God, we will recognize the needs in God's kingdom and respond to them wherever we may be. Service is the responsibility of every Christian.

What do we mean when we talk about service? The word *servant* in the Bible refers to a slave or bondman. A servant is one who gives himself to another's will, one who is devoted to another with disregard for his own interests. We truly need to be servants of Christ.

The proper mentality for service comes out of a heart full of love for God because of all He has done for us. However, there are some things we can do to encourage service in the next generation. For example, when your children help with the dishes, are they doing it "as unto the Lord"? Help them develop a keen awareness of the needs around them.

The Bible calls Moses the servant of God; Paul, the servant of God; and James, the servant of God. Someone has said, "We like to be thought of as a servant, until someone *treats* us as a servant." Being a servant of God is really being a servant to others. Be in service for the Lord by responding to the needs around you.

Mark Webb, Hicksville, OH

Bible Reading: Luke 22:24-30
One Year Bible Reading Plan:
1 Corinthians 12:1-19
Psalms 148–150

Christ taught us to serve the Father by serving the least of our brothers.

Jesus Christ—Wonderful Counselor

. . . and his name shall be called Wonderful, Counsellor . . .
Isaiah 9:6

Isaiah 9:6 is a prophetic Scripture which lists a number of titles for the coming Messiah. Among these are *Wonderful* and *Counselor.* However, since the original Hebrew did not have punctuation, some scholars feel that these two words are to be taken together as one title for Jesus Christ: Wonderful Counselor. Whether that is the case or not, it is nonetheless true that He *is* a Wonderful Counselor.

He speaks to us through our conscience when we err. He speaks with a still small voice when we meditate. Sometimes, He speaks to us through our friends, or perhaps through those who differ with us. He speaks to us through the events of the day, but mostly He speaks to us through His Word. We need to cultivate a sensitivity to His counsel.

When He gives counsel, it may be a rebuke: "Thou art the man" (2 Samuel 12:7), or words of comfort: "I will never leave thee, nor forsake thee" (Hebrews 13:5). It may be advice: "This is the way, walk ye in it" (Isaiah 30:21), or a wake-up call: "Get thee up. . . Israel hath sinned" (Joshua 7:10-11).

Our own vision is limited, hindered by earthly considerations. We see matters from a skewed earthly perspective. We often indulge in wishful thinking to confirm the choices we make. We need someone to counsel us from a heavenly perspective, so we can make decisions that count for eternity. We need a Wonderful Counselor. That Wonderful Counselor is Jesus Christ. Let us heed His counsel.

Bible Reading: Isaiah 30:8-21
One Year Bible Reading Plan:
1 Corinthians 12:20-31
Proverbs 1, 2

Enos D. Stutzman, London, OH

Have you listened to the Wonderful Counselor today?

September 4

The Coming of Christ

For yet a little while, and he that shall come
will come, and will not tarry.
Hebrews 10:37

When have you last thought of Christ's second coming? Do you catch yourself hoping that He will hold off for a little while, because there is still something you want to do? Too often we forget that Jesus says in Revelation 22:12, "And, behold, I come quickly; and my reward is with me, to give every man according as his work shall be."

Christ's coming should be the greatest expectation of the Christian. It will free us from the curse of sin and place us in the very presence of God Himself. There will no longer be any sickness, sorrow, or fighting. Instead, there will be perfect health, joy, and peace. Yet, we often find ourselves not even preparing for His coming. We simply expect that when He comes, we will be ready.

"Seeing then that all these things shall be dissolved, what manner of persons ought ye to be in all holy conversation and godliness, looking for and hasting unto the coming of the day of God, wherein the heavens being on fire shall be dissolved, and the elements shall melt with fervent heat?" (2 Peter 3:11, 12). It is important that we prepare ourselves now for that day, because when He comes, our destiny will be final. The rewards will far exceed the small and insignificant trials we face here. "For I reckon that the sufferings of this present time are not worthy to be compared with the glory which shall be revealed in us" (Romans 8:18). The opportunity to praise God throughout eternity for all He has done for us is something to which all Christians can look forward with eager anticipation.

Bible Reading: Hebrews 10:32-39
One Year Bible Reading Plan: 1 Corinthians 13
Proverbs 3, 4

Steve Smucker, Lott, TX

Even so, come, Lord Jesus.
Revelation 22:20

Where Is Hell, Anyway?

The wicked shall be turned into hell,
and all the nations that forget God.
Psalm 9:17

Odd question, is it not? Let us think about it. Generally we think of heaven as being up and hell as being down. Is hell in the center of the earth? The earth has a mantle, a crust of varying thickness, and a fiery molten core. Some Bible scholars think the increase of earthquakes and volcanic activity is a literal fulfillment of Isaiah 5:14, where it speaks of hell "enlarging" itself. What is it enlarging itself for? Those scholars say it is for the coming Judgment. The devil, his demonic cohorts, and unredeemed mankind will then be hurled into hell. So, is hell in the center of the earth? We can only speculate.

A country church held revival meetings, and a young man responded to the altar call. He marvelously experienced the cleansing blood of Christ. Two old buddies on horseback stopped by the next day. They tried to discourage the young man from keeping his new faith. As they mounted their horses to leave, one mockingly asked, "Where is heaven? Where is hell?" Laughing and jeering, they galloped off.

It had rained during the night, and the dirt road had a layer of slippery mud on it. As they rounded a sharp turn in the road, one of the horse's feet slipped. Horse and rider spun head over heels! The horse landed with terrible force on the young man's chest. There were a few gasping breaths, and then an awful silence. At that curve in the road, a wicked young man learned where hell is.

Where is hell? Let us try to answer that question again. Hell lies at the end of an unrepentant and Christless life. Friends, that is no speculation.

Jim Yoder, Clarkson, KY

Bible Reading: Luke 16:19-31
One Year Bible Reading Plan:
1 Corinthians 14:1-20
Proverbs 5, 6

The one principle of Hell is "I am my own."
—George MacDonald

Through a Cloud of Smoke

But he that glorieth, let him glory in the Lord.
2 Corinthians 10:17

We like our family doctor. He has often helped us with our children's sicknesses. However, it appears that he smokes. He has that unpleasant smoke smell about him.

We all know that smoking is not good for one's health. It causes cancer and emphysema and other health problems. It causes yellow teeth. A bad smoke smell hangs about the smoker like a cloud.

Why would a doctor smoke? A doctor knows all the statistics. He has seen people die because of smoking. He has probably even told certain patients that smoking caused their sicknesses.

Sometimes Christians do the same thing. We know sin will not be in heaven, but we still find it hard to let go of a grudge or ill feelings. It is very hard for us to let go of our pride. Self-pity, a defensive spirit, a critical attitude, or impatience toward our family are elements of pride. It is easy to neglect our Bible reading and take less and less time for praying. Even looking down on those who smoke reveals a self-righteous attitude, which Jesus condemned in Matthew 5:20.

We need to pray for a transparency of spirit so that we can see through the smoke clouds in our own hearts and be cleansed.

Bible Reading: Romans 2:17-29
One Year Bible Reading Plan:
1 Corinthians 14:21-40
Proverbs 7, 8

Jason Bontrager, Chilton, TX

_____

Therefore to him that knoweth to do good,
and doeth it not, to him it is sin.
—James 4:17

The Power of the Word of God

_For the word of God is quick and powerful and
sharper than any two-edged sword._
Hebrews 4:12

Boys like to compare muscles or have a wrestling match to see who is the most powerful. Men like to compare tractors or trucks. We like power. We like powerful cars and trucks or great big earthmoving equipment. The bigger and more powerful it is, the more impressed we are. Recently I had my first ride in a jet, and I enjoyed the feeling of tremendous power at takeoff. Consider the great power of an atomic bomb, which can destroy whole cities in a matter of seconds. All this power, and yet it is not half as powerful as the Word of God.

Manufactured power can have great effects on our physical bodies, but the biggest machine ever built cannot change the heart of a man. However, when we apply the Word of God to our lives, it changes our inner being; it makes us whole and softens our hearts.

What power can remove sin from one's life? What power can make a new man of the alcoholic or the drug-addict? What power can change sinful habits? What power can help a person live a holy and righteous life? Only the power of the Word of God can do these things.

Allow the power of the Word of God to be applied to your life. You will enjoy the difference.

Bible Reading: Hebrews 4:1-13
One Year Bible Reading Plan:
1 Corinthians 15:1-32
Proverbs 9, 10

Inspired by a sermon by L. J. Helmuth
HDY

Saturate your heart with God's Word.
—Theodore Cuyler

The Invitation

Come unto me, all ye that labor . . .
Matthew 11:28

Recently, we received an invitation to attend the wedding of a former neighbor's daughter. Earlier we had heard of the young couple's engagement and wondered, will we, or will we not, be invited. Our uncertainty was laid to rest when finally the invitation arrived. How nice, how very nice!

A world of fulfillment is contained in the words, "will you come," or "we desire your presence," for they speak of friendship, or family ties, or both.

Even a simple request to be guests in a friend's home for food or fellowship addresses one of the basic needs of man—being accepted and loved. This is the glue of human relationships. Who would dare to spurn this highest form of tribute?

The Lord was quite aware of all this when He spoke those gracious words, "Come, ye blessed of my Father." We, who were once, in the apostle Paul's words, "aliens from the commonwealth of Israel, are brought nigh by the blood of Jesus." He wants you and me, who were numbered among the highway travelers mentioned in today's text, as His guests. Oh joy! We are invited, not only for a one time occasion, but forever and ever in heaven!

Bible Reading: Matthew 22:1-14
One Year Bible Reading Plan:
1 Corinthians 15:33-58
Proverbs 11, 12

Jerry Yoder, Auburn, KY

The most sastisfying definition of heaven:
Jesus' words, "Where I am."

The Glory of God

But we all . . . are changed into the same image from glory to glory.
2 Corinthians 3:18

Have you ever wondered what God is like? He is full of glory. We see a little of His glory in the sunsets, the sun, moon, stars, the Swiss Alps, and pure white snow, in awesome lightning, and the intricate flower. The children of Israel beheld His glory on the Mount. Moses talked with God. When he came back to address the people, his face shone so brightly that he had to cover it with a veil.

The glory that we see in Christ is far greater. Renown, splendor, radiant beauty, glorious light all describe the glory of God in Christ.

How can we reflect that glory? Not by standing in front of a mirror and fixing ourselves up, but by looking at Jesus. I have heard people say that the longer husbands and wives live together, the more they resemble each other. So it is with you and Jesus. The more you think about Jesus and talk with Him, the more you will reflect His wonderful glory.

Bible Reading: 2 Corinthians 3
One Year Bible Reading Plan:
1 Corinthians 16
Proverbs 13, 14

My friend, come very close to Jesus and let His glory shine on your face and life.

Sam Nisly, Cullman, AL

---

*The glory that the saints will have
is the same glory that the Lord possesses.*
—Spurgeon

September 10_____

A Morning Meditation

My voice shalt thou hear in the morning, O LORD;
in the morning will I direct my prayer unto thee, and will look up.
Psalm 5:3

In our Bible reading, we see that Jesus was busy doing good at the beginning of His ministry. After a day packed with activities, He arose early in the morning to go out to pray by Himself. If He, the Son of God, needed that quiet time alone with the Father, how much more do we? Family devotions, public worship, and other inspirational group activities all have their place, but there is no substitute for time spent alone with God. Schedules may make it difficult, and unforeseen circumstances may hinder, but each day should begin this way. This will form a solid foundation upon which the day's activities can be built. Then we will be fortified for whatever the day might bring and empowered for effective service to the Lord. Discouraging circumstances and the attacks of the evil one need not hinder us, for we can reflect upon our early meditation, and draw strength from it for whatever may come. If we have asked the Lord to sustain us, He will certainly supply every need as it comes along.

Enos D. Stutzman, London, OH

In this quiet morning hour,
Lord, endue me with Thy pow'r
Give me courage for this day;
Fill me, Lord, I pray.

In the East appears a glow,
As a fire that's burning low.
In my heart, O Lord, I pray,
Build a fire today.

Now the radiant morning light
Hides the shadows of the night.
In my spirit, may I be
Filled with light from Thee.

If, throughout this coming day,
Wounded souls should cross my way,
Help, O Lord, that I may be
Pointing them to Thee.

If this day should be my last,
And my time on earth be past,
Grant, O Lord, that I may be
Walking close to Thee.

Bible Reading: Matthew 14:1-23
One Year Bible Reading Plan:
  2 Corinthians 1
  Proverbs 15, 16

I have set the LORD always before me.
—Psalm 16:8

The Purpose of Discipline

No chastening for the present seemeth to be joyous . . . nevertheless,
afterward it yieldeth the peaceable fruit of righteousness.
Hebrews 12:11

At times we resist God's discipline because we feel sorry for ourselves or that we do not deserve such treatment. We must remember that God loves and cares about us more than we do ourselves.

A certain women was visiting in Switzerland and came to a sheepfold on one of her daily walks. Venturing in, she saw the shepherd seated on the ground with his flock around him. Nearby, on a pile of straw, lay a single sheep which seemed to be suffering. Looking closely, the woman saw that its leg was broken. Her sympathy went out to the suffering sheep, and she looked up inquiringly at the shepherd, as she asked how it happened. "I broke it myself," said the shepherd sadly, and then explained. "Of all the sheep in my flock, this one was the most wayward. It would not obey my voice and would not follow when I was leading the flock. On more than one occasion it wandered to the edge of a perilous cliff. Not only was it disobedient itself, but it was leading other sheep astray. Based on my experience with this kind of sheep, I knew I had no choice, so I broke its leg. The next day I took food to it, and it tried to bite me. After letting it lie alone for a couple of days, it not only eagerly took the food, but it licked my hand and showed every sign of submission and affection. Now let me say this, when this sheep is well, it will be the model sheep of my entire flock. No sheep will hear my voice so quickly nor follow so closely. Instead of leading others away, it will be an example of devotion and obedience."

Bible Reading: Hebrews 12:1-11
One Year Bible Reading Plan:
2 Corinthians 2
Proverbs 17, 18

So it is with us. Through our suffering, God seeks to teach us obedience and reliance on His care.

Daniel B. Miller, Middlebury, IN

Discipline is not God's way of saying, "I am through with you,"
or a mark of abandonment by Him. Rather, it is
the loving act of God to bring us closer to Him.

I Am Following You

Be ye followers of me, even as I also am of Christ.
1 Corinthians 11:1

It was another lovely day. My upper grade students and I were outside enjoying a game. The object of the game was to cross between two lines of students without getting caught by those who were "it" in the middle. I was on one side looking across, when I heard one of my students remark to me, "I'm going to follow you, Brother Josh, because I think that you know the safe way across." Thinking back, I recalled having seen him behind me on more than one run across the gravel. Not giving it much more than a passing thought, I continued playing.

Later the incident returned to my mind, and with the memory came the sobering realization of the power of influence. There is no dodging the fact that we are being observed, and no minimizing the responsibility that accompanies it. There are eyes watching us in utter confidence that we know the safe way across. Where are we headed?

May God help us rise to the duty before us! There is not merely a game at stake, but a soul. In case the value of a soul has diminished in our minds, let us refresh our memories with John 3:16. Words fail to express the deep love God has for His only Son. What then is the price tag attached to the souls for whom God was willing to sacrifice His Son? They are perfectly priceless! We dare not thoughtlessly blight them by careless detours on the exits of materialism, excessive busyness, and other temporal pursuits.

A courageous resolution to always radiate a virtuous example is at best a shaky foundation (Romans 7:18). The answer is found only in Jesus. The only life that can consistently point others to the safe way across is that life which "is hid with Christ in God" (Colossians 3:3).

Joshua Yoder, Clarkson, KY

Bible Reading: Matthew 18:1-15
One Year Bible Reading Plan:
2 Corinthians 3
Proverbs 19, 20

Suppose that we would echo Paul's appeal in 1 Corin͏*ians 11:1, and that others would precisely obey us. Would Satan* ·*frown?*

A Heart Experience

For with the heart man believeth unto righteousness; and
with the mouth confession is made unto salvation.
Romans 10:10

"Having a form of godliness, but denying the power thereof: from such turn away" (2 Timothy 3:5). Is it not true that we are surrounded today by people who have a form of godliness, but lack a true heart experience? They profess to be Christians, yet their heart is far from God. God told Isaiah in our Bible reading, that the children of Israel drew near with their mouths and lips, but removed their hearts from Him. The fear of God that they professed was by the precepts or rules of man—only a form.

The enemy of our souls does not mind if we give lip service to God. Hypocrites do a lot to aid the devil's program. How is it in your relationship with God? Are the words you use when you pray or testify coming from your heart, or only from your lips? Do you fear God because of the rules of the church or man, or because of a heart experience with Almighty God? May God help each one of us to have a heart-to-heart relationship with God and not just lip service.

When we have a heart experience with God, we cannot help but confess it with our mouths. What a blessing it is to know God, and that His mercies are new every morning! The Apostle Paul writes in Philippians 3:10-11, "That I may know him, and the power of his resurrection, and the fellowship of his sufferings, being made conformable unto his death; if by any means I might attain unto the resurrection of the dead."

Bible Reading: Isaiah 29:7-24
One Year Bible Reading Plan:
2 Corinthians 4
Proverbs 21, 22

Mark Webb, Hicksville, OH

Schedule a heart checkup today.

261

September 14_____

Spiritual Growth

. . . Desire the sincere milk of the word, that ye may grow thereby.
1 Peter 2:2

In 1965 I stood and gazed in awe at the gigantic General Sherman Tree. "The largest living thing on earth; enough lumber to build a village of forty-five houses, including shingles for the roofs and cabinets in the kitchens; around 4,000 years old," commented the park ranger, trying to help us grasp its magnificence. Then he asked if we had questions.

"Are there any seedling Sequoia trees? Are they still propagating themselves?" was my question.

The ranger pointed to two young trees nearby, one about thirty feet tall, the other a mere eight feet.

"They were both planted in 1932," said the ranger.

"Then, why the huge difference in size?" asked someone.

"We don't know," he answered, "but probably the larger one has found a better supply of nutrients and water. Nevertheless, both trees are healthy and growing."

"Yet one is growing four times as fast as the other," I thought to myself.

As I went on with that trip, and often since, I have been reminded that people are much like those two trees. Some find rich sources of food for their spirits to feed on, others feed on the spiritual crumbs discarded by others. The big difference is that we as creatures of choice are accountable for what we feed on. If we feed on spiritual poison, it is because we have chosen to do so. If we are to grow tall and strong and become a brace for other, weaker ones to lean against and find shade and shelter from life's storm, we must feed on the rich food of God's Word and avoid the spiritual poisons of anger, envy, covetousness, jealousy, bitterness, and hatred.

Bible Reading: 1 Corinthians 3
One Year Bible Reading Plan:
2 Corinthians 5
Proverbs 23, 24

Dan Schmucker, Franklin, KY

_____

The growth of a saint is the work of a lifetime.

The Israelite Experience—
From Proud to Humble

Humble yourselves in the sight of the Lord, and he shall lift you up.
James 4:10

Moses was a zealous young man. He could not bear to see an injustice go unpunished. However, in his pride, he thought he could handle the problem on his own, and no one would know. The young man Moses said, "I can."

Years later, we see a different person. Moses still had the same burden for his brethren back in Egypt, but now he realized that he could not lift the burden on his own. Now he was in a condition that the Lord could use him. The older Moses said, "I can't, but God can."

What changed Moses? Two things had a humbling effect on his life. First, the Lord frustrated his proud, heroic ambitions. His sin was found out, and he had to flee for his life. Often the plans that we make with a proud, selfish attitude come to naught. If we learn from our failures, it will quickly humble us.

Second, the time on the backside of the desert helped to bring Moses to a useful condition. There, he had plenty of time to think about what he had done, to consider his own weakness, and to spend time with the Lord. If you desire more humility, try spending more time alone with God.

We should desire and seek after humility. Only when we are empty of ourselves are we really useful to God.

Bible Reading: Exodus 2:11-15; 4:1-14
One Year Bible Reading Plan:
2 Corinthians 6
Proverbs 25–27

Henry Yoder, Clarkson, KY

Other things may be the worse for breaking,
yet a heart is never at its best until it is broken.

*September 16*_____

The Gospel of the Face

But we all, with open face . . . are changed into the same image.
2 Corinthians 3:18

Sitting in a restaurant lately, my attention was drawn to the expression on a man's face. It impressed me that he could have snapped in two a ten-penny nail with ease. His past was vague to me, but what came out of his mouth was a clear indication of his problem.

Someone has rightly said we can't help the expression we were born with, but at mid-life, it's our fault. This angry man was a cute little boy at one time.

Did you ever notice that what is on the inside of us works its way onto our faces? Loss of virtue, greed, lust, selfishness, and rebellion surface on our faces for all the world see. How sad to see the "light" go out on a young person bent on doing their own thing.

How blessed then, how encouraging, how spiritually stimulating it is to see someone at mid-life or even older with clear eyes and the glory of the Lord on their faces.

It is said of Fenelon that after his communion with God often his face shone. Lord Peterborough, a skeptic, was once compelled to spend a night with Fenelon at an inn. In the morning he hurried away saying, "If I spend another night with that man, I shall be a Christian in spite of myself." Fenelon's manner, voice, and face reflected so perfectly the glory of Christ, that he was irresistibly attractive to even the worldliest man and woman.

Bible Reading: 2 Corinthians 3:1-18
One Year Bible Reading Plan:
2 Corinthians 7
Proverbs 28, 29

R. O., Auburn, KY

The serene, silent beauty of a holy life is the most powerful influence in the world—next to the might of God.
—Blaise Pascal

Be a Man

But Daniel purposed in his heart that he would not defile himself.
Daniel 1:8

Daniel was taken captive as a teenager and carried away to the wicked city of Babylon, where he was separated from the godly influence of his parents and family. Renamed after a heathen god, he was enrolled in a godless education program. Most of his peers who had been taken captive with him rejected their upbringing and accepted new heathen customs. In addition, Daniel faced painful suffering at the hands of cruel and merciless men. If anyone had reason to be bitter against God and reject the moral standards by which he was raised, it was Daniel. Instead, Daniel became one of God's most outstanding examples of standing alone for scriptural convictions.

Each time Daniel stood alone, it looked as though he would lose; but God used the struggles that Daniel experienced to give him greater honor and spiritual insight. In every age, God is looking for Daniels—men and women who understand scriptural principles and have purposed to stand for them whatever the cost. "The LORD is on my side; I will not fear: what can man do unto me?" (Psalm 118:6). Daniel had great confidence in God. "Be not afraid of sudden fear, neither of the desolation of the wicked, when it cometh. For the LORD shall be thy confidence, and shall keep thy foot from being taken" (Proverbs 3:25, 26). God shut the lions' mouths, and Daniel experienced no harm in the lions' den. He was a strong man for God, because of his great faith.

Bible Reading: Daniel 1:1-17
One Year Bible Reading Plan:
2 Corinthians 8
Proverbs 30, 31

Simon Overholt, Auburn, KY

_____

Courage is the love of truth more than life.

In Search of a City

For here have we no continuing city, but we seek one to come.
Hebrews 13:14

More than forty years ago I had my first experience serving as a pallbearer. The occasion was the funeral of my thirteen-year-old cousin, who was taken from this life in a truck accident. I especially remember our key verse being used by the minister who spoke at the home the night before the funeral.

The fact that we have no continuing city should cause us to "live soberly [seriously], righteously, and godly in this present world; looking for that blessed hope, and the glorious appearing of the great God and our Saviour Jesus Christ" (Titus 2:12, 13).

Today, many professing Christians give little thought to the brevity of life and are often involved in activities that leave us wondering if in truth they are looking "for a city which hath foundations, whose builder and maker is God" (Hebrews 11:10).

God has given us the road map in His Word and also has given us His Spirit to show us the best route to ensure our safe arrival in the city that has sure foundations.

If we are bound for that city, let us declare plainly by our lifestyle that we are strangers and pilgrims on the earth, desiring a better country, that is a heavenly one. "Wherefore God is not ashamed to be called [our] God: for he hath prepared for [us] a city" (Hebrews 11:16).

Bible Reading: Hebrews 11:1-16
One Year Bible Reading Plan:
2 Corinthians 9
Ecclesiastes 1–3

Robert Overholt, Auburn, KY

Hold loosely all that is not eternal.
—Royden

Be Still

*Be still, and know that I am God: I will be exalted
among the heathen, I will be exalted in the earth.*
Psalm 46:10

"Be still, and know that I am God." What a relaxing thought! In today's world, such stillness is almost unheard of. Our schedules are too full to let us take this verse to heart. All of our evenings are taken up with activities that keep us up late, and then the next morning it is hard to meditate and pray.

Often we miss blessings because we do not take time to be still. Jesus, our perfect example, was able to take some time off from being around the crowds to be still. At the end of a busy day, Jesus would go into the mountains alone to pray. Sometimes the Lord brings things into our lives to slow us down, so that we have more time to meditate on Him. It takes effort to be still long enough for God to work in our lives as He would like to.

Sometimes we wish the Lord would come and talk to us in an audible voice, but I believe the Lord would rather speak to us in a still, small voice as He did to Elijah after the Mount Carmel experience. Elijah was discouraged and tired, feeling like he was the only one left who feared the Lord; and now his life was at stake. As Elijah was talking with the Lord, He passed by. First, there was a strong wind, followed by an earthquake, and then a fire; but the Lord was not in those. The Lord then came in a still, small voice. Let that still, small voice speak to you.

Bible Reading: Psalm 46:1-11
One Year Bible Reading Plan:
2 Corinthians 10
Ecclesiastes 4–6

Dwayne Beachy, Free Union, VA

Take time to be quiet; it is the opportunity to seek God.

September 20

Heaven

But now they desire a better country, that is, an heavenly
Hebrews 11:16

Job 14:1 tells us that man is full of trouble. In this life we have death, sorrow, crying, pain, disappointments, discouragements, fears, sickness, and loneliness. Life is just not always easy. This may seem like a dark picture of this world, but Jesus said, "In the world ye shall have tribulation: but be of good cheer; I have overcome the world."

Praise God, we can have a bright outlook on life and have the blessed hope of eternal life in heaven, if we have Jesus, the Way, the Truth, and the Life. Are you looking forward to that great day when Jesus will come back again to take His children home to be with Him forever in heaven?

You may have heard the story of the slave who was told that his master had gone to heaven. Thoughtfully, he said, "I doubt it. Whenever my master took a trip to any other place, he always talked about it and planned for it a long time beforehand. I never heard my master talk about going to heaven."

Are we making plans to go to heaven? "Seek ye first the kingdom of God." "For where your treasure is, there will your heart be also." "Rejoice and be exceeding glad: for great is your reward in heaven." "But he that shall endure unto the end, the same shall be saved." Let us keep pressing toward that great reward, heaven!

Bible Reading: Psalm 15; Revelation 21:1-7
One Year Bible Reading Plan:
2 Corinthians 11:1–15
Ecclesiastes 7–9

Ernest Stoll, Odon, IN

Heaven is not only the reward but the natural effect of a religious life.
—Addison

Remain Faithful!

Blessed be the God and Father of our Lord Jesus Christ,
which according to his abundant mercy hath begotten us again unto
a lively hope by the resurrection of Jesus Christ from the dead.
1 Peter 1:3

I am very thankful for God's abundant mercy. Where would we be without it? We would be miserable and utterly without hope; but God has regenerated us and has given us a living hope through the death and resurrection of His Son Jesus Christ. He has given us an inheritance that will never pass away; a priceless gift from God reserved for those who are faithful. God has made sure that we will receive our inheritance, if we accept His salvation and are faithful and obedient to Him.

We can rejoice greatly, even though we go through some very heavy trials and manifold temptations. The trial of our faith makes it like gold, when it is purified with fire; but our faith is much more precious in God's sight than gold. If our faith remains strong through trials, it will bring praise, honor, and glory at the coming of our Savior Jesus Christ.

Although we have not seen Him, yet we love Him and trust Him, and rejoice with joy unspeakable, because we will receive the salvation of our souls if we are faithful.

We need to stir up our minds and be sober and hope to the end, as obedient children forsaking our former life. As Jesus who has called us is holy, so we need to be holy in our walk of life.

We are commanded to pass our time here in fear because God will judge us according to our works. We are not going to be redeemed with corruptible things, like silver and gold but with the precious blood of Christ. Let us remain faithful!

Bible Reading: 1 Peter 1:3-21
One Year Bible Reading Plan:
2 Corinthians 11:16–33
Ecclesiastes 10-12

Marv Garber, Crozet, VA

_____

Firm . . . was the faith they possessed
for it was followed by works of faith.
—Clement of Alexandria

Unnecessary Fears

It is better to trust in the LORD than to put confidence in man.
Psalm 118:8

One morning our daughter told us that she had heard something during the night. In fear, she put her hands over her ears. Soon she saw a shadow in the doorway, and she quickly closed her eyes. Later, she learned that it was her older sister coming into the room.

We smile at this, but it is a reminder to us that often, when we are confronted with difficulties, we try to cover and protect ourselves with our own means. The Christian has many promises he can claim during times of trial, or when he sees the corruption and evils of the world around him.

If we dwell in the secret place of the Most High, we come under a divine overshadowing and refuge, and we can put our trust in God. He promises deliverance from the snare of the devil and a covering which we can trust for protection from the terror by night and also from the arrow that flies by day. Psalm 91:9 and 14 give the conditions of our protection. Because we have made the Lord our habitation, no evil shall befall us. He gives His angels charge over us to keep us in all our ways. We must set our love on God and call on Him when in trouble, and He will deliver and satisfy us with long life and show us His salvation.

Bible Reading: Psalm 91
One Year Bible Reading Plan:
2 Corinthians 12
Song of Solomon 1–3

Benuel S. Stoltzfus, Parkesburg, PA

If a care is too small to be turned into a prayer,
it is too small to be made into a burden.

Choose Today

_And if it seem evil unto you to serve the LORD, choose you
this day whom ye will serve; . . . but as for me and
my house, we will serve the LORD._
Joshua 24:15

Whom will you serve? The question comes to all of us alike. Before his death, Joshua gathered the people of Israel together to admonish them. He started with the fear of the Lord, and instructed them to serve Him in sincerity and in truth. He did not force them to serve God, but he said if it did not seem right to them to serve God, then they should choose without delay whom they would serve, but, he added, "As for me and my house we will serve the Lord."

Whom will you choose? The people recognized that God had done many great things for them. They chose to follow God, but Joshua said to them, "Ye cannot serve the LORD: for he is an holy God; he is a jealous God; he will not forgive your transgressions nor your sins. If ye forsake the LORD, and serve strange gods, then he will turn and do you hurt." The people answered, "Nay, but we will serve the LORD." Joshua replied, "Ye are witnesses against yourselves that ye have chosen you the LORD."

Are you a witness against yourself of your profession of faith to serve Jesus Christ? Have you confessed with your mouth that Jesus Christ is the Son of God? Have you been living up to your confession? If not, then you are a witness against yourself of your wrong.

The words of Joshua are still challenging. Choose today whom you will serve! God is no respecter of persons. Just because you were baptized does not mean that all is well between you and God. God must be served in all sincerity and in truth.

Bible Reading: Joshua 24:14-28
One Year Bible Reading Plan:
2 Corinthians 13
Song of Solomon 4, 5

Joe Miller, Belleville, PA

Choose today; not tomorrow.

Are You a Keeper?

To be discreet, chaste, keepers at home, good, obedfient to
their own husbands, that the word of God be not blasphemed.
Titus 2:5

Millions of children all over America come home from school every day to an empty house. Millions more spend several hours after school each day in day care centers. Their mothers are at work, keeping full time jobs outside the home. This is how I grew up. I had a key to our house and let myself in after school. There were times, however, when I forgot my key and had to wait outside until my mother came home. Home sweet home?

In Titus 2:5 the Lord instructs mothers to be "keepers at home." According to *Strong's Concordance*, a "keeper at home" is a "stayer at home." What a beautiful phrase. Only those mothers who stay at home can fully tend to the affairs of the home. Notice that in verse five, these things are done so that the Word of God is not blasphemed. There are many mothers who don't work outside the home, but they are not true keeprs at home. They don't stay at home enough. They are always running around, always on the go.

The virtuous woman of Proverbs 31 was a keeper. Verse 27 says, "She looketh well to the ways of her household." Mothers, are you staying home and looking well to the ways of your household? If you are, your children will call you blessed, and your husband will praise you!

> **Bible Reading:** Titus 2
> **One Year Bible Reading Plan:**
> Galatians 1
> Song of Solomon 6–8

Terry Lester, Montezuma, GA

_____

The bearing and the training of a child are woman's wisdom.
—Tennyson

Watch With Christ

What, could ye not watch with me one hour?
Matthew 26:40

The suffering, death, and triumphant resurrection of Jesus is the basis for everything of eternal value. Consider these lines from the familiar song, "Go to Dark Gethsemane," written by James Montgomery in the 19th century:

Go to dark Gethsemane, ye that feel the tempter's pow'r,
Your Redeemer's conflict see; watch with Him one bitter hour:
Turn not from His griefs away; learn of Jesus Christ to pray.

Our Savior's conflict in Gethsemane involved several eternal choices: removing the "cup" or drinking it; living for the immediate or the future; choosing physical comfort or sacrificial torture; embracing life or death. We cannot fathom the intensity of His struggle or the sweetness of His victory, for it was here in the Garden that Christ decided our eternal fate. In a sense, our future was more vulnerable in the Garden than on Calvary, for when Christ had resigned Himself to completing the Father's plan, it was as good as done.

Being human, Jesus desired companionship at this critical time. Imagine His disappointment at finding the disciples asleep after he had requested that they watch with Him. By extension, His request to "watch with me" is given to us. How faithful am I to hear His heartbeat and to pray fervent intercessory prayers on behalf of His people, and those who might be His? The prayers of Jesus in the Garden were accompanied by sweat and blood. What measure of intensity does my watchful praying reflect?

Ken Kauffman, Falkville, AL

Bible Reading: Matthew 26:36-46
One Year Bible Reading Plan:
Galatians 2
Isaiah 1–3

Prayer is the Christian's vital breath . . .
He enters heaven with a prayer.
—James Montgomery

Miry Clay

He brought me up also out of an horrible pit, out of the miry clay.
Psalm 40:2

Are you stuck in some miry clay? We think of David as a great man of God, but David many times faced difficulties, and even periods of depression. In our Scripture reading for today, we see David right after one of these experiences, when God had brought David out of a horrible pit, out of despondency and depression, and put his feet on the solid rock, and put a new song in his heart.

Praise God! Today we too can receive deliverance if we ask and wait on God. For our "God, who is rich in mercy" toward us, and "is able to do exceeding abundantly above all that we ask or think" is able to deliver us out of our troubles.

"Great is the Lord, and greatly to be praised." Even now, as I write and think of this verse, I feel the greatness of our Lord and Savior. Yet, because of some things I am experiencing, some of the trials I am facing, I find it hard to voice my praise.

Satan is real and wants nothing more than to see the children of God suffer and even fall away. God is just as real but even more powerful, and He is always able and willing to help us in times of difficulty. If you feel like Satan is hiding behind every bush waiting to snare you, remember that God is on your side of the bush ready to keep you from the snare. All you need to do is look to Him and ask Him to help you.

Bible Reading: Psalm 40:1-17
One Year Bible Reading Plan:
Galatians 3
Isaiah 4–6

Joe Miller, Belleville, PA

God is an ever-present help in trouble.

When Reality Strikes

The fear of the LORD is the beginning of knowledge:
but fools despise wisdom and instruction.
Proverbs 1:7

In our Bible reading for today, Uzziah lived the first part of his reign fearing God, until he became strong and arrogant. Uzziah overstepped his authority, for he thought he was more important than he actually was.

Many of the disappointments I experience in my walk with the Lord result from false ideas I have about God's character and nature. These false ideas cause me to expect the Lord to perform in some certain manner, or perhaps to overlook some disobedient area of my life. The Lord teaches me that He will not submit to my concept of Him. When I am confronted with the reality of the situation, I become disappointed. But God does not want us to be surrounded by walls of our own private illusions. He wants us to live in reality. He wants us to know Him for who He is, thereby seeing ourselves more clearly for what we are.

We often dictate to God what we expect Him to be, but we can only approach the Lord on His terms. King Uzziah learned this lesson in a very painful way. Every time Uzziah saw his own reflection and viewed himself covered with leprosy, he was reminded of God's sovereignty. We, too, can learn from this episode. Perhaps our prayer today should be that we may be freed from all illusion of our supposed self-importance. May God use the rod of disappointment to heal us from all false conceptions we may have of Him and of ourselves. By this we may grow to know Him in a more real and intimate way.

Bible Reading: 2 Chronicles 26
One Year Bible Reading Plan:
Galatians 4
Isaiah 7–9

Shannon M. Latham, Guys Mills, PA

Christ works among the pots and pans.
—Teresa of Avila

Get in the Wheelbarrow!

Trust in the LORD with all thine heart; and lean not
unto thine own understanding.
Proverbs 3:5

Suppose, for a moment, that you have a friend who is a tight-rope walker. He has trained for this precarious art from a very young age and is now well experienced. He performs great feats, which draw large crowds. Many times you have seen him walking the ropes with ease.

One day you are with this good friend as he prepares to push a wheelbarrow across a rope, strung at an awesome height, high above the mighty Niagara Falls. You stand with him and view the scene. One wrong move and he will be dashed on the rocks below or drowned in the churning water. But you are not anxious for his well-being, for he has done this many times before.

He turns to you and asks, "Do you believe I can do it?"

"Oh yes," you reply, "You've done it before, and there is no doubt in my mind that you can do it today."

"Okay," he says, "Then get into the wheelbarrow and allow me to push you across."

You, of course, quickly and emphatically refuse such a proposal.

Often we respond to the Lord in this way. We say we believe without a doubt that He spoke the entire creation into being; that He parted the Red Sea; that He sent His Son, who died on the cross, rose again, and ascended to heaven; and we say we believe that He can and will take care of us today. Yet when it comes to actually trusting Him with our very lives, we hesitate. What the Lord really wants is for us to get into His wheelbarrow and allow Him to push us across those high and terrifying places in life.

Henry Yoder, Clarkson, KY

Bible Reading: Genesis 6:22; 7:11–8:4; Hebrews 11:7
One Year Bible Reading Plan:
Galatians 5
Isaiah 10–12

Faith is not believing that God can, it is knowing that He will.

The Body

Now ye are the body of Christ, and members in particular.
1 Corinthians 12:27

When we think of the body, we think of our own hands, feet, and legs. Is it not amazing how our bodies work, each part always looking out for the other members? If something goes wrong with a member, the head tells the other parts to treat that member in a special way.

The church is much the same. Christ Jesus is the Head. Then we have elders, who serve as the nervous system of the church, helping to communicate the will of the Head to the body. However, a head and a nervous system by themselves are not much of a body, are they? We need teachers, prophets, servers, exhorters, and missionaries. Do we have a complete body yet? No, far from it! We also need prayer warriors, those who minister to the sick, and others. What would it be like if they did not do their jobs?

The story is told of a carpenter who hit his thumb with a hammer. Oh, how it hurt! It made him so mad he just up and hit it again. Is that the way we care for our members? The carpenter had an uncontrolled temper. Sometimes we find ourselves with an uncontrolled attitude. When we see that a brother in the church is discouraged or hurting, do we just say, "He'll get over it sooner or later," or do we give him special prayer and attention to help him heal?

Bible Reading: 1 Corinthians 12:13-31
One Year Bible Reading Plan:
Galatians 6
Isaiah 13–15

Too often we are too busy to notice that a fellow member is in trouble or has been bruised, and we do not encourage him (or her) as we should. Today, think of a member who may be facing a struggle and pray for that person.

Michael Mast, Auburn, KY

_____

A member disconnected from the body will soon die.

The Righteous Are Bold
as a Lion

The wicked flee when no man pursueth:
but the righteous are bold as a lion.
Proverbs 28:1

"A lion which is strongest among beasts, and turneth not away for any" (Proverbs 30:30). The lion's strength is not only legendary, it is real. A lion can clear fences twelve feet high, leap twenty feet in a single bound, drag twice its own weight, crush bones in its vice-like jaws, and charge at speeds up to fifty miles per hour. The male lion is considerably larger than the female. In his prime, the king of the beasts grows to about eight feet in length and may weigh as much as five hundred pounds. Only males grow a mane, which protects the lion's head and neck during combat. The lion also lies out in open fields because he is not afraid.

"The righteous are bold as a lion." Sin makes men cowards, but God needs men today who will speak the truth with holy boldness. In Acts 5:40, the apostles were beaten for preaching the Word and commanded not to speak in the name of Jesus. Did this stop them? No! They boldly went into the temple and into every house, and ceased not to teach and preach Jesus Christ (Acts 7:51).

Stephen was a martyr for his boldness. James was also a martyr for his holy boldness, speaking out for Christ. The apostle Peter was put in prison for boldly speaking out for Christ. Paul and Silas were, also. Today God needs you and me to be bold as lions, speaking forth the truth, the Word of God. "Now when they saw the boldness of Peter and John, and perceived that they were un-learned and ignorant men, they marvelled; and they took knowledge of them, that they had been with Jesus" (Acts 4:13).

Bible Reading: Acts 6:8-15
One Year Bible Reading Plan:
Ephesians 1
Isaiah 16–18

Simon Overholt, Auburn, KY

_____

Often the test of courage is not to die but to live.
—Vittorio Alfieri

White as Snow

Purge me with hyssop, and I shall be clean:
wash me, and I shall be whiter than snow.
Psalm 51:7

There are few things that fascinate me more than waking up in the morning and finding the world covered with a fresh blanket of snow. What were open fields of plowed ground or corn stubble the evening before, are now covered with a fresh blanket of pure whiteness. Then the clouds break, and the sun shines through, and everything seems to sparkle and glitter with a million diamonds and pearls.

It reminds me that we were lost in sin, and our lives were as the barren fields—so hard and cold, so undesirable. When we came to the Lord and asked Him to forgive us, cleanse and free us from our sins, He cleansed and purified our hearts, and made us white as snow.

Bible Reading: Psalm 51
One Year Bible Reading Plan:
Ephesians 2
Isaiah 19–21

"Come now, and let us reason together, saith the LORD: though your sins be as scarlet, they shall be as white as snow; though they be red like crimson, they shall be as wool" (Isaiah 1:18).

Tim Yoder, Reedsville, PA

Your life lies before you as a field of driven snow;
Be careful how you tread on it, for every track will show.

Crippled Prayers

Likewise, ye husbands, dwell with them according to knowledge, giving honour unto the wife, as unto the weaker vessel, and as being heirs together of the grace of life; that your prayers be not hindered.
1 Peter 3:7

As a young lad, I heard an elderly Mennonite man tell a group of boys that he and his wife had never exchanged cross words. This impressed me so much that I made it a goal of my married life, too.

How can our prayers be hindered? Well, it is the desire and prayer of all sincere Christian parents that their children not drag through the gutter of sin, but that they would, in their early years, make a commitment to the Lord Jesus. But what if Mom or Dad step out of their roles and start setting each other straight in the children's presence? Such disorder may very well hinder parents' prayers for their children. There is room for mistakes, and for differences between husband and wife, but it is best if all such corrections and reproofs be made in the absence of the children.

Of course, we need to confess to our children when we are in error, but what if we tell our children that the error is our partner's fault? We may rob our children of their needed security. We may be "crippling our prayers." Notice again 1 Peter 3:12 from our Bible reading for today. Be very careful lest you create evil in your home, for "the face of the Lord is against them that do evil."

Bible Reading: 1 Peter 3:1-12
One Year Bible Reading Plan:
Ephesians 3
Isaiah 22, 23

Andy Miller, Leitchfield, KY

---

*One way to correct your children
is to correct the example you are setting for them.*

Why Run?

But Jonah rose up to flee unto Tarshish, from the presence of the LORD.
Jonah 1:3

Years ago, a car was stolen in California. The police staged an intense search for the vehicle and the driver, even placing announcements on local radio stations to contact the thief. On the front seat of the stolen car sat a box of crackers that were laced with poison. The car owner had intended to use the crackers as rat bait. Now the police and the owner of the car were more interested in apprehending the thief to save his life, than to recover the car.

Whenever we run from God to escape being restricted, we are actually eluding His rescue. God forbid that you should run from Him, whether you are an unconverted sinner feeling the condemnation that sin brings, or a fearful child of God unwilling, as Jonah was, to do God's bidding. God wants to save us from condemnation. He wants to lead us to greener pastures and to the true happiness that can only be found in trusting Him and doing His will.

Consider the life of Jonah. God told him to go to Nineveh, but fearing for his life, Jonah fled, only to endanger the very life he was trying to save! Jonah had to experience great trials because he ran from God. Some folks spend their lifetime trying to fool God, to elude Him, but in the end they will learn Jonah's lesson, only it will be too late. Turn to Christ, who wants to apprehend you in order that He might save you.

Bible Reading: Jonah 1, 3
One Year Bible Reading Plan:
Ephesians 4
Isaiah 24–26

Kevin Miller, Auburn, KY

Though we can ignore God, we can never get away from Him!

Two Sides of David

Woe to them that are at ease in Zion. . . .
Amos 6:1

I have often read the account of David and Goliath and have told the story to my children many times. It is fresh each time I read it; I glean something different every time.

I can imagine the beating of David's heart as Goliath challenged the army of Israel for a champion fighter. That ruddy-faced lad was deeply moved at the giant's verbal attacks. Of all the men in Israel, David alone accepted the challenge, and he prevailed over the Philistine with a sling and a stone. It is a beautiful story of God's hand upon a man after God's own heart.

I have read also the amazing story of David and Bathsheba. I have asked myself, "Is this the same person who killed the giant? How can a man after God's own heart stoop so low and fall into such sin?"

It was the time of year when the kings went out to battle. However, King David stayed home, at ease in his palace in Zion. He had progressed from shepherd boy to king. He no longer had to sleep in the fields and tend sheep. David slept soundly in his soft bed, while his army fought the soldiers of Ammon. Such was David's state when he looked upon Bathsheba.

What had happened to Israel's champion? Where was the man after God's own heart? David was at ease. He had let his guard down. That hurts me deeply, for I too am like David. Today God wants us to go forth in spiritual combat. Brethren, let us hastily run toward the giant and not take up our ease in Zion.

> **Bible Reading:** 1 Samuel 17:40-51; 2 Samuel 11:1-5
> **One Year Bible Reading Plan:**
> Ephesians 5
> Isaiah 27, 28

Terry Lester, Montezuma, GA

Quit you like men.
—1 Corinthians 16:13

Influence—Sweet or Bitter?

Nevertheless my brethren that went up with me made the heart of the people melt: but I wholly followed the LORD my God.
Joshua 14:8

God's people are called to holiness (Leviticus 20:7; Ephesians 1:4). To walk holy before God, we must obey His Word and commands, even if at times it causes fear in our hearts, or we cannot understand what God desires to accomplish in our lives.

In Numbers 13:17-20, Moses commanded the spies to spy out the land and bring back a report of the strength of its inhabitants. I suppose they went fully intending to obey.

The sorrow and tragedy was only begun when the spies came back, and ten of them gave an evil report to the people. The remarkable influence of ten men on hundreds of thousands of people was agonizing. It brought much grief, sin, and death in the wilderness.

The influence that we have on others, especially on our own families, children, and neighbors, is great.

Brethren, let us take courage to stand for the truth, even if the majority does not. Caleb and Joshua lived to see the land that God had promised to His people, while many others died in the wilderness because they were influenced by a few who reported to them in unbelief.

Bible Reading: Numbers 13:26–14:10
One Year Bible Reading Plan:
Ephesians 6
Isaiah 29, 30

Lester Stoltzfus, Honey Brook, PA

A man who sets a bad example may repent, but he cannot be certain that those he has drawn into sin by his example will repent. It is often otherwise.
—Henry

Our God Is Matchless

Among the gods there is none like unto thee, O Lord;
neither are there any works like unto thy works.
Psalm 86:8

Many gods vie for our attention and devotion: pleasure, affluence, fashion, sports, and amusements are just a few. Of course, most people would never admit to worshiping them, yet they constantly chase after these allurements. They are never satisfied, but are still foolishly bowing to them in helpless addiction.

What about me? Is it possible that a child of God could become entangled in such things? The Scriptures repeatedly warn against falling into sin, for the enemy of our souls would like nothing better than that.

But our God is greater than all! The gods of this world may offer fun, excitement, or prestige, but all the while they subtly bring one into bondage, depression, and despair and, finally, eternal ruin. Serving the Lord may not be popular or glamorous, but the blessings far surpass the cheap alternatives of the world. When we surrender our lives to the lordship of Christ, we have freedom from the power of sin, peace and joy within, and a glorious future in store!

Our God is the One who created this marvelous universe by a spoken word. It was He who parted the waters, protected from the fire, delivered from the lions, and showed Himself mighty in countless other incidents throughout the course of history. He still does wonders in the lives of people today. Why would anyone turn away from such a wonderful God to follow the dead gods of this world?

Bible Reading: Psalm 86
One Year Bible Reading Plan:
Philippians 1
Isaiah 31–33

Allen Beiler, Stuarts Draft, VA

Who can know with certainty the
nature of God, except God Himself?

Of Presidents and Garbage Collectors

And the eye cannot say unto the hand, I have no need of thee:
nor again the head to the feet, I have no need of you.
1 Corinthians 12:21

Who is more important, the President or a garbage collector?

In March of 1981, President Ronald Reagan was shot by John Hinckley, Jr., and was hospitalized for several weeks. Although Reagan was the nation's chief executive, his hospitalization had little affect on the nation's activity—government continued on.

On the other hand, suppose the garbage collectors in this country went on strike, as they once did in Philadelphia. That city was a literal mess; the piles of decaying trash quickly became a health hazard. As one writer put it, a three week nationwide strike would paralyze the country.

In the body of Christ, seemingly insignificant members are urgently needed. As Paul reminds us, the eye cannot say to the hand, "I have no need of you," nor again the head to the feet, "I have no need of you." On the contrary, those parts of the body that seem to be weaker are indispensable! There is an important place for every child of God to fill, whether it be in open view or behind the scenes.

If you are filled with the Holy Spirit of God, and you are serving where God has called you, be faithful in that, until God calls you to a larger field. You do not have to be a preacher to study God's Word. You do not have to be a prophet to hear God's voice, and you do not have to be a renowned physician, to apply the healing balm of love. Neither must you be of excellent speech or ability to be used of God. If you desire to do great things for God, you must prove yourself faithful in small things!

Bible Reading: 1 Corinthians 12
One Year Bible Reading Plan:
Philippians 2
Isaiah 34–36

Kevin Miller, Auburn, KY

God has no larger field for the man who is not
faithfully doing his work where he is.

Go for the Gold

*But these are written, that ye might believe that Jesus is the Christ, the
Son of God; and that believing ye might have life through his name.*
John 20:31

Speaking of the tabernacle of Moses, the writer of Hebrews
says that in the Holiest of all there dwelt the cherubim of glory. He
continues to say, "of which we cannot now speak particularly"
(Hebrews 9:5). The great attraction in the Holy of Holies was the
ark of the covenant. Even the cherubim looked at the ark, as if
attempting to gaze into its mysteries.

The ark was made of shittim wood and entirely covered with
gold. As one looked at the ark, he could not see the wood, which
decays with age. Likewise, Christ came in the flesh and lived in the
flesh (John 1:14). He ate, slept, spoke, cried, and experienced other
things that men experience. However, we do not worship Him as a
man of flesh. As we look at the ark, we see gold: its glory. As we
look at Jesus, we see His glory, but it is the glory of the man who
humbled Himself and became obedient unto death before he was
exalted above all.

As our eyes roam the length, the width, and the height of the
ark, they come to focus on the mercy seat. We catch our breath, and
our eyes brim with tears as we lovingly gaze at it. Praise and
adoration well up in our hearts as we bow and worship our God.
We know that the interior of the ark contains the tables of stone, the
pot of manna, and Aaron's rod that budded; but for now we gaze at
the golden mercy seat.

How can we claim a life in Christ and not see a glorious Jesus?
How can we see a glorious Jesus and live our lives in the flesh?
When we have the Spirit of God, we perceive the things of the
Spirit. The things of the Spirit are deeper than our natural understanding and have to be under-
stood by His Spirit in us. The
more we exercise living in the
Spirit, the hungrier we will get,
and the more we will see. Let us
become heavenly minded and
worship the Lord our God.

Bible Reading: Hebrews 9
One Year Bible Reading Plan:
Philippians 3
Isaiah 37, 38

Alvin Mast, Millersburg, OH

When Christ is the center of your focus, all else will come into perspective.

Be Ye Kind

And be ye kind one to another.
Ephesians 4:32

The kindness of the little Israelite maid toward her master was so outstanding that God inspired the writer of 2 Kings to record it for our inspiration and example.

Would the little maid not have had ample reason to think that Naaman got just what he deserved for taking her away from her family and friends into a strange country with strange customs?

Because Naaman had leprosy, he would have to be banished from society. Apparently, the little maid wanted her master to receive the honor that the king wanted him to have. Luke 4:27 says, there were many lepers in Israel during that time, but only Naaman the Syrian was cleansed. How remarkable! But his healing came about because of the kindness of one little girl.

Would it make a difference in our families, in our churches and schools, and in our neighborhoods if we would put this attitude of unselfish kindness into practice?

God is ready to help us if we are willing.

Bible Reading: 2 Kings 5:1-14
One Year Bible Reading Plan:
Philippians 4
Isaiah 39, 40

Andy Miller, Malta, Ohio

Kind words . . . kind acts . . . these are the means of grace when men in trouble are fighting their unseen battles.
—John Hall

In Prison

And the Spirit and the bride say, Come. And let him that heareth
say, Come. And let him that is athirst come. And whosoever will,
let him take the water of life freely.
Revelation 22:17

Hard concrete. Steel doors slamming. Loud, raucous laughter. Angry words. Cursing. Weeping. This was prison, and I was in it. For two and a half years I went into the prison to minister to the down and out. The hopelessness and despair were very real, but it was the noise that almost drove me crazy.

Contrast this to the gentle breeze blowing across my face. The birds are singing cheerily from the treetops. The finches add their own melody and color as they playfully dart about. The beef cattle are grazing in contentment. The pigeons are cooing happily, and the game rooster bursts forth his crow of delight. Ah, this is home, and I love it!

So many about us are in the prison of despair. They are walking in darkness, with no hope of ever getting out. Release is possible, but they are walking in the vanity of their hearts. Even now, God is holding out the key to light and calling them to rest (Matthew 11:28-29). When I see a person trapped in sin, I can almost hear the prison noise, for that is where he is. He is serving his time because he is committing his sin.

I know that as I step out into the world today, the noise of sin will beckon loudly. I know that the stench of sin will be real and will attempt to overwhelm me. I also know that amid the noise there will be quietness, for God will whisper beautiful things to my heart while I listen. After He speaks, He will listen as I whisper my love to Him.

Bible Reading: Isaiah 42:1-9
One Year Bible Reading Plan:
Colossians 1
Isaiah 41, 42

Alvin Mast, Millersburg, OH

The chains of sin are too light to be felt
until they are so strong you cannot break them.

Firmly Stand

Who knoweth whether thou art come to the
kingdom for such a time as this?
Esther 4:14

The high waters had receded after the past night's rain. As I approached the little creek bridge, I saw that some planks were missing. Just around the bend there stood a young tree at just the right place to catch the planks and keep them from their downstream course.

I was glad for that young tree, not merely because it saved my planks, but because it taught me a deeper appreciation for young people who are serious about their commitment to God and the church.

For such a time as this, young person, you have a purpose and God is counting on you. Maybe the flood of worldward drift brings you under pressure to conform. Someone puts on a tape with inappropriate music. A faithful word from you may help someone return to a Scriptural stand. Remember, your testimony in word or life may keep others from becoming mere driftwood, and they may be restored to the useful place God intended for them.

You may feel alone, but God will give you courage.

I was encouraged recently by two young men who sat at our table. They easily conversed about spiritual things from God's Word. Young brother or young sister, when you "delight thyself . . . in the LORD" (Psalm 37:4), it is a great encouragement to those who observe your life.

When in the assembly I see young people with upturned faces giving full attention to the message, it seems to me they are saying to God, "Yes, Lord, that is for me, I want to live my life for You." That is so encouraging.

As you go forth today, sing the song "Be ye strong in the Lord and the power of His might." Remember, God is counting on you.

Bible Reading: Esther 4:1-17
One Year Bible Reading Plan:
Colossians 2
Isaiah 43, 44

Clayton Weaver, Linneus, MO

God is able to make you stable.

Where Are Your Roots?

That Christ may dwell in your hearts by faith;
that ye, being rooted and grounded in love.
Ephesians 3:17

I helped harvest timber on a swampy lot of several acres. Even though the ground conditions were not the best, there was some good quality timber on the lot.

The trees stood close together and were very tall, but their roots did not go down very deep. When we took the big trees out, the wind hit the younger ones harder and uprooted some of them.

I had to wonder, *Am I, a young Christian, like these trees? How well am I rooted?*

"Study to shew thyself approved unto God, a workman that needeth not to be ashamed" (2 Timothy 2:15). If we study God's Word, and put our roots down deep into it, we will not have to fear the wind. The more we study, the deeper our roots will go.

When we try to uproot a well-rooted tree, pulling at the top, it breaks off above the ground. The man who feeds on God's Word is immoveable. He can suffer and even give his life for Christ, but he cannot be uprooted.

"Heaven and earth shall pass away: but my words shall not pass away" (Luke 21:33).

David Kauffman, Allensville, PA

Bible Reading: Ephesians 3:14-21
One Year Bible Reading Plan:
Colossians 3
Isaiah 45–47

_____

When you read God's Word, you must constantly be saying
to yourself, "It is talking to me, and about me."
—Søren Kierkegaard

True Friendship

*A man that hath friends must shew himself friendly:
and there is a friend that sticketh closer than a brother.*
Proverbs 18:24

Many people do not know the meaning of real friendship. They have "friends," but when a misfortune or death occurs, they do not really have anyone to go to or lean on. This often brings discouragement or even depression into their lives.

The Christian has God as his best friend. But we also need close friends on this earth. How do we attain friends? The Bible says that in order to have friends, we need to be friendly. You know those people who make you feel at ease and comfortable around them. They stop in unexpectedly at your house or out on the job. They help out with whatever job you are doing, not expecting anything in return. They bring a cold drink or an ice cream bar on a hot day, just to see how things are going.

I often wonder how these people do it. Maybe they know that the way to another's heart is acceptance. They look at others for who they are, and not what they think another should be. They do not condemn but encourage. When a person like that takes me into his heart, it is really hard for me to keep him out of mine.

To whom should we be friendly? We need to be a friend to our brother and neighbor or anyone else who needs a friend, for we all need encouragement to live the Christian life. We can be the ones who help others through their good and bad times.

Bible Reading: 1 Samuel 18:1-9
One Year Bible Reading Plan:
Colossians 4
Isaiah 48, 49

Titus Troyer, Middlebury, IN

It brings comfort to have companions in whatever happens.
—John Chrysostom

*October 14*_____

Simplicity

But thou, O Daniel, shut up the words, and seal the book,
even to the time of the end: many shall run to and
fro, and knowledge shall be increased.
Daniel 12:4

We live in a complex world. The "computer age" is also the "aspirin age." The increase in technology and modern conveniences has not brought greater satisfaction to people. The naturalist, Henry David Thoreau, observed years ago, "Most men live lives of quiet desperation!" This is increasingly true today.

The best things in life are simple. The Gospel is simple, and yet so profound it will engage our wonder throughout all eternity. The Sermon on the Mount was simple. It consisted mainly of one and two syllable words. Simple pleasures make the best memories. It is in the simple home that travelers feel the most welcome. The simple dress looks more noble than the glamorous. The best things in life are simple.

We are sometimes described as a "simple people." (Hmm . . . is that really true?) Simplicity is freedom from distractions and complexity. Are we a simple people then? Our faith, our homes, businesses, our life styles? How many acres, employees, vehicles, and toys are simply a "must" for us? Should we take the crew to the Bahamas, or elk hunting in Montana? I simply fill out form 40-B, or was it form 50-C? Remember that appointment with the IRS? Or was it the U.P.S. or the S.O.S.? This is getting to me—pass the aspirin. Or should I take Tylenol, Advil, or Anacin?

Simplicity: freedom from distractions and complexity. In this age of much running to and fro, can we maintain a quietness of spirit? This quietness comes when we enjoy peace with God, peace with man, and peace with ourselves. May this quietness manifest itself in an uncluttered, simple life of service.

> **Bible Reading:** 2 Corinthians 1:8-12; 2 Corinthians 11:3
> **One Year Bible Reading Plan:**
> 1 Thessalonians 1
> Isaiah 50–52

Jim Yoder, Leitchfield, KY

_____

Happy are the simple, for they shall enjoy much peace.
—Thomas á Kempis

True Greatness

He that is greatest among you, let him be as the younger;
and he that is chief, as he that doth serve.
Luke 22:26

In the book *Character Sketches* (volume 2), the author states, "In order to achieve true greatness, we must first discard our ideas of what it is." Jesus explicitly taught us this truth in Luke 22, when He set aside man's idea of greatness—being in a position of power—and exalted God's concept of greatness—being in a position to serve.

Consider the great men in the Bible: Moses, Daniel, David, and Joseph. These men were great rulers, but ruling did not make them great. Rather, God allowed them to rule because they had first become great by serving and meeting the needs of others.

Moses tried to become great by using man's methods, and God had to take him into the wilderness, where he was subjected to the rigorous school of serving. Only after learning to meet the needs of others was Moses fit to be a leader.

We become so intent on meeting our own needs—or, often, our own desires—that we forget our Lord's instruction to serve. True joy comes in serving, not in being served. The paradox is that as we meet the needs of others, we find our own needs are being met.

> **Bible Reading:** Luke 22:20-30
> **One Year Bible Reading Plan:**
> 1 Thessalonians 2
> Isaiah 53–55

Michael Overholt, Isabella Bank, Belize

O Divine Master, grant that I may not
So much seek to be consoled as to console;
To be understood as to understand;
To be loved as to love;
For it is in giving that we receive;
It is in pardoning that we are pardoned;
And it is in dying that we are born to eternal life.
—Francis of Assisi

When We See Christ

That he might present it to himself a glorious church,
not having spot, or wrinkle, or any such thing.
Ephesians 5:27

It was his wedding day. Today he would be united with his beloved. Today they would start out together on the path of life. Today he would have his first sight of her whom he loves.

He had been blind. He had undergone surgery to regain his eyesight. The beautiful wedding day dawned. At the church waited the eye specialist who had been scheduled to remove the bandages the morning of the ceremony.

The bandages were removed. To his joy, he saw clearly. Stepping into the sanctuary, he saw his beloved. It was a tensely joyous moment as the couple met at the altar. The love they had known—he sightless, she seeing—was deepened, because this was the first time they had beheld each other.

Think of another wedding day—of Christ being wed to His church. Both are preparing for the Great Day, when the church will be presented to Christ as His bride. Imagine the anticipation in glory. Christ is preparing all things for His bride. Their home is nearly complete. The marriage supper is nearly ready. Do you not think that Christ may be getting impatient to return for His own?

When we see Christ, we shall behold Divine Perfection. What will be seen in us? God forbid that we should have any spot, wrinkle, or anything marred by sin. Christ, who is preparing glory for the church, is also preparing the church for glory.

Bible Reading: Revelation 19:6-10; 22:10-17
One Year Bible Reading Plan:
1 Thessalonians 3
Isaiah 56–58

Josh Bechtel, Estacada, OR

Surely, I come quickly.
—Revelation 22:20

Your Speech Betrayeth You

For by thy words thou shalt be justified, and
by thy words thou shalt be condemned.
Matthew 12:37

In our everyday language, we sometimes let words slip that are not edifying. Are we willing to let the Holy Spirit discipline our speech, so that we may speak that which is edifying to others?

Many years ago, I worked on a government dairy farm. One morning I was talking with one of the herdsmen, who was a fine Christian man. I let a word slip which was very unseemly for a Christian to speak. The herdsman sidled up close and said, "Amos, what did you say?" Needless to say, my face burned with shame! It was a lesson I never forgot. Such speech casts a shadow over our testimony, but if we truly repent, God is faithful and will forgive us.

"But I say unto you, that every idle word that men shall speak, they shall give account thereof in the day of judgment" (Matthew 12:36). Do you believe these words of Jesus? We should refrain from using worthless words and from jesting, "which are not [fitting]: but rather giving of thanks" (Ephesians 5:4). It is needful that we practice carefulness in our speech. Let us repent of careless speech and encourage one another to continue in the faith, being rooted and grounded in Christ.

We are living in the day of grace, but we do not want to frustrate the grace of God. "For he that will love life, and see good days, let him refrain his tongue from evil, and his lips that they speak no guile" (1 Peter 3:10). God calls His children to a holy life, and that includes the way we speak. "But as he which hath called you is holy, so be ye holy in all manner of conversation" (1 Peter 1:15).

Bible Reading: Matthew
26:31-25, 69-75
One Year Bible Reading Plan:
1 Thessalonians 4
Isaiah 59–61

Amos Graber, Rosebush, MI

There is a grace of kind listening
as well as a grace of kind speaking
—Frederick Faber

*October 18*_____

Dragging Crumbs

Go to the ant, . . . consider her ways, and be wise.
Proverbs 6:6

While eating lunch at work one day, I noticed a few ants that seemed to be pretty interested in some crumbs that had fallen from my sandwich. I saw an ant pick up a little crumb and scurry away with it, and soon there were other ants gathering to look for more.

I wondered what would happen if I gave them a larger piece, so I tore off a piece of bread considerably larger than the ants. Soon I noticed an ant tugging at the piece, with little success. However, it did not give up but kept tugging and pulling. A little later, another ant came and took hold, and together they started moving the crumb. After they started moving it, two more ants came along to help with the project. They began pushing, and soon the crumb was moving along at a brisk rate. Knowing that the crumb was far too large to go down into an ant nest, I followed the little procession.

I watched with amusement as two of the little ants disappeared down the hole. The crumb came to an abrupt halt. Soon the ants underneath pushed it up, and they tried again but to no avail. Did they give up? Absolutely not! They tore that crumb apart and carried it down the hole bit by bit, until it was all gone and stored away.

If the ants at either end would have pulled against each other, they would have gotten nowhere. But, because they worked together, they were able to accomplish much more than one ant could have managed working alone. It is so beautiful to see Christians helping each other along in life. It strengthens our relationships with each other, and we are able to walk together in unity for the same goal. When we cooperate with one another, we can accomplish more than any one of us can do on his own. We are working with souls headed for eternity, and our help may make a difference in the destiny they reach.

Vernon Troyer, Clarkson, KY

Bible Reading: Galatians 6
One Year Bible Reading Plan:
1 Thessalonians 5
Isaiah 62–64

Look not every man on his own things,
but every man also on the things of others.
—Philippians 2:4

The Freedom of Forgiveness

For I will be merciful to their unrighteousness, and their sins
and their iniquities will I remember no more.
Hebrews 8:12

Have you ever considered what life would be like if God had not promised total forgiveness of our sins? First John 1:9 assures us that He will not only forgive all our sins, but that He will also cleanse or deliver us from the power of sin that has in the past driven us to sin.

When an individual commits a crime and is sentenced to punishment, this does not mean that the court cannot again refer to this crime, if later he appears in court for committing further crimes. The judge will often refer to previous records in order to draw a conclusion about just punishment.

Praise the Lord, when we face up to our sins and confess them at the foot of the cross, we have the confidence that our Judge will not cover our sins until we again need forgiveness, but He will remove our iniquities from us, as far as the east is from the west. Hebrews 8:12 gives us the confidence that He will not remember once forgiven sins.

This is real freedom, which enables us to live a life of purpose and meaning. Jesus' words in John 8:36, "If the Son therefore shall make you free, ye shall be free indeed," direct us to the only way we can experience real freedom.

Bible Reading: Psalm 103
One Year Bible Reading Plan:
2 Thessalonians 1
Isaiah 65, 66

Andy Yoder, Stuarts Draft, VA

Real freedom is not the liberty to do what I want,
but the power to do what I ought.

Am I Honest?

. . . in all things willing to live honestly.
Hebrews 13:18b

Recently a sister stopped at the bank. The teller, a new employee, gave the sister too much money. As the sister went on with her business in town, she discovered that she had too much money. She went right back to the bank. As she got to the counter, some of the ladies said, "We knew you would be back." They then told her that when the new teller had found her mistake, she made quite a fuss about it; but they had told her, "She'll be back."

Some time ago we delivered some products to a customer and accidentally overcharged him. Later, when we realized our mistake, I went back to the customer to return some of his money. I explained our mistake. His remark was, "Thank you, but most people wouldn't do this."

Please allow me to paraphrase the teaching of Christ in Matthew 5:16: "Let men see your honest works, and glorify your Father which is in heaven."

Can people sense that we are pilgrims and strangers looking for a better country, or do they see us coveting earthly possessions, following after worldly pleasures and entertainments, and influenced by changing fads and technologies?

Have we honestly yielded our lives to the will of God? Let us be honest examples of Scriptural living, for Jesus promises that when we are, our lives will glorify the Father.

Bible Reading: Matthew 19:13-26
One Year Bible Reading Plan:
2 Thessalonians 2
Jeremiah 1, 2

David Borntrager, Monticello, KY

The man who is not honest will not trust others.

Come, Lord Jesus

Even so, come, Lord Jesus.
Revelation 22:20b

Our lives are often so busy that we forget Christ is coming again. Oh, we would like to go to heaven when we die, but we want a little more time here on earth. There are so many good things we would like to do that we forget that He said, "Behold, I come quickly."

Several months ago our girls were praying the little bedtime prayer, "Now I lay me down to sleep." The second line says, "I pray the Lord my soul to keep." They prayed it this way, "I pray the Lord my soul to take." Their mistake really spoke to me. How often do I pray for the Lord to come for me?

Can we say in the morning when we get up, I sure hope the Lord comes today? Or, in the evening, perhaps tonight? We have it so nice here in America that we fail to realize that this life is temporal. We live as though we plan to be here forever! Remember, Christ has prepared a place for us. Let us set our sights on the eastern sky and pray as the apostle John did, "Even so, come, Lord Jesus."

Mark Webb, Hicksville, OH

Bible Reading: Revelation 22
One Year Bible Reading Plan:
2 Thessalonians 3
Jeremiah 3, 4

What a beautiful day for the Lord to come again.

Follow the Leader

And he saith unto them, Follow me, and
I will make you fishers of men.
Matthew 4:19

Cloudy was just an ordinary Holstein dairy cow of unknown ancestry, but she possessed one unusual characteristic, which she exemplified throughout her entire bovine life. Her previous owner had warned us that even in inclement weather, Cloudy would, without fail, be the leader of the herd out to the back pasture and into the dairy barn for each milking every day. Though occasionally other herd mates challenged her, it seemed that Cloudy had earned her position, and she was respected as she dutifully followed the well-worn paths each day.

To be a follower is not a very popular idea in an age characterized by the compelling desire to live out one's own selfish agenda. But leadership that is not encompassed by a life of obedience and self-denial often creates frustration and confusion. When Jesus sought suitable leadership for the early church, He simply asked four laboring fishermen to follow Him. Without asking any questions or offering excuses, the four immediately left their nets and followed Him. *Following* sounds quite elementary, and perhaps a little too simple, yet it is the only way, if we are to become effective fishers of men.

Endeavoring to follow in the Christian life does not mean that we simply blunder aimlessly along in blind obedience, but it means crucifying our personal desires and choosing through faith to commit our way to God. We can be assured that God always has our best interests in mind when He leads us through situations we do not understand.

The direction in which God leads us may not always be the shortest or the easiest way; but we can be sure it is the safest way, because He is leading the way!

Bible Reading: Matthew 4:12-25
One Year Bible Reading Plan:
1 Timothy 1
Jeremiah 5, 6

Phil Hershberger, Abbeville, SC

God will never lead us where His grace cannot keep us.

Overhauled, But Still Broken

*The dog is turned to his own vomit again; and the
sow that was washed to her wallowing in the mire.*
2 Peter 2:22

I used to do some mechanic work in a small shop beside our house. A brother from the church brought to me a truck with a bad head gasket. It already had been overhauled and repaired once. I replaced one head and both head gaskets.

Several weeks later, the same brother returned. His truck had the same problem again. This time we decided to replace the entire engine, so that it wouldn't happen again. We bought a rebuilt engine. At the same time we replaced the transmission, because the brother wanted an automatic instead of the manual transmission it had.

After driving the truck about one hundred and fifty miles, the new engine developed a bad rod knock and needed to be replaced again! By this time I was so frustrated I wished never to see the truck again. To top it all off, the new transmission had to be replaced several months later.

It is very frustrating to have to repair the same problem more than once. This was an especially bad experience for the brother who owned the truck. Not only were the repair costs high, but, also, the truck was not available for him to use. How it must grieve the Lord when we return to our old sinful ways after He has saved us, renewed us, replaced our old man, and made us new creatures. Consider what it cost the Lord to save us from sin. Consider how it saddens Him when we are not available for His use because we have returned to wallow in the mire of sin.

Bible Reading: 2 Peter 2:15-22
One Year Bible Reading Plan:
1 Timothy 2
Jeremiah 7, 8

Henry Yoder, Leitchfield, KY

If we are ruled by sin, we shall inevitably be ruined by it.

Facing Discouragement

*The L*ORD *is with you, while ye be with him; and if ye seek him,*
he will be found of you; but if ye forsake him, he will forsake you.
2 Chronicles 15:2

Do you ever feel that God has forsaken you, that He no longer cares about you, or that He allows things to happen just to make life hard for you? Every person faces discouragement at times. Jesus tells us in Luke 11:10, "Every one that asketh receiveth; and he that seeketh findeth." Notice the words ask and seek. God wants us to ask Him for help. He wants us to seek His guidance. Sure, God allows us to experience trials, but He will help us through them if we allow Him to.

Once an old man was captured by a group of bandits. One day he managed to get on a raft and escape down a river. After days of floating down the river with nothing to eat, he became too weak to help himself. Finally, the raft floated past a town, but the man was too weak to bring his raft to shore. After floating past the town unnoticed, he raised his hand in one last attempt to be seen. A man washing his horse in the river saw the old man raise his hand. The man took notice, and soon the old man was rescued.

If you feel like giving up, raise your hand to God. He will notice. He will not force His help upon you. He wants you to humble yourself and seek Him.

Roman Yoder, Belvidere, TN

Bible Reading: Luke 11:5-13
One Year Bible Reading Plan:
1 Timothy 3
Jeremiah 9, 10

He that planted the ear, shall He not hear?
—Psalm 94:9

Where Is That First Love?

Nevertheless I have somewhat against thee,
because thou hast left thy first love.
Revelation 2:4

In the Scripture reading today, God remembers when Israel followed Him with her whole heart. He remembers how she had followed Him through the barren wilderness with nothing in mind but to enter with Him into the promised land of Canaan. God revealed His love to Israel when He delivered her from Egypt and led her to Canaan. As long as Israel loved Him with her whole heart, she was holy before Him. She was His special nation. Those who offended her, God dealt with.

But Israel's love waned. Though God protected her fiercely and spared her many times, she began to long after the idols of the people of the land. Finally, Israel quit loving and seeking after the Lord. She soon became ignorant and unwilling to learn about God. Her once glorious inheritance became an abomination to God.

All Israel did at first was to be satisfied with less than her first love. This led to her ruin. This same loss of love will also ruin us, if we continue in it. We must love and seek for the Lord with all our hearts. He longs to have that first love relationship with us. How is your first love?

Bible Reading: Jeremiah 2:1-9
One Year Bible Reading Plan:
1 Timothy 4
Jeremiah 11–13

Chris Beiler, Auburn, KY

Thou shalt love the Lord thy God with all thy heart.
—Matthew 22:37

On Guard for Spiritual Danger

Abstain from all appearance of evil.
1 Thessalonians 5:22

It was a beautiful, sunshiny day with barely a cloud in the sky when a group of young people started out for a hike in the Virginia mountains. They were a happy, carefree bunch, as young people usually are, and eager to make the most of this special day. Little did they know the tragedy that would befall them before the day was through.

They started on their way, and though the path was rugged and steep, they finally made it to the top, where they could see for miles and miles.

The group was standing a safe distance from the edge of a sheer drop-off. One of the girls, curious to see down over the cliff, decided to get a little closer to the edge. The rock ledge, which was slightly sloped, looked safe enough, being covered over with moss. But she did not know that there was water underneath. Before anyone realized what was happening, she began slipping and sliding toward the edge, and there was nothing for her to grab on to. With a scream, she disappeared out of sight, landing in a stream of water over one hundred feet below. By the time the others reached her, she was drawing her last breath, and her life on this earth was over.

What a tragedy for such a sweet girl, so full of youth and vitality, to be snatched from this life in such a way. How much more tragic it is to see someone living a careless life, getting too close to the "edge."

Satan offers many things that are covered over with "moss." They may look ever so harmless, but we must be on guard for the "water" underneath, which will cause us to slip and fall! There is safety only in the Rock of Ages.

Bible Reading: 1 Thessalonians 5:8-28
One Year Bible Reading Plan:
1 Timothy 5
Jeremiah 14–16

Abner Overholt, Auburn, KY

Watch out for temptation. The more you see of it, the better it looks.

Nail Holes

_I acknowledged my sin unto thee, and mine iniquity have I not hid.
I said, I will confess my transgressions unto the Lord;
and thou forgavest the iniquity of my sin. Selah._
Psalm 32:5

All sin carries a price tag. Whether the sin is small or great, somebody always pays.

I heard a story about a boy whose father pounded a nail in the barn door every time the boy did something wrong. After some time the barn door held quite a number of nails. One day the boy accepted Christ into his heart. To impress upon his son the wonder of being forgiven, the father took his son out to the barn and pulled out every nail. "This is what it means to have all your sins forgiven," he said. "They are gone forever."

The boy was deeply impressed. Then, looking at the door, he asked, "But Father, how can I get rid of the holes?"

"I'm sorry," said the father, "but they will remain."

How many times have we pounded a nail in the door without thinking about the gaping hole it would leave behind? Some holes may not be as big as others, but they still will leave a permanent scar. Those scars do not have to haunt us. Even though they are there, we can still have victory. How? Because of God's forgiveness.

David paid dearly for the sin he committed with Bathsheba. Even though he confessed his sin, and God removed the nail, David carried with him a deep sorrow. But this did not rob him of the blessedness of forgiveness.

Bible Reading: 2 Samuel 12:1-23
One Year Bible Reading Plan:
1 Timothy 6
Jeremiah 17–19

Even though we may have to suffer consequences for our sins, we can rejoice in His unfailing forgiveness. Praise the Lord!

Joseph Gingerich, Free Union, VA

Never is a nail too rusty, too big, or too small to pull out.

Where's the Fruit?

But the fruit of the Spirit is love, joy, peace,
longsuffering, gentleness, goodness, faith.
Galatians 5:22

A farmer climbs aboard his combine and heads for the field. This is the time for which he has been waiting. All summer long he has been observing the corn through its various stages of development. Other than some curling during a dry spell in July, the plants have appeared quite healthy and vigorous. Now the stalks and leaves are brown, and the grain is ready for harvest. Eagerly the farmer guides his combine along the stately rows.

One round . . . two rounds—alas! The grain bin is still not full. Mr. Farmer's heart sinks with disappointment. He is painfully aware of the investment that went into this crop. He recalls the careful preparation and planting. He remembers the cost of the seed, the fertilizer, and the pesticide. Now there may not be enough return to cover the expenses, let alone enough to make a profit.

Our heavenly Father also has invested heavily in the human race. He gave His only Son to save us from eternal destruction. He sent another part of Himself—the Holy Spirit—to guide us into all truth. To further provide for spiritual growth and security, we can hold in our hands His precious, eternal Word. Many other blessings have been poured out upon us. Truly the prophet Isaiah asks, "What could have been done more to my vineyard?"

What return does God have in my life for all His goodness? Let us not disappoint Him with shriveled lives and puny fruit. May our hearts be soft and warm, overflowing with gratitude and fruit, and bringing glory to His name!

Bible Reading: Isaiah 5:1-7; Galatians 5:22-26
One Year Bible Reading Plan:
2 Timothy 1
Jeremiah 20–22

Allen Beiler, Stuarts Draft, VA

Where there is no life, there will also be no fruit.

Beware of Naaman's Attitude

But Naaman was wroth, and went away, and said, Behold, I thought, . . .
2 Kings 5:11

Naaman was stricken with leprosy. In his era, there was no medicine or doctor able to cure him. By the providence of the Lord and a girl's words, Naaman was led to a prophet in Israel who could heal him.

When Naaman finally arrived at the prophet's house with all his horses, chariots, and servants, he must have been excited. He stopped at Elisha's door, and the prophet sent a messenger with instructions that Naaman should dip himself in the Jordan River. Naaman did not like those instructions. Dip himself in the muddy Jordan? Why, the rivers in Damascus were much better than any water Israel had! He turned away in anger.

Water was not Naaman's problem. His problem was that he thought he knew how the prophet would heal him, and that it would take a great miracle. He said, "Behold, I thought, He will surely come out to me, and stand, and call on the name of the LORD his God, and strike his hand over the place, and recover the leper" (2 Kings 5:11).

His servants saw Naaman's pride and asked him if he would do a great thing to be healed, how much more willing should he be to simply wash and become clean? Naaman recognized the reasonableness of this, and he went to the Jordan River, washed seven times, and was clean.

I cannot be too hard on Naaman. I think in the same ways. I think my present situation will take a great miracle, and it will. What I forget is that it is God who does the miracle, not I. This does not mean that I sit back and relax. I need to do what He tells me to, little as it may seem. Maybe it is a prayer, a helping hand, a word of encouragement, or witnessing for Christ. Let us not have Naaman's attitude.

Bible Reading: 2 Kings 5:1-19
One Year Bible Reading Plan:
2 Timothy 2
Jeremiah 23, 24

Timothy D. Miller, Farmington, NM

No one can possibly go forth in the strength of the Lord
until he has first learned to stand still in his own helplessness.

Feed My Sheep

Teaching them to observe all things
whatsoever I have commanded you.
Matthew 28:20a

As Jesus met with His disciples for one of the last times before returning to His Father in heaven, He gave Peter some important instructions concerning the thousands of people who would come to know Jesus in a different way than they ever had known Him before.

He asked Peter about his love for Him. In reply to Peter's response, Jesus instructed him to feed His lambs (John 21:15) and to feed His sheep (John 21:16, 17). At this time the disciples probably did not yet realize the great work that was being laid at their feet. Jesus, knowing that His return to heaven was at hand, tried to help Peter see his responsibility to supply spiritual direction and food for the souls of those who would soon believe.

A pastor once told me that as he prepares a message, he wants to make sure it is a complete meal. If his listeners are hungering and thirsting after righteousness (Matthew 5:6), there must be something in the message that will fill them.

God looks down today at His followers. He wants His church to continue on nurturing and feeding one another spiritually. The concern of Jesus' heart still stands for all ministers, Sunday school teachers, parents, schoolteachers, and all His servants to continue meeting the needs wherever we have been asked to teach or minister God's Word.

Bible Reading: John 21:11-25
One Year Bible Reading Plan:
2 Timothy 3
Jeremiah 25, 26

Lester Stoltzfus, Honey Brook, PA

Grant me Thy grace for every task
Until Thy face I see,
Then ever new shall be that joy
In service, Lord, for Thee.
—Edith Witmer, 1937

"Teach Me Thy Truth, O Mighty One," Edith Witmer, 1937, *Life Songs II*, Copyright by Eastern Mennonite Publications. Used by permission.

Joy

Thou wilt shew me the path of life: in thy presence is fulness of joy;
at thy right hand there are pleasures for evermore.
Psalm 16:11

Ungodly people can be happy, but they can never have godly joy. Godly people can be happy and also have godly joy. There is a vast difference between happiness and joy. Happiness can be canceled without further notice. Godly joy carries a lifetime warranty. Circumstances can bring happiness, or take it away. Godly joy is not derived from and not dependent on circumstances; therefore, circumstances cannot take it away.

When Ezra read the book of the law, the people wanted to weep. They were told not to weep but to rejoice, for it was a holy day (Nehemiah 8:9). You can have joy only when your day is a holy day. When God orders a holy day, He requires rejoicing (Philippians 3:1, 3; Romans 5:2). To live in a holy day without rejoicing is displeasing to God.

The joy of the Lord brings strength (Nehemiah 8:10). Joy is a motivating factor that propels us up and over the rough terrain we so often have to travel over. If the pressures of circumstances disrupt our relationship with God and take away our good feelings, then maybe we are relying upon happiness, rather than true joy. If those same pressures do not disrupt our joy but drive us to God, then we know that we have real joy (Hebrews 12:2).

The peace of God in us is the result of meeting God's conditions. Joy is the effect of that peace. Praise God for Jesus, and for every day that we are allowed to live redeemed in Him. Rejoice in Him every day, for every day in Him is a holy day!

Bible Reading: Nehemiah 8:1-12
One Year Bible Reading Plan:
2 Timothy 4
Jeremiah 27, 28

Alvin Mast, Millersburg, OH

Joy is the echo of God's life within us.
—Columba Marmion

Dead—Yet Alive

Therefore if any man be in Christ, he is a new creature:
old things are passed away; behold, all things are become new.
2 Corinthians 5:17

I had just finished cutting down a stump in our front yard. I hauled the chunks of wood to the wood pile and was about to unload them. About that time I saw green leaves growing on a piece of poplar I had cut the previous winter. It should have been dead; but a few factors changed that.

I noticed that the wood was still green. There was still life somehow. Although severed from the life-giving roots, there was still potential for life and growth.

There was contact with water because of all the rain during the previous weeks. Water encouraged growth even in an unlikely setting. Potential plus water equaled new life.

We believe that the spirit, under the domain of sin, is dead or dormant. There is no sign of life; although much potential is hidden. But let God get hold of the spirit and breathe His life into it, and you have a new creature! This new life becomes active and bears fruit.

Just what empowers the Christian? The world did not give him this new life; so he gets no help from it now. It is the grace of God that enables Christians. As we by faith appropriate this grace, it imparts spiritual life evidenced by our works.

Bible Reading: Job 14:6-9; 2 Corinthians 5
One Year Bible Reading Plan: Titus 1, Jeremiah 29, 30

Thank God for His abundant provisions of grace!

Josh Bechtel, Estacada, OR

God provides a full Christ for empty sinners.

Is He Not Wonderful?

O come, let us worship and bow down:
*let us kneel before the L*ORD *our maker.*
Psalm 95:6

Recently, while listening in church to a devotional from Psalm 144, I was reminded of all God means to me. I went home and did some meditating and reading and put together a list. This list is by no means exhaustive, but I trust it may encourage you to dig deeper into God's Word and count your blessings.

Think about the blessing of salvation. Christ is my Lord, my Savior, my Salvation, and my Redeemer. He is my Portion, my Hope, my Passover, and my Peace. Thank you, Lord, for saving my soul!

I am thankful that He is even now at the right hand of the Father interceding in my behalf. What a privilege to have such a High Priest, Advocate, and Mediator! He cares for me!

I know that I can rest in Him. God is the strength of my heart. He is my Fortress, my High Tower, my Defense, and my Refuge. He is my Deliverer, my Buckler, my Shield, my Help, and the Rock of my Refuge. What a strong habitation and hiding place! The Lord is my Shepherd, and I rest in Him. I will fear no evil.

Who is so great a God as our God? God is my Lamp. God is my Glory, my Delight, and my Beloved. He is my Creator, my Father, and my King. He is my Song. He is King of kings and Lord of lords.

Is it not exciting to think about what God means to you? It is wonderful to think about our salvation. How satisfying and peaceful to consider how He cares for us and protects us. I trust God means all this to you and more. Take some time right now to thank Him for what He means to you.

Mark Webb, Hicksville, OH

Bible Reading: 2 Samuel 22:29-37
One Year Bible Reading Plan:
Titus 2
Jeremiah 31, 32

He is worthy of all our praise.

November 3

Tragedy to Triumph

*. . . I will build my church; and the gates of hell
shall not prevail against it.*
Matthew 16:18

The world called it a waste. Christians around the world were shocked when five young, dedicated missionaries were speared to death in 1956 by Auca Indians in the jungles of Ecuador.

Recently, as a group of us stood on Palm Beach, where the missionaries were killed, tears of sorrow and gratitude flowed down our cheeks. We felt sorrow at the loss of the lives of five young men. We also felt gratitude, because out of this tragedy grew a determination to bring the Gospel to a group of people that knew very little about God.

The Gospel of Jesus Christ triumphed over darkness as the New Testament was translated into a language the people could understand. Lives were changed by the power of God. Spearing and jungle superstitions gave way to an understanding of God's Word, and peace now flows through the lives of these people.

A highlight for our group came the following Sunday morning. One of the men who had participated in the spearing of the five missionaries shared a sermon in a small thatched-roof church along the Curary River in the Amazonian jungle.

The older generation once knew spearing as a way of life. Spears have been exchanged for real values and a forgiving attitude. The Aucas' love for the Word of God has taken the Gospel to other areas, at the risk of their own lives.

Jesus reminded us in John 12:24, "Except a corn of wheat fall into the ground and die, it abideth alone: but if it die, it bringeth forth much fruit."

As we thank God for turning tragedy into triumph, may our hearts respond with a deeper dedication and love for God.

Bible Reading: Matthew 16:13-28
One Year Bible Reading Plan: Titus 3
Jeremiah 33–35

Henry Petersheim, Abbeville, SC

God's Word brings changes that nothing else can.

In My Name

And whatsoever ye shall ask in my name, that will I do,
that the Father may be glorified in the Son.
John 14:13

A farmer wished to go overseas to do evangelistic work. His friend offered to take care of his dairy farm while he was gone. But how was he to handle the financial aspects of his business?

The solution was to give "power of attorney" to the friend who was to take care of the farm. This legal document authorized the friend to write checks, pay bills, buy supplies, sell cows, even to borrow money, all in the name of the man who was overseas. Of course, he was accountable for the way he conducted the missionary's business. Naturally, one does not give this authority to another unless one trusts him completely.

In John 14, Jesus gives us the power to do business in His name, and He promises to honor our commitments. This is a tremendous honor and responsibility, as well as a privilege. In fact, in the parable of the talents, we get the impression that we are commanded to exercise this authority. Even the fear of making mistakes does not excuse us from trying to bring gain and honor to the Kingdom of Heaven. Jesus even promises to take our mistakes and work them over for good.

Only to do nothing with that which God gives us brings condemnation.

Bible Reading: Acts 19:13-20; John 14:12-14
One Year Bible Reading Plan:
Philemon
Jeremiah 36, 37

Dan Schmucker, Franklin, KY

Think less of the power of things over you
and more of the power of Christ in you.

Spiritual Pride

. . . For God resisteth the proud, and giveth grace to the humble.
1 Peter 5:5

An unusual pearl was found in Australia. It was perfect in shape, in color, and almost an inch in diameter. Though it was practically priceless, the pearl could not be sold, for it was too large to be used as a ring setting, and few other pearls could be found to match, so that it might be part of a necklace.

So it is with the proud and haughty Christian; he may have more than ordinary abilities, be well versed in God's Word, and possess a fine personality. But pride, selfishness, condemnation of others, and boasting render his otherwise invaluable service value-less, and he is set aside, while God uses a more humble, obedient servant with less abilities to perform His work.

An article in the *Gospel Herald* reminds us that generally, plants grow only in certain soils, or at certain heights, or under certain lines of latitude. Pride, however, like a weed, taking root in every heart, grows at all elevations, in the humblest as well as in the highest callings in life.

A writer in the *Sunday School Times* tells the story of a young pastor who once asked an old farmer what was the greatest step to spiritual growth and happiness. "Would renouncing our sinful self be the most important?" suggested the pastor. "No," replied the old farmer, "the greatest step is to renounce our righteous self."

Bible Reading: 1 Peter 5:1-10
One Year Bible Reading Plan:
Hebrews 1
Jeremiah 38, 39

Rudy Overholt, Auburn, KY

Pride is the only poison that is good for you when swallowed.

Remember!

Only take heed to thyself, and keep thy soul diligently,
lest thou forget the things which thine eyes have seen.
Deuteronomy 4:9

The memory is our capacity for storing information and later bringing it back to the conscious mind for use. Many, if not all, the events of our lives are stored somewhere in our memory. Some we frequently think about, some only occasionally, and some never.

Throughout the Scripture, God commanded His people to do things to help them remember important events and experiences. The Feast of the Passover was instituted to help the Israelites remember their deliverance. And when they passed over the Jordan River, they were commanded to set up twelve stones as a memorial of their crossing. When Jesus instituted the breaking of the bread and the drinking of the cup He said, "This do in remembrance of me."

Much of the information that our memory retains can be valuable for everyday living. Of special value to the child of God is memorized Scripture. There are several ways in which memorizing Scripture can be a blessing to us. It can help us to overcome temptation. Jesus used Scripture in this way to withstand Satan during His temptations in the wilderness. When we are tempted in a certain area, thinking about Scripture that pertains to that particular thing can help us overcome. Memorizing Scripture is also a means of comfort, encouragement, and pure thinking. When we are thinking about the Word, we are thinking God's thoughts. Scripture memorized is a help in teaching, preaching, or sharing with others, too. Paul and Peter were familiar with the Old Testament and able to include portions of Scripture to back up the truths they wished to teach.

Committing Scripture to memory makes it available to us at anytime without the need to open the Book. May we make good use of the Sword of the Spirit, which is the Word of God.

Bible Reading: 2 Peter 1:1-21
One Year Bible Reading Plan:
Hebrews 2
Jeremiah 40–42

John E. Glick, Gap, PA

The object of opening the mind, as of opening the mouth,
is that I might shut it again on something solid.
—G. K. Chesterton

315

Four Hundred and Ninety Times

Blessed are the merciful: for they shall obtain mercy.
Matthew 5:7

Peter was concerned about how often he should forgive someone who had sinned against him. He wondered if seven times was enough. Jesus said we need to forgive 490 times. It is hard to imagine that someone would come 490 times in one day to ask forgiveness. Jesus tells us that our willingness to forgive must be boundless. We cannot forgive too often.

Jesus gives us an example of how to forgive. As I read Matthew 18:23-27, I picture myself being called before God to give an account of what I have done. I stand before God. He begins telling me all the things that are written under my name. He says, "You did not help that fallen brother. You kept for yourself that which belonged to Me. You have laid aside your first love, Me." As He continues speaking, I fall on my face before Him, and cry out, "Lord, forgive me; have patience with me. I will change my life. I will make right all that in which I have wronged you." The Lord replies, "I will forgive you all."

As I go out from the Lord's presence, I find a brother who has wronged me. I tell him, "You have cheated me. You need to make this right with me." This brother asks for patience and time until he can make this thing right. I do not have patience with him but cast him aside, and even hate him.

Our fellow brethren see what I have done to this brother, and they come before the Lord and tell Him what I have done. The Lord returns to me and says, "Oh, you unmerciful and unforgiving servant. After I forgave you, should you not also have forgiven your brother? I will be against you until you are willing to forgive your brother."

Joe Miller, Belleville, PA

Bible Reading: Matthew 18:21-35
One Year Bible Reading Plan:
Hebrews 3
Jeremiah 43–45

Freely ye have received, freely give.
—Matthew 10:8

The Lord, Our Refuge

God hath spoken once; twice have I heard this;
that power belongeth unto God.
Psalm 62:11

In this Psalm David encourages us to trust deeply in our God. For He really is our Rock and our Defense, our Salvation and our Glory. We can trust Him at all times, for He is also our Refuge.

A refuge is a place of safety. It takes a powerful God to keep us safe from the darts of the evil one. Verse 11 says that power belongs to our God.

Those who have witnessed the power and force of a tornado have a good understanding of the word *refuge*. Recently a tornado came through our area, and our church helped to clean up the mess. Household items, trash, debris, and many trees were cleaned up. Many of the people we met were in a state of shock, but they acknowledged that the power within the tornado is far beyond man.

How many times has God shown Himself powerful right before our eyes? God may be speaking to our inner need for courage through catastrophe, sickness, or death.

Let us be open to God to receive His instruction and counsel.

Bible Reading: Psalm 62
One Year Bible Reading Plan:
Hebrews 4
Jeremiah 46–48

William Troyer, Huntland, TN

God's mighty hand the world sustains,
And everything that it contains.
—Heinrich Albert

Contentment

Not that I speak in respect of want, for I have learned
in whatsoever state I am, therewith to be content.
Philippians 4:11

Can you identify with Paul? Recently I was reminded that a large percentage of the world's population lives in poverty. Many do not have their basic needs met, yet they are happy and content.

We have been abundantly blessed, but we often invent needs because of our lifestyle. Our wants become our needs. We think if only we could have a certain "thing," we would be happy. Yet things never bring true happiness.

What does bring true happiness? Taking one day at a time, trusting, and seeking God's will brings real peace and contentment. Paul says, "I have learned in whatsoever state I am, therewith to be content" (Philippians 4:11). May our attitude, our expression, and even our lifestyle reflect peace and contentment.

> **Bible Reading:** 1 Timothy 6:1-12
> **One Year Bible Reading Plan:**
> Hebrews 5
> Jeremiah 49, 50

Philip Yoder, Whiteville, TN

Contentment consists in being happy with what
we have, and with what we don't have.

White Elephants

*But they that will be rich fall into temptation and a snare,
and into many foolish and hurtful lusts, which
drown men in destruction and perdition.*
1 Timothy 6:9

The King of Siam wished to destroy a person he disliked, so he gave him a gift: a white elephant. A white elephant was a very valuable and sacred animal, and a person who refused to receive the gift would appear ungrateful, incurring the wrath of the king. But accepting the gift meant the man's ruin, because the king's enemy was poor. It took all of his time, energy, and resources to support the white elephant, so that there was nothing left for his family.

The world values highly a lot of sacred "white elephants." The prince of this world, wishing to destroy us, offers them to us as gifts, knowing that if we accept them, they will bring about our spiritual ruin. Accepting the world's value system, means devoting all of our time, energy, and resources to maintaining that system, at the expense of our souls. Jesus said, "For what shall it profit a man, if he gain the whole world and lose his own soul?" (Mark 8:36).

In today's Bible reading, the young ruler's "white elephant" was his riches. Wasn't he foolish to forfeit eternal life so that he could feed his "white elephant" for a few short years?

Melvin Troyer, Clarkson, KY

Bible Reading: Mark 10:17-31
One Year Bible Reading Plan:
Hebrews 6
Jeremiah 51, 52

He who knows the world best will love it least.

Following the Shepherd

My sheep hear my voice, and I know them, and they follow me.
John 10:27

When I was a young boy, my grandfather owned two pastures that were at a distance from his home. On one he kept his young cattle during the grazing season. On the other, which was in a different direction, he kept his sheep during the summer. Both the cattle and the sheep were taken to their pastures yearly on foot. To take the cattle to their pasture, Grandpa always needed help because the cattle usually scattered out over the whole width of the road. Grandpa always walked along behind to prod the stragglers. Occasionally, we helpers had to run ahead to keep the cattle from straying into people's driveways, or to keep them going in the right direction at crossroads.

When Grandpa took the sheep to their pasture, he needed no helpers. He simply opened the door of the sheepfold and called for them to come. Down the road he walked, with the sheep following. When he passed someone's driveway or needed to turn at a crossroad, he simply said, "Come sheepy, sheepy, sheepy." The sheep would respond with a joyous, "Baa, baa." They always stayed close together, and as close to Grandpa as they could. When Grandpa opened the gate to the pasture and led them in, the sheep immediately spread out and filled up on the luscious grass. By the time Grandpa had checked the fence and had the windmill running to pump water, the sheep were ready to lie down in their green pasture, and the still waters were available when they were thirsty.

Some Christians are like cattle that need to be prodded along and need a guard at each gap and crossroad. Instead, let us give heed when Jesus our Shepherd calls, and follow Him gladly. We, too, will be led beside the still waters and made to lie down in green pastures.

Bible Reading: Psalm 23
One Year Bible Reading Plan:
  Hebrews 7
  Lamentations 1, 2

Moses Gingerich, Middlebury, IN

Where He leads, I'll follow. Follow Jesus every day.
—W. A. Ogden

On Time

And that, knowing the time, that now it is high time to awake out of sleep: for now is our salvation nearer than when we believed.
Romans 13:11

I was traveling I-65 recently, when the slogan of a commercial freightline caught my eye: "On time, every time." Quite an ideal to strive for in the business world, but the writer of Ephesians goes deeper. Ephesians 5:16 tells us to "redeem the time." This short phrase is especially noteworthy following the condemnation of sin in the preceding verses.

The best gift I can give anyone is my time. If I give you money, I am really giving you the time it took to earn that money. If I give you a gift, I am giving you the time it took to earn the money with which I bought the gift. Life is time. When someone is killed, the time he would have lived is taken from him. The time I spend writing this devotional cannot be spent doing anything else. Prisoners talk about "doing time," and I think they have a proper concept of what we are trying to say. So, what shall we do with our time?

Suppose you had a bank account that was credited with $86,400 every morning. No overdrafts were allowed, and every evening whatever was left in the account was canceled, what would you do? You would draw it out and apply it to some good use. Now, with 86,400 seconds in every day we have something more valuable than money. We ought to apply each second to some good use!

Usually we develop a sense of urgency about something after we see that there is only a limited amount of it left. When the bank account gets low, we suddenly sense it is time to get back to work. So it is with time. The Psalmist had something like this in mind when he wrote Psalm 90:12: "So teach us to number our days, that we may apply our hearts unto wisdom."

Bible Reading: Ephesians 5:1-21
One Year Bible Reading Plan:
Hebrews 8
Lamentations 3–5

Jerry Yoder, Auburn, KY

Time is so precious that it is dealt out to us only in the smallest possible fractions—one tiny moment at a time.
—Irish Proverb

"Just Happen?"

And we know that all things work together for good to them that
love God, to them who are the called according to his purpose.
Romans 8:28

The accident happened about a week after school let out for the summer. The surgery that repaired my severed big toe required that I lie at home on my back, with my left foot elevated, for about a week.

One day, there was a knock at the door. Since we were not a Christian family, one of us said in a loud whisper, "It's a preacher!" With that warning, three other children fled for hiding places, leaving Mom and me to defend ourselves alone. The preacher was looking for children to attend Summer Bible School and said he would provide transportation.

"Well," Mom said, "I don't think any of the children are interested."

"What about the young fellow with the bandaged foot?" he asked.

I really did not want to go, but to a seven-year-old, lying on the couch for a week was not fun, either. The next thing I knew, I was off to Bible school for two weeks. There I heard many Bible stories and learned about a man called Jesus. This experience left so great an impression on me that it never left my memory. It became a constant reminder that my life was lacking something. I also had many unanswered questions about Jesus. Fourteen years later, this experience had a real bearing on my decision to follow Christ.

Did I just happen to have an accident? Did a preacher just happen to stop by? I do not believe so. God was and still is in control of my life. These events were part of His plan to show me the way of salvation. It was a part of the "all things" of Romans 8:28 that worked together for good for me.

What about your flat tire, your stay in the hospital, or an embarrassing situation? Blessings in disguise! Trust God today!

Jerry Akins, Guys Mills, PA

Bible Reading: Genesis 50
One Year Bible Reading Plan:
  Hebrews 9
  Ezekiel 1–3

There are no "oops" with God.

The Mind of Christ

For I say, through the grace given unto me, to every man that is among you, not to think of himself more highly than he ought to think.
Romans 12:3

In Christ we find purpose and self-worth, but our old Adamic nature still wants to be looked up to and to gain superiority over our fellow man. Today's reading says that we are to have the mind of Christ. He is the Son of God, and yet He humbled Himself to save and serve sinful man. He died as a criminal at the mercy of those who rejected His offer of pardon and eternal life! If I possess this mind of Christ, I will look for ways to serve my brother, or my neighbor, instead of concentrating on proving my point of view or having matters go my way. Even if my convictions or practices seem to me to be more Scriptural than the church's practices, I can hinder the very cause I seek to promote, if I have a better-than-thou attitude. We need the mind of Christ to be able to speak the truth in love.

How do I humble myself and obtain more of the mind of Christ? Verse 13 says that God gives us the desire and the power to do His will. But verse 12 tells us that we also play a part in working out our salvation. We must allow God's work within us by the Holy Spirit to flow out through us and bring God's grace and love to those with whom we rub shoulders each day.

When Isaiah saw the Lord he responded, "Woe is me! for I am undone." When upright Job heard God's message personally, he declared, "I abhor myself, and repent in dust and ashes." The mind of Christ is ours as we experience the presence of God, which causes us to humbly seek to hear His voice and do His will.

> **Bible Reading:** Philippians 2:1-16
> **One Year Bible Reading Plan:**
> Hebrews 10:1-23
> Ezekiel 4–6

Amos Beiler, Stuarts Draft, VA

Humility before God is nothing if not proved in humility before men.
—Andrew Murray

*November 15*_____

What Mean These Stones?

*. . . that when your children ask their fathers in time
to come, saying, What mean ye by these stones?*
Joshua 4:6

In Joshua 3 and 4, we read about the children of Israel crossing the Jordan River. The Jordan was an obstacle to them. They set up twelve stones as a memorial of their victory over their obstacle.

We also meet with obstacles of various descriptions, and only by the grace of God can we overcome them. These obstacles may be in the form of temptations, difficulties, or actual failures to overcome temptations. By sharing our victories with others, we can help them realize that God can also give them victories over their obstacles. Our testimony may become witness stones—a memorial of the grace of God, which overcomes every obstacle.

"Let the redeemed of the LORD say so, whom he hath redeemed from the hand of the enemy" (Psalm 107:2). Who is better qualified to sing the praise of victory over Satan and sin than the victorious? Satan wants to deceive and destroy whomever he can. We need to stand together and encourage one another. What greater love can we show our brother or sister than to encourage them in the way of righteousness, truth, and holiness?

Bible Reading: Joshua 4:1-18
One Year Bible Reading Plan:
Hebrews 10:24-39
Ezekiel 7–9

Dan Chupp, Stuarts Draft, VA

_____

I must have encourgement, just as much as the crops must have rain.
—Gerard Manley Hopkins

Tender Loving Care

But we were gentle among you, even as
a nurse cherisheth her children.
1 Thessalonians 2:7

All human hearts hunger for tenderness. We are made for love—not only to love, but also to be loved. Harshness pains us. Gentleness is like a genial summer to our life. Beneath its warm, nourishing influence, beautiful things grow in us.

I am reminded of the time we were trying to establish a uniform pecan grove. One of the trees was broken off below the graft, and it started to grow from the root which had not been grafted in. So, I proceeded to graft a bud in the root stock. One day, while I was spraying the trees, I noticed that this bud had taken hold and was growing. It had a very tender shoot, about six to eight inches tall. I felt really good about the accomplishment and trimmed away the other limbs around it. As I was about to return to the tractor, I carelessly nicked the tender little shoot and broke it. As the husbandmen of the orchard, I should have been more careful with the young, tender shoot, and it probably would have grown and produced fruit in later years.

Many people have special needs for tenderness. We cannot know what secret burdens those about us are carrying. Some of those with whom we mingle every day have hidden griefs in their hearts. Not all grief wears the outward garb of mourning; sunny faces oftentimes veil heavy hearts. We remember how our Master himself longed for expressions of love when He was passing through His deepest experience of suffering, and how He was disappointed when His friends failed Him.

We can never do amiss in showing gentleness. There is no day when it will be untimely, and there is no place where it will not find welcome. It will harm no one, and it may save someone from despair.

Bible Reading: 2 Timothy 2
One Year Bible Reading Plan:
  Hebrews 11:1-19
  Ezekiel 10–12

Lloyd Swartzentruber, Montezuma, GA

Thy gentleness hath made me great.
—Psalm 18:35

_____

The Tramp's Treasure

. . . As Esau, who for one morsel of meat sold his birthright.
Hebrews 12:16b

Mr. Betts, the owner of a music shop, glanced up from his work. There in his doorway stood the most awful looking tramp he had ever seen. On the tramp's face was a look of utter despair; he seemed to have given up all hope in life. "I'm starving," said the man. "Will you please buy this violin from me? I'll sell it for $5.00."

Mr. Betts felt like it was a fair deal, and after the tramp left, he put the violin upon a shelf. Evening came, and he was about to close his shop when he remembered the violin. He took it down, tightened a few strings, and tuned it up. Now, Mr. Betts was a first class musician. He knew how to get the most out of an instrument, and soon he recognized that he held a real treasure in his hands. Never had he played a better sounding violin. Turning it over, he read the label, "Made by Antonia Stradivari, A.D. 1704."

If the tramp had only known the value of his possession, he could have been a rich man. Mr. Betts sold the violin for $5,000, and the man who bought it from him was offered $25,000, but he would not sell it for any price.

We have a treasure in our earthen vessels that is worth far more than any violin. The Bible tells us that one soul is worth more than the whole world, yet we often value it very little.

Many people live careless lives, selling their souls for drink, fornication, drugs, or other worldly pleasures. Esau sold his birthright for a mess of porridge, and "afterward, when he would have inherited the blessing, he was rejected: for he found no place of repentance, though he sought it carefully with tears" (Hebrews 12:17).

Bible Reading: Hebrews 12:7-17
One Year Bible Reading Plan:
Hebrews 11:20-40
Ezekiel 13–15

Abner Overholt, Auburn, KY

What would you give in exchange for your soul?

Rotten at the Core

. . . Ye make clean the outside of the cup and of the platter,
but within they are full of extortion and excess.
Matthew 23:25b

Several years ago we purchased a bakery and bulk food store and proceeded to give it some facelifting. Over a period of several years we replaced the suspended ceiling tile, tiled the concrete floor, painted the walls, changed the windows, and installed a new lighting system. On the outside we stuccoed and painted the block walls, covered the wood with vinyl, put a metal roof over the leaking shingled roof, and paved the parking lot. Our customers commented favorably about the changes.

One day recently, I noticed a sag in the ceiling, which was getting worse. Upon inspection, I discovered that the problem was not that the suspended ceiling hangers were tearing loose, but that the very joists themselves were rotten! Some joists were held to the beam by only one nail! The sheetrock was holding them in place. Had not immediate action been taken, the ceiling would have collapsed! Lives could have been lost.

We can cover up sin for many years. People may never suspect what is inside our hearts. We can speak well, act respectably, and wear the right clothes.

But there is One who will not be deceived. At the day of judgment, the one who has covered up inner rottenness will collapse, unless a complete change takes place.

Bible Reading: Matthew 23:25-39
One Year Bible Reading Plan:
Hebrews 12
Ezekiel 16

Lloyd Mast, Whiteville, TN

God will not be fooled.

November 19

How Shall We Come?

I have called upon thee, for thou wilt hear me,
O God: incline thine ear unto me, and hear my speech.
Psalm 17:6

In *Spiritual Disciplines for the Christian Life*, Charles Spurgeon wrote, "I cannot imagine any one of you tantalizing your child by exciting in him a desire that you did not intend to gratify. It would be a very ungenerous thing to offer alms to the poor, and then when they hold out their hand for it, to mock their poverty with a denial. . . . Where God leads you to pray, He means for you to receive."

Notice that statements in Luke 18:14 and Hebrews 4:16 seem to contradict each other. One suggests that we must approach God humbly. The other instructs us to come boldly. How can the two agree?

It all has to do with the perspective. Because of who we are, we can never come into God's presence demanding that He do our bidding. Romans 3:23 says, "For all have sinned, and come short of the glory of God." We must come to Him in humble prayer, depending on His mercy.

However, because of who God is, we do not have to shrink back in fear. God's compassion will not allow Him to turn a deaf ear to our cries. His love is the ground on which we confidently stand whenever we approach Him.

As we approach God humbly, we have the confidence that He will answer our prayers.

Ryan Good, Amanda, OH

> **Bible Reading:** Luke 18:9-14;
>   Hebrews 4:14-16
> **One Year Bible Reading Plan:**
>   Hebrews 13
>   Ezekiel 17–19

Approach God humbly in prayer
and confidently await His answer.

Go Through Samaria

And he must needs go through Samaria.
John 4:4

It was necessary to pass through Samaria when traveling from Judea to Galilee. The time and distance of the journey required that one buy food along the way and pause to rest. The delay might have been a nuisance to some; however, the Lord knew that a Samaritan woman would come to the well near Sychar while He waited and rested there. A beautiful conversation followed which resulted in the conversion of that woman. The Gospel was preached to Samaritans for the first time.

Eventually, the Samaritans asked Jesus to stay and preach, which he did for two days. "And many more believed because of his own word; and said unto the woman, Now we believe, not because of thy saying: for we have heard him ourselves, and know that this is indeed the Christ, the Saviour of the world" (John 4:41, 42).

Sometimes, seemingly pointless intrusions interrupt our day-to-day activities. Sometimes, God intervenes in our lives through these intrusions, so that we will be at the right place and time for small services for Him.

Bible Reading: John 4:1-42
One Year Bible Reading Plan:
James 1
Ezekiel 20, 21

Dan Schmucker, Franklin, KY

No event occurs by chance, but in accordance with a plan so carefully considered that it does not overlook even the number of the hairs of the heads.
—Origen

November 21

Does That Light Guide Your Path?

In him was life; and the life was the light of men.
John 1:4

Jesus is the light of the child of God. Jesus is that bright light shining into our hearts if we let Him. There was a time in my life when I rejected His light. Oh, how miserable everything was! It is so dark when we do not have Jesus shining in our hearts. After I laid down my self-life and let Jesus shine in my heart, the joy and peace was indescribable. When we flip on the light switch in a dark room, darkness has to flee. It is the same way when we give our hearts to Jesus; the darkness has to flee.

The sun shines so brightly that we cannot look at it without hurting our eyes. Jesus is much brighter than the sun. The Bible says that when we get to heaven, we will have no need of the sun, for Christ Himself will be the light there. Let us allow Jesus to shine in and through our lives now, that we may not miss seeing His bright shining Light for eternity.

If you have not given Him all of your life, give it to Jesus today. You will see that bright shining Light in your heart, and it will also shine out to others and help them find Christ.

Marlin Wagler, Cottage Grove, TN

Bible Reading: Ephesians 5:6-19; John 12:35, 36
One Year Bible Reading Plan:
James 2
Ezekiel 22, 23

No day is dark when the Son is shining.

God's Grace to Me

And he said unto me, My grace is sufficient for thee:
for my strength is made perfect in weakness.
2 Corinthians 12:9

I want to share how God's grace was sufficient for me.

As a boy, I found school to be very easy. My parents fostered high expectations for my future. In the third grade, however, my school work began to suffer because of eye problems. When I was ten, the problem was tracked to a brain tumor. With God's help, the doctors successfully removed the tumor.

But the tumor and the resulting operation had a major effect on my life. The tumor damaged my eyesight. As a result, I am unable to drive. An important gland was also removed. This stopped my physical development. It soon became apparent that I could never marry like most young men and raise a family. Three years later, I started having seizures. I battled with discouragement: did I have to accept all this?

As I look back now, I see that God's grace was at work. He helped us find the medicine I needed to control the seizures. Often I had questioned, "What can I do for an occupation?" The options seemed rather limited. God answered that, too. He called our family to the mission field, where I could serve as a bookkeeper. What an answer to prayer! Most importantly, He gives me daily strength to take my gaze off the handicaps and fix it on the Lord. This is the ultimate evidence of grace.

Bible Reading: 2 Corinthians 11:18-31; 12:6-10
One Year Bible Reading Plan:
James 3
Ezekiel 24–26

I can see that God's grace allowed this situation in my life. Without this experience, I might never have learned to depend completely on God. This has helped me keep things in proper perspective, and I thank God for it.

Nathan L. Yoder, Poperinge, Belgium

To see God's hand in everything is the evidence of growth in grace.
—Charles Finney

The Samaritan's Testimony

I said, LORD, be merciful unto me . . .
Psalm 41:4

The day began as all days had for a long season—painful and lonely, with no hope lingering in my being. My only friends were those who suffered the same condition I did. My eyes could see nothing but death approaching. I was a helpless, doomed leper. Until I met Jesus. Oh, praise be unto the most high God who rules heaven and earth! For He sent His only Son, of whom I am so unworthy!

Jesus entered our village. Having heard of His fame, of the great things He had done, we began to cry out with one voice (as if our lives depended on Him; for surely they did): "Jesus, Master, have mercy on us!" And, glory to God, He did! Suddenly I felt within my own body a departure of all pain and sickness. Health surged through my body; hope through my heart and soul. Wonderful! My steps hastened toward the village priest's house. Suddenly, I stopped. Wait. I must thank this wonderful Healer for this marvelous work of grace!

I raced down the street, ignoring the stares of those who knew me to be a leper. I must go back and thank Him. Upon reaching Him, I fell to my knees and worshiped Him, giving thanks and praise to God. Jesus asked about the other nine. He said I was the only one to come back and thank Him. I wondered why. I wondered if the others were even thankful? "Oh that men would praise the LORD for his goodness, and for his wonderful works to the children of men!" (Psalm 107:8).

Bible Reading: Luke 17:11-19
One Year Bible Reading Plan:
James 4
Ezekiel 27, 28

Kevin Miller, Auburn, KY

No duty is more urgent than that of returning thanks.

Be Ye Thankful

In every thing give thanks: for this is the will
of God in Christ Jesus concerning you.
1 Thessalonians 5:18

Whether we are thankful or unthankful, we have an influence on those around us.

As I was growing up, I had two neighbors who made a lasting impression on me. The first neighbor always spoke negatively in our conversations. It was always too dry for him, or his garden was not doing well, or the government was going from bad to worse, and on and on. I would leave his presence feeling depressed and blue. The second neighbor had more than his share of knocks in life. Financial and physical problems plagued him most of his life. Never did I hear him complain. When I asked him how he was doing, he typically responded with a genuine smile, "I have a lot to be thankful for." He showed by his example that thankfulness does not depend on one's having an abundance of things. He gave thanks in everything, as 1 Thessalonians 5:18 commands.

Yes, our key verse is more than a mere suggestion. A thankful attitude is the spontaneous result of experiencing God's goodness within. When it is hard to find something for which to be thankful, we need to take another look at Calvary and ponder the provisions God has made for us.

Let us make it a point to consider our blessings and thus be able to say, "Yes, I have a lot to be thankful for." Remember that your thankfulness will very likely influence someone else's life.

Phil Schrock, Stuarts Draft, VA

Bible Reading: Colossians 3:15; Psalm 135:1-16
One Year Bible Reading Plan:
James 5
Ezekiel 29–31

If you are thankful to the brim, let it show by praising Him.

Thanksgiving

*By Him therefore let us offer the sacrifice of praise to God
continually, that is, the fruit of our lips, giving thanks to His name.*
Hebrews 13:15

I can just smell the aroma of fresh baked pumpkin pie cooling on the counter, while Mother busily prepares the rest of the meal. There is a feeling of anticipation as we await the arrival of Grandma and Grandpa and aunts and uncles and cousins we haven't seen for some time. It's a day of drawing family and friends closer together, a day of bonding. And as we gather around the table laden with delicious food, we pause to reflect upon the past year.

The canning shelves are full, and the crops have been harvested and are in the grain bin. Whether you've had a banner year or a crop failure, whether everyone is enjoying good health or there is am empty seat at the table, we must still humbly acknowledge the goodness and faithfulness of God. He has met our needs and helped us through the tough times.

Or is your day just another day of complaining: the pie crust was burnt; Uncle Georges are late again as usual; I just wish one time we could have mashed potatoes that weren't cold and stiff; cattle prices are down again, another bummer. . . .

Someone has said, "If you want gratitude, the only place you will find it is in the dictionary." We live in an ungrateful society. But the Scripture reminds us: "When thou hast eaten and are full, then thou shalt bless the LORD thy God for the good land which he hath given thee" (Deuteronomy 8:10).

Bible Reading: Psalm 103
One Year Bible Reading Plan:
  1 Peter 1
  Ezekiel 32, 33

Melvin Troyer, Clarkson, KY

The man who has forgotten to be thankful has fallen asleep in life.
—David McCarthy

God Is Creator

He was in the world, and the world was made
by him, and the world knew him not.
John 1:10

There is hardly anything as enjoyable as sitting quietly in the woods and observing nature and wondering how God created everything.

We reason back from the leaf to the trunk and from the root to the seed. What caused the seed? Another plant. As we go back along the chain of causation, we finally come to the first seed and face the cause of its existence.

All nature abounds in questions, which no atheist has ever been able to answer. There is a law that substances are expanded by heat and contracted by cold. One among very few exceptions is found in the fact that when water approaches its freezing point, it begins to expand. So ice forms on top of the water, instead of sinking to the bottom. This keeps rivers and lakes from forming solid masses of ice on their bottoms, which no single summer sun could ever melt. Who designed this wise exception? Or is it simply a freak happening?

Similar thoughts confront us as we behold the starry heavens, the earth, and the seas, and all that is in them The inevitable question arises, "Where do they come from?"

How do we account for the origin of matter? What about the origin of life, the origin of species, and the origin of man?

There must be a first cause. This first cause we call God.

To believe in a God without beginning or end, who with His infinite power called all things visible and invisible into existence, requires less credulity than to believe that all these things came into being by mere chance (Romans 1:20).

James Mast, Caneyville, KY

Bible Reading: Genesis 1
One Year Bible Reading Plan:
1 Peter 2
Ezekiel 34, 35

Nature is but a name for an effect whose cause is God.

Lord, Teach Us How to Pray

And when thou prayest, thou shalt not be as the hypocrites are.
Matthew 6:5

Here we find two kinds of people whom we must not copy, yet we can learn from their errors.

A hypocrite is one who has a false appearance of virtue or religion. Do hypocrites pray? Apparently they do, but only when other people can see or hear them. Their reward is only earthly.

A heathen is one who does not acknowledge the God of the Bible. Do heathens pray? Apparently they do. A good example of this is in 1 Kings 18:21-29, in the experience of Elijah and the prophets of Baal. The prophets of Baal prayed from morning till noon. They leaped upon the altar. Elijah told them to cry louder. They even cut themselves with knives. There must have been much commotion. Through all this, their god still did not answer. Do we need such commotion to get God's attention? No. God is not interested in a great commotion, but in a meek and quiet spirit.

When we have only the audience of God and His holy angels, we will experience the deepest rewards of quiet prayer. Our heavenly Father knows what we need before we ask Him.

Bible Reading: Matthew 6:5-15
One Year Bible Reading Plan:
1 Peter 3
Ezekiel 36, 37

Andy Miller, Malta, OH

Prayer requires more of the heart than of the tongue.
—Adam Clarke

Our Reasonable Service

*I beseech you therefore, brethren, by the mercies of God,
that ye present your bodies a living sacrifice, holy,
acceptable unto God, which is your reasonable service.*
Romans 12:1

The compelling call of Romans 12:1 to present our bodies as living, holy, and acceptable sacrifices echoes God's call for unblemished sacrifices in the Old Testament. Under the new covenant, His focus is on our bodies, which He desires us to present to Him as acceptable sacrifices. It is reasonable for Him to claim us.

"The maker is the rightful owner" is an unspoken, almost universal, rule. Since God is the creator of man, this rule declares God to be the rightful owner of all people (Psalm 24:1). By right of Creation, God's demand that we present our bodies to Him is reasonable.

Because of man's rebellion and resulting alienation from Him, God's rights of ownership of mankind have been assumed by Satan (John 8:44; 2 Corinthians 4:4; Acts 26:18). However, He is "not willing that any should perish . . ." under Satan's control (2 Peter 3:9). Therefore, at heaven's highest price He redeemed us with the blood of His Son. Our redemption renders it reasonable to present our bodies to God.

Bible Reading: Romans 12:1-8
One Year Bible Reading Plan:
1 Peter 4
Ezekiel 38, 39

By dual rights of creation and redemption God has a claim on our lives. Let us gladly and unreservedly abandon our lives to Him. To do so is only our reasonable service.

Ken Kauffman, Falkville, AL

Presenting our bodies is not giving God a present, but a surrender.

Has Your Name Been Changed?

And the disciples were called Christians first in Antioch.
Acts 11:26

Have you ever wondered why people have the names they have? Names usually have meanings, and people receive their names for various reasons. Some people are named after their fathers or grand-fathers, and others after famous people or close friends.

Some people change their names. Frequently, members of the Hollywood crowd change their names so that they will sound more glamorous. People of other religions sometimes change their names to accommodate the traditions of that religious sect. Others may change their names because of marriage or adoption.

The Bible has something to say about people having their names changed, as we can see in our Bible reading. God changed Abram's name to Abraham, and He changed Jacob's name to Israel. Further reading reveals others who also had their names changed. Simon's name was changed to Peter, and Saul's to Paul. These name changes in the Bible occurred after the people had an encounter with the Lord.

Peter encountered Christ, the Son of the Living God. Paul met Christ on the road to Damascus. The believers at Antioch had an encounter with the Lord. All of them had met the Lord.

Bible Reading: Genesis 17:1-8; 32:24-32
One Year Bible Reading Plan:
1 Peter 5
Ezekiel 40

Have you met the Lord? If not, there is still time to have your name changed from stranger to Christian.

Terry Lester, Montezuma, GA

Is your new name written there?

Eternity

Let us hear the conclusion of the whole matter: Fear God,
and keep his commandments: for this is the whole duty of man.
For God shall bring every work into judgment, with every
secret thing, whether it be good, or whether it be evil.
Ecclesiastes 12:13, 14

What is eternity? We cannot really comprehend what eternity is, but let us try.

This world is 25,000 miles around. Let us suppose that the whole world was all sand, and a little bird would come at the end of each million years and carry away one grain of sand.

Even by this inconceivably slow process, this big pile of sand finally would be removed. But eternity would be no nearer to an end. Eternity has no end; it is forever. We are all headed for eternity, and there are only two destinations for all people. Heaven is for the saved, and hell is for the lost.

Someone has said if all water was converted into ink and all steel into pens, the glories of heaven could not be written, nor half the horrors of hell portrayed.

May God help us to realize the truth of His Word. Hebrews 9:27 says, "And as it is appointed unto men once to die, but after this the judgment." "But the end of all things is at hand: be ye therefore sober, and watch unto prayer" (1 Peter 4:7). Let us tell the world about Jesus. Time is running out. Today is the day of salvation.

> **Bible Reading:** Ecclesiastes 12
> **One Year Bible Reading Plan:**
> 2 Peter 1
> Ezekiel 41, 42

Ernest Stoll, Oden, IN

Eternity—where? Oh, eternity—where?

December 1 _____

Meditations at the Footbridge

All the words of my mouth are in righteousness;
there is nothing froward or perverse in them.
Proverbs 8:8

I sit on the footbridge pondering the movement of the creek below me. The swiftly-moving water chuckles merrily as it rushes over the rocks into the pool.

I notice a contrast between the one side of the bridge and the other. Upstream, the shallow water moves swiftly. Below the bridge, the water slows when it reaches a large pool. The shallow water makes much noise when it encounters an obstacle. An observer can easily detect its shallow depth. In contrast, the movement of the pool is barely noticeable. Its depth conceals the fact that the same volume of water is flowing through it. The water quietly flows over every obstacle in its path, making no fuss about them.

Our lives are like a stream. Am I like the shallow water? Do I make lots of commotion when I face an obstacle in life? In incessant action and speech the possibility of sinning increases dramatically (Proverbs 10:19). Or is my life like the deep pool? Do I evidence a deep, inner peace that is unaffected by outward circumstances? Strong character can accept unpleasant experiences peacefully.

That depth of character does not mean stagnation. It means deep, rich character overflowing into practical areas of life.

Others can readily discern the depth of my character. Will they be challenged by what they see, or will they be discouraged by my lack of godly character?

Matthew Mast, Mountain View, AR

Bible Reading: Proverbs 8:1-19
One Year Bible Reading Plan:
2 Peter 2
Ezekiel 43, 44

Your words may hide your thoughts,
but your actions will reveal them.

Peace

These things I have spoken unto you, that in me ye might have peace.
John 16:33

Two artists were asked to paint a picture of their own choosing to illustrate peace. One artist painted a scene with a quiet brook flowing through a meadow. Chipmunks were chirping from the base of a stately oak, from whose branches songbirds were sounding their song. Butterflies were floating among the fragrant wildflowers along the banks of the creek. The sun cast its balmy rays upon the vegetation and foliage, wet with sparkling droplets from the recent spring shower. The clouds that had dropped the rain lazily floated in the distant sky. Now, that is peace!

The other artist painted the scene of a calm eagle, nested in the heavy branches of a weather-proven poplar, high in the crevice of a rocky cliff. The cliff dropped off hundreds of feet to the canyon below. A storm was raging against the canyon wall. Heavy thunderclouds were draped from sky to earth. Lightning was flashing and the thunder was rolling. Heavy beads of rain were drenching the earth, while rushing streams fell from the heights. Now, that is peace!

But which is peace? Oh, we desire the calm meadow scene. That is our experience at times. We find it among beloved brethren in fellowship and worship. Sometimes we experience it during a relaxing vacation in some secluded spot, away from the hustle and bustle of life. But often, we must live in the grind of life and experience storms that, at times, almost overwhelm us. We do not know what this day may bring forth. Maybe the morning will begin bright and clear. As the day advances, the clouds may darken, and the storm come upon us with its violent blow. Even then we can be secure, just like the eagle perched on the cliff, because Jesus, our Rock, is a safe retreat. Now, that is peace!

Bible Reading: John 14
One Year Bible Reading Plan:
2 Peter 3
Ezekiel 45, 46

James Yoder, Lewisburg, PA

In the midst of the storm, peace, be still!

Rejoicing in Suffering

And if children, then heirs; heirs of God, and joint-heirs with Christ; if so be that we suffer with him, that we may be also glorified together.
Romans 8:17

Suffering is not an exciting word. When life is going well, the last thing I want to think about is hardship. Rejoicing in suffering seems out of the question. What good reason could there be for God to allow difficulty to roll my way?

Suffering comes in many forms: financial loss, health problems, or the death of a loved one. Many Christians endure persecution because of their faith. People even suffer because of others' sins.

Our hearts may cry out, *How can these things be good? How could I ever rejoice in this? What is your purpose, Lord?*

I praise God that behind every single difficult thing we might experience, He has a purpose. Our God desires to give us beauty for ashes. Whether He can or not depends on our response. If we become bitter toward God, or toward any person who has a part in our experience, we will miss God's whole purpose, and we will reap the consequences of bitterness.

If we can continue to trust in God's marvelous love for us, we will be able to accept our suffering. God desires that which is best for us. From His eternal perspective, He sees our whole life. If we will simply trust Him, He can give us inner joy in the midst of sorrow and peace in the midst of pain.

God's blessing will continue as we remain faithful. Our lives will never be the same, and over in glory, our reward will be beyond our grandest dreams!

Lovell King, Harrison, AR

Bible Reading: Hebrews 12:1-15
One Year Bible Reading Plan:
1 John 1
Ezekiel 47, 48

---

*The deeper the valley, the more rugged the climb,
the more glorious the peak!*

A Clean Heart

Create in me a clean heart, O God; and
renew a right spirit within me.
Psalm 51:10

Once, while driving through an area away from home, I observed a rare sight. It had been extremely dry and dusty, and the roads were grimy and gritty. Suddenly, the sun went behind the clouds, and it became very dark. Great drops of rain began to fall harder and harder, until the rain was pouring down. In the distance, the sun started to shine. As I continued driving, I noticed rainbow colors on the wet pavement as well as in the spray from the tires. The sight was beautiful. I looked up, and to my amazement, there was a bright, beautiful, double rainbow in the sky.

I drove for another hour, but the rainbow continued to move with me. Never before had I seen a rainbow so bright for a complete hour. It was awesome!

Our lives are like a dirty road under a cloudy sky, until the transforming "rain" of Jesus washes the grime away. The rainbow is His extended promise of another opportunity to let His "rain" cleanse our lives.

Join me in bowing at the feet of the Master to implore Him for a clean and transformed heart.

Stewart Gerber, Millbank, Ontario

Bible Reading: Psalm 51
One Year Bible Reading Plan:
1 John 2
Daniel 1, 2

God looks where man looks least — at the heart.

Our Savior's Love

Who his own self bare our sins in his own body on the tree,
that we, being dead to sins, should live unto righteousness:
by whose stripes ye were healed.
1 Peter 2:24

Our Savior was a man of sorrows, well acquainted with grief. He was despised and rejected in the darkest night in history. The power of darkness ushered in the darkest day in the entire world. The seed of the serpent then bruised the heel of Him who healed the brokenhearted. And he, in whom was life and the power to raise the dead, tasted death for every man. The holy Son of God, who like a lamb without blemish and without spot, shed His precious blood to atone for your sins and mine.

What moved the Savior to pay such a great price? The joy that was set before Him enabled Him to endure to the end. It was love, which would melt men's hearts, that took Him to the cross. His delight was to bring forgiveness and peace to troubled souls.

Does the night seem extra dark for you? Is your day dark and bleak? Remember that Jesus went through a darker night and a darker day; not for His own griefs, but for our sins He suffered. He finished the work and rose triumphantly from the grave, so that we can live in the light of a new day!

Clayton Weaver, Linneus, MO

Bible Reading: Luke 22:39-53
One Year Bible Reading Plan:
1 John 3
Daniel 3, 4

He died that I might live.

Growing, Growing, Gone

But speaking the truth in love, may grow up into him
in all things, which is the head, even Christ.
Ephesians 4:15

Proper diet and exercise are two necessary factors for growth and development. We need both, not just one or the other. A good diet without exercise may cause growth, but probably not the kind of development we want. Exercise is needed to help us develop and to keep us fit. On the other hand, exercise without a substantial diet will cause us to become burned out and unable to function.

How can one grow and develop spiritually? It will take more than simply reading a devotional every day. However, a thought provoking article, along with a dose of God's Word, can be the core of a healthy diet for a Christian. We need to daily digest God's Word! What else do we need to feed on? Philippians 4:8 tells us to think about things that are true, honest, just, pure, lovely, and of good report. Also, we should think about what God has done for us personally.

Do you want to stay fit spiritually? Practice what you know. Keep doing right, regardless of what happens. Make use of your diet of God's Word. Draw strength from it to exercise your faith.

Exercise is work, and getting a well-balanced, healthy diet can be difficult. They require sacrifice. Nevertheless, they are rewarding.

Carving out time to meditate on God's Word may be challenging at times, but look at the benefits! We can develop our relationship with God, sharpen our vision for the lost, receive strength to do God's will, and grow in Him.

As you eat and work today, keep this prayer in mind: "Thank you, Lord, that you have made all the necessary provisions for my spiritual growth and development. Help me to keep on growing, growing in You, until You call me home at the time of the great harvest. Amen."

Bible Reading: 2 Peter 1:3-18
One Year Bible Reading Plan:
1 John 4
Daniel 5, 6

Michael Webb, Grabill, IN

Warning: Neglecting God's Word will be
hazardous to your spiritual health.

December 7

"You Are Invited to Attend . . ."

Blessed are they which are called unto the
marriage supper of the Lamb.
Revelation 19:9

There is a wedding supper being planned. We invite you to join us as we eagerly await this special occasion. We are not certain of the date or the time this marriage supper will take place. We encourage you to prepare yourself so you will be ready at any moment. It will be announced suddenly, without warning. When the supper is ready, the Groom will come for you. If He does not find you ready, He will go on and leave you behind, and you will miss out on the supper forever. There will be no other chance, no other supper to attend. It will be forever too late.

This wedding supper is the marriage supper of the Lamb (Revelation 19:9), when God will send His Son Jesus to bring His people home to be forever with Him in glory. At that time, those who are not ready will cry for the rocks and the mountains to cover them (Revelation 6:16).

Are you prepared? What must we do to prepare ourselves? Jesus said in Matthew 4:17, "Repent: for the kingdom of heaven is at hand." And Paul added in Romans 10:9, "That if thou shalt confess with thy mouth the Lord Jesus, and shalt believe in thine heart that God hath raised him from the dead, thou shalt be saved." Praise God!

Joe Miller, Belleville, PA

Bible Reading: Revelation 19
One Year Bible Reading Plan:
1 John 5
Daniel 7, 8

Many are called; but few are chosen.
—Matthew 22:14

Obstacles

For I reckon that the sufferings of this present time are not worthy to be compared with the glory which shall be revealed in us.
Romans 8:18

This morning the weather seemed perfect. As I was sitting in my study, the sun strained to shine its light through a dense fog. The fog was so heavy that only a few beams of light got through. The beauty of the morning was not in the fog, nor the sun, but in the sunbeams that crowded their way through the trees and the fog. However, the sunbeams would not have been possible without those obstacles.

Our lives are not made in a crisis. A crisis only shows who we truly are. Many times we see lives expressing the beauty of holiness, which have been purified by obstacles.

Did you know that you need those people who gossip about you and ridicule you? How would you develop patience, longsuffering, tenderness, and forgiveness if not for obstacles? When we are in need of patience, God puts us in situations that require patience.

God wants to form the character of Christ in each of us. Suffering will do just that, if we are willing to endure it. The servant is not greater than his master. If Christ had to suffer, then we should expect also to suffer as Hebrews 5:8 and 1 Peter 4:1 remind us. The next time there are obstacles in your path, do not complain about them; thank God for them and watch for the sunbeams to break through the fog!

Bible Reading: Acts 16:19-31
One Year Bible Reading Plan:
2 and 3 John
Daniel 9, 10

Alvin Mast, Millersburg, OH

_____

Thank you, Lord, for the night, for it reveals the stars.

December 9

Who Was Andrew, Anyway?

Sir, we would see Jesus.
John 12:21

Most of us do not possess the silver tongue of Apollos. Most of us will not plant churches as Paul did. Few share Peter's leadership ability. None of us expects to experience a vision as John did on the Isle of Patmos. Our attempts at writing seem pale and shallow when compared with Luke's inspired writings. On and on we could compare ourselves! But before we get discouraged, let's take encouragement from Andrew.

Who was Andrew, anyway? He was a relatively unknown person, who took the back seat to his outspoken brother, Peter. In the Scriptures we do not see Andrew displaying spectacular gifts. I suspect he was a "common Joe" and a "regular person," just like you and me. Perhaps his friends called him "Andy." However, upon examining the life of Andrew, you will find a blessed habit. Andrew quietly led people to Jesus (John 1:42; 6:8, 9; 12:22).

In the Scripture reading for today, Andrew brought a small boy to Jesus. This boy's humble lunch was the material for a great miracle that day. We never know the far-reaching effects when we point someone to Jesus. Keep a liberal supply of gospel tracts on hand. Pass them out, or plant them in obvious places. Tracts are reasonably priced, and opportunities are endless. Invite non-Christian friends to church. In your workday conversations, begin to develop an "Andrew" habit of pointing people to Jesus. Welcome spiritual discussions. (We are not required to know every answer immediately.) And remember, your banker needs Jesus just as much as your garbage collector does.

Bible Reading: John 6:1-15
One Year Bible Reading Plan:
Jude
Daniel 11, 12

Jim Yoder, Leitchfield, KY

Those on the road to heaven will not be content to go there alone.

Rejoice or React

*In every thing give thanks: for this is the will
of God in Christ Jesus concerning you.*
1 Thessalonians 5:18

The story is told of a small seacoast village of fishermen and their families. One day, all the men and the older boys went on a fishing trip. Everything was going very well for them. They were a long way from shore when they suddenly noticed storm clouds forming, and soon the storm was upon them. They lost all sense of direction and had nothing to guide them. It was late in the day, and darkness overcame them.

At home in the village, the wives and children were in great agony. They walked up and down the coast, hoping, watching, and praying for some little sign of the fishermen's return.

On top of this, after dark a house caught on fire. With no men around to help, nothing was saved; everything burned to the ground. When daylight finally came, the wives and children trudged to the beach to look for some sign of the men returning. At last, they spotted them! When the boat finally came ashore, all safe and sound, there was a happy reunion with praises, thanksgiving, and tears of joy.

One woman, however, met her husband with a sad look and told him the unhappy story of having lost their house and all their possessions by fire. His response was, "Praise the Lord! It was the light of that fire that guided us home."

The fisherman saw immediately what we usually discover only later: that God works to bring good out of apparent tragedy. His response should be our response by faith—Praise God! He will use this sad event for a much greater good!

Kore Yoder, Belleville, PA

Bible Reading: Job 1:13-22;
4:3-4
One Year Bible Reading Plan:
Revelation 1
Hosea 1–4

Encourage someone along the way today.

The Unspeakable Gift

Thanks be unto God for his unspeakable gift.
2 Corinthians 9:15

The gifts of God are rich and free. Sometimes we are told, "Count your blessings," and we should. Yet who could finish enumerating every blessing and gift that God freely has given to us? The Psalmist says, "If I would declare and speak of them, they are more than can be numbered" (Psalm 40:5).

When we think of the gifts that God has given to us, our minds quickly go to the gift of salvation. We remember the guilt of sin, and the blessedness of forgiveness. We stand in awe of the gift of divine grace. The Holy Spirit within our hearts is a gift from God, and is a seal of our inheritance (Ephesians 1:14). When we think of the inheritance that awaits the children of God, we get just a little homesick for the things that our Father has in store for us in glory.

The greatest and best gift of all, the supreme and most excellent gift, far beyond the ability of man to write or tell, is the gift of God's Son, the Lord Jesus Christ. He is the Alpha and Omega of the gifts of God. Jesus is the supreme superlative of all that God has given for the whole human family.

Have you received God's unspeakable gift?

Bible Reading: Ephesians 2:1-10
One Year Bible Reading Plan:
Revelation 2
Hosea 5–8

Eli Kauffman, Montezuma, GA

All my theology is reduced to this narrow compass—
Christ Jesus came into the world to save sinners.
—Alexander of Hales

Random Acts of Kindness

And be ye kind one to another, tenderhearted, forgiving one another,
even as God for Christ's sake hath forgiven you.
Ephesians 4:32

We hear so much today about hatred, killing, racism, and abuse, that it is refreshing to hear about an act of kindness. Whenever we hear about someone's kindness, it is an inspiring reminder that people have the ability to be generous, merciful, caring, and of service to others. There are endless opportunities to be kind, yet we tend to save them up for big occasions such as death, crop failures, sickness, or the loss of a job. While kindness is imperative at these times, we also have the ability to practice kindness as a part of our everyday lives.

Many of us grew up with Ephesians 4:32 and the parable of the Good Samaritan firmly etched in our minds. Yet when opportunity presents itself, we shy away. We would never want to appear too bold. What if we go out of our way, and our kindness is not acknowledged?

True kindness has no price, and nothing is expected in return. So let's make kindness a part of our daily lives by:

- Making kindness a priority. Make a commitment that in all you do, you will be kind, live, act, and speak kindly.
- Not procrastinating. Our best intentions do not get the job done. Send a card, write a letter, or make a phone call today. Kindness delayed is kindness denied.
- Loving the unlovely. Kindness is easily shown to those we love. Make an effort today to be kind to an enemy.

Jim Bontrager, Middlebury, IN

Bible Reading: Luke 10:25-37
One Year Bible Reading Plan:
Revelation 3
Hosea 9–11

Be kind—everyone you meet is fighting a battle.

Effective Prayer

The effectual fervent prayer of a righteous man availeth much.
James 5:16

Why do you pray? Do you pray because you know that as a Christian you should pray? I hope not. When we pray out of mere obligation, our prayers go no higher than the ceiling.

Prayer is communion with God. It is pouring out our hearts to God in adoration, thanksgiving, and confession. It is being still before God and allowing Him to speak to us. Prayer is the Christian's vital breath. God wants us to speak to Him, and He promises us that He will answer us if we ask Him. Over and over God affirms His desire to answer prayer.

"And I say unto you, Ask, and it shall be given you; seek, and ye shall find; knock, and it shall be opened unto you" (Luke 11:9). "If ye shall ask any thing in my name, I will do it" (John 14:14). "If ye abide in me, and my words abide in you, ye shall ask what ye will, and it shall be done unto you" (John 15:7). "Again I say unto you, That if two of you shall agree on earth as touching any thing that they shall ask, it shall be done for them of my Father which is in heaven" (Matthew 18:19).

What beautiful promises! Do you believe them?

God places one condition on receiving His promises: faith. "But let him ask in faith, nothing wavering" (James 1:6). Faith is not only believing that God can, it is believing that God will.

Are you tapping into the power of prayer? Do you have a loved one who is lost and headed for hell? What are you doing about it? May God help us to believe His Word, claim His promises, and give our lives over to the ministry of prayer: interceding for those who are lost, in need, or backslidden, those on the mission fields, and for the church of Jesus Christ.

Lawrence Overholt, Russellville, KY

Bible Reading: James 5:7-20
One Year Bible Reading Plan:
 Revelation 4
 Hosea 12–14

Prayer is the power that moves the hand that rules the world.

Mirrors or Windows?

But we all, with open face beholding as in a glass the glory
of the Lord, are changed into the same image from
glory to glory, even as by the Spirit of the Lord.
2 Corinthians 3:18

There is an elegant cathedral in Florida that has beautiful stained-glass windows. Each window portrays an important event in the life of Jesus. I imagine that the first window shows the birth of Jesus at the stable in Bethlehem, and each window thereafter shows some important incident during the subsequent life and ministry of Jesus.

However, God is not looking for windows in a church to tell this great story; rather, He is looking for the people in the church to live lives that are a reflection of Jesus Christ!

Even as those cathedral windows could not decide which event in the life of Christ they would portray, so we, too, have no right to pick and choose which character qualities of Jesus we will portray. Many Christians want to reflect only the effortless or advantageous qualities of Christ, but when it comes to being a true disciple, they fall short of this test.

A mirror reflects the true representation of the person or object in front of it. We, too, as children of God, are called to be true images of His dear Son. God wants us to represent the life, ministry, suffering, death, and resurrection of Jesus Christ! "For if we have been planted together in the likeness of his death, we shall be also in the likeness of his resurrection" (Romans 6:5).

Will you try to impress people today with your own arrangement in the window of your life, or are you willing to be a mirror that gives a pure and faithful reflection of the Lord Jesus Christ?

Bible Reading: 2 Corinthians 3
One Year Bible Reading Plan:
Revelation 5
Joel

Jason Kauffman, Cullman, AL

Can the world see Jesus when they look at me?

Faith

Now faith is the substance of things hoped for,
the evidence of things not seen.
Hebrews 11:1

Do you have faith? If so, on what is your faith based? Of what does it consist? Does your faith affect the way you live?

There are many different kinds of faith. All around us there are Hindus, Muslims, Catholics, Protestants, Mormons, and even atheists. Members of these religions are often dedicated to their cause and believe that their religion is the correct one.

How about you? Maybe your grandfather and father are dedicated Muslims. Is that a good enough reason for you to be a Muslim? Maybe they are Christians. Does that make you a Christian? No! Faith needs to come from the heart. We need to have a personal faith of our own. It does us good to look at why we believe as we do, and to be sure that we are not deceived like so many people around us are.

If you share my faith in Jesus Christ, then you believe that God created the world and all that is in it. You know that the Bible is God's truth, and that God's Word can never change. You know that Jesus is the Son of God, and that He died that we might live eternally. If you share my faith, you believe that you were placed on the earth to bring glory to God and to win lost souls who do not know Christ.

Will you, with God's help, be true to your faith in Jesus Christ today?

Clifford Horst, New Hamburg, Ontario

> **Bible Reading:** Hebrews 11:1-16
> **One Year Bible Reading Plan:**
> Revelation 6
> Amos 1–3

We walk by faith, not by sight.
—2 Corinthians 5:7

Just Happened to Be Lucky

*Praise ye the LORD: for it is good to sing praises unto our God;
for it is pleasant; and praise is comely.*
Psalm 147:1

Someone just happened to drive by and help us when we ran out of gas. We were lucky to have avoided an accident.

Sometimes I find myself guilty of making statements like these. I forget to give God the credit for helping me out of a bind, or for keeping me safe. We should be ready to give God the glory, rather than just passing events off as luck, or saying that something "just happened."

Maybe when we are speaking to non-Christians, we feel a little bit awkward saying that it was the Lord's will that certain things took place. In Mark 8:38, Jesus says, "Whosoever therefore shall be ashamed of me and of my words in this adulterous and sinful generation; of him also shall the Son of man be ashamed, when he cometh in the glory of his Father with the holy angels."

We let Jesus down when we make comments that fail to give Him the glory for the circumstances. When we give God the glory for the trials that come our way, it may be that we will cause someone to think more seriously of God, and we will be a means of bringing them to the Savior.

We need to see God even in the smallest aspects of life, and I believe we will have a deeper appreciation for life, and for what God does for us.

Bible Reading: Psalm 136
One Year Bible Reading Plan:
Revelation 7
Amos 4–6

Galen Lengacher, Caneyville, KY

No happening in the Christian's life is a chance experience.

Lord, Refine Me

Behold, I have refined thee, but not with silver;
I have chosen thee in the furnace of affliction.
Isaiah 48:10

It was a beautiful Sunday morning. This particular morning a young sister (we will call her Anna) felt a need to be refined. She brought her request to her heavenly Father, "Lord, refine me."

On this Sunday morning Anna's family was taking a gallon of milk along to church to share with one of the other families. The milk would be placed in the refrigerator, and after the service, the other family would then take it home. Seven minutes before the service started, Anna was taking the milk to the refrigerator. Midpoint across one side of the main auditorium, she had an accident. Crash! Splash! Glass shattered; milk splattered. Very soon, a brother came with a mop, and a sister came with some other supplies. The brethren pitched in and soon had the mess cleared away, greatly relieving poor Anna's dismay!

Later on, Anna shared how God had answered her request. This unpleasant experience was God's way of humbling her, thereby refining her heart. Anna's response to this unpleasant blessing not only helped to refine her own heart but was also a blessing to others. People are watching us. May our response to unpleasant blessings bless their hearts, as we allow these unpleasant blessings to refine our hearts!

Bible Reading: Daniel 3:8-30
One Year Bible Reading Plan:
Revelation 8
Amos 7–9

John Dale Yoder, Belvidere, TN

Each must make, ere life is flown,
A stumbling block or a steppingstone.
—R. L. Sharp

A True Friend

My little children, let us not love in word,
neither in tongue; but in deed and in truth.
1 John 3:18

The life and ministry of Jesus was filled with acts of love and compassion for humanity. He reached out to the sick and hurting around Him. He taught His disciples to love like this: "That a man lay down his life for his friends." Jesus did this when He gave His life for us on the cross.

How can we lay down our lives for our friends? If we are in union and fellowship with Christ, and ask Him to direct our lives daily, He will reveal opportunities to reach out to those around us. So easily we become too busy and so wrapped up in our own interests that we grow insensitive to the hurting around us. A word of encouragement, a card, or a handshake can do much to lift a spirit that is down.

Sometimes God takes us through experiences to help us learn how to minister to others (1 Corinthians 1:4). When we lost our oldest son in an accident, we learned that it is not the amount of words you say that ministers the most to others, but just being there and showing you care. Yet we treasure the memories of the kind words and deeds of our friends, church, and family. Even after twenty-eight years, receiving cards around the date of his death is very precious. Are we sensitive to those around us?

Bible Reading: 1 Samuel
20:30-42
One Year Bible Reading Plan:
Revelation 9
Obadiah

Laban Hochstetler, Middlebury, IN

A friend comes in when the rest of the world goes out.

The Parable of Bears and Mosquitoes

*Behold, I am the L*ORD*, the God of all flesh:*
is there anything too hard for me?
Jeremiah 32:27

A man of God was traveling through the forest. Suddenly, his horse shied at a grizzly bear and the man was thrown to the ground. There he lay, facing the oncoming bear. He prayed fervently to God for deliverance. Then, miraculously, he was able to evade the bruin, mount his horse, and gallop away at full speed.

That evening he marveled at the grace of God that had spared his life, and his heart was lifted up with gratitude. As he lay meditating, a lone mosquito found its way into the cabin. It circled the man of God and prepared for a landing. The man swiped and missed. Again the hungry mosquito circled. For hours the duel continued. The man of God had a fitful, restless night.

The next morning he awoke with a sour, moody disposition. Now, what was wrong? Then it dawned on him that with the bear he knew he needed divine help, but he thought he could handle the tiny mosquito himself!

How many times do we behave in the same way? Oh, sure, we know that God divided the Red Sea. But this little pesky problem that annoys me, I'll handle it myself. Psalm 37:1 says, "Fret not." Most of our problems are not big bears, but little pesky mosquitoes. Yet, they can sap us of our spiritual vitality and leave us irritable and fretful. Consider God's question in today's key verse, "Is there anything too hard for me?"

Bible Reading: Matthew 10:29-31; 1 Peter 5:5-9
One Year Bible Reading Plan:
Revelation 10
Jonah

Rudy Overholt, Auburn, KY

God is our help in trouble; if you worry you are on your own.

Mother's Prayers

My son . . . forsake not the law of thy mother.
Proverbs 6:20

For a year after my wife and I were married we lived with my mother at the homeplace, in Ohio. From there we moved to Indiana, where my wife's folks lived.

We hadn't lived in Indiana very long before one night I couldn't sleep. I was thinking about my mother, and feeling badly about how much trouble I had been in her life. I wrote her a letter and told her how much she meant to me and that I was sorry for the way I had treated her.

After my mother died, the family was going through her things and dividing them, when someone found the letter I'd written, nearly twenty years earlier. It was soiled from her handling it so much, and I knew then that she'd prayed often for the one who sent it. I believe she sent many prayers heavenward on my behalf, and those prayers are still reaching me today. Somehow, by some spiritual understanding, she must have known I would need supreme help further down the road, and so I did.

Sixteen years ago I had a very serious accident. The doctors all told me that it was a miracle that I was still living, as no one had had such a severe brain concussion and lived. I believe Mother's prayers were still having an effect on my life.

Never take your mother for granted. Honor her, respect her, and care for her. You will never miss your mother, until she is gone.

Leroy R. Overholt, Blountstown, FL

Bible Reading: Proverbs 3:1-20
One Year Bible Reading Plan:
Revelation 11
Micah 1–4:8

The best monument a child can raise to his mother's memory is a clean, upright life.

Comforting

For I was an hungred, and ye gave me meat: I was thirsty,
and ye gave me drink: I was a stranger, and ye took me in.
Matthew 25:35

Recently I was a visitor at another church. A kind young man and his little boy invited me to sit with them. Since I was alone and enjoy having children sit beside me, I gladly accepted his hospitality. As I observed this young boy beside me, my curiosity was aroused, so I quietly asked him his name. Next I inquired about his age, and with the tender innocence of youth, he looked up and said, "I'm nine."

As swift as a dart, it pierced into my innermost thoughts. I remembered holding a baby boy in my arms nine years ago, as he drew his last breath. As the memory of that whole scene flooded in upon me, I did what Jesus did. I wept.

Why did I weep? A loved one had been taken from me—one who would now be the age of this young boy beside me.

Tears are an expression from the heart. Some people weep for lost friendships; some for lost companions. Sometimes we weep for lost souls of friends and relatives. Some weep for love lost from their companion. Tears are also a wonderful way to express our sympathy. One family we hardly knew came the day before the funeral of our little son and stayed all day. They spoke few words, but shed tears. What a comfort!

One of our children was born with a closed tear duct. A physician needed to open that passage. Maybe we need to ask the Great Physician to open the tear ducts of our hearts, so that we can express our love to our fellowman, by weeping with those who weep, so that we can better rejoice when they rejoice. May we diligently seek those who need comfort.

Stephen Miller, Loyal, WI

Bible Reading: John 11:31-44
One Year Bible Reading Plan:
Revelation 12
Micah 4:9–7

God does not comfort us to make us comfortable,
but so that we can comfort others.

The Romans Road to Salvation

These things have I written unto you that believe on the name of the Son of God; that ye may know that ye have eternal life, and that ye may believe on the name of the Son of God.
1 John 5:13

"As it is written, There is none righteous, no, not one" (Romans 3:10). "For all have sinned, and come short of the glory of God" (Romans 3:23). "For the wages of sin is death; but the gift of God is eternal life through Jesus Christ our Lord" (Romans 6:23). "But God commendeth his love toward us, in that, while we were yet sinners, Christ died for us" (Romans 5:8). "That if thou shalt confess with thy mouth the Lord Jesus, and shalt believe in thine heart that God hath raised him from the dead, thou shalt be saved. For with the heart man believeth unto righteousness; and with the mouth confession is made unto salvation" (Romans 10:9, 10). "For whosoever shall call upon the name of the Lord shall be saved" (Romans 10:13). "There is therefore now no condemnation to them which are in Christ Jesus, who walk not after the flesh, but after the Spirit" (Romans 8:1). "The Spirit itself beareth witness with our spirit, that we are the children of God" (Romans 8:16). "For if ye live after the flesh, ye shall die: but if ye through the Spirit do mortify the deeds of the body, ye shall live" (Romans 8:13).

Helping someone to salvation is one of the greatest blessings a Christian can experience outside of his own salvation. It is one of the fruits of the true children of God. It is a work in which we should all be engaged.

Bible Reading: Romans 10:1-17
One Year Bible Reading Plan:
Revelation 13
Nahum

We can point the Way to the hungry and the seeking, but it is up to the individual to repent and exercise faith. At that point, we have to stand back and simply pray and let the Lord do His work. Let us seek to help some soul today.

James Yoder, Richfield, PA

Men may be able to polish men,
but only the blood of Jesus can cleanse them.

Father-Son Relationship

And the Word was made flesh, and dwelt among us,
(and we beheld his glory, the glory as of the only
begotten of the Father,) full of grace and truth.
John 1:14

A son is born. The God of the Old Testament becomes a Father in the New Testament, because Jesus is born into the world. Jesus was incarnated, that is, He was born in the flesh. Two great revelations were given at Christ's birth: God is the Father and Jesus Christ is the Son of God. This Father-Son relationship is clearly evident throughout all New Testament Scripture.

Jesus extends this relationship to all believers. "But as many as received him, to them gave he power to become the sons of God, even to them that believe on his name" (John 1:12). "Ye have received the Spirit of adoption, whereby we cry, Abba, Father" (Romans 8:15). "And because ye are sons, God hath sent forth the Spirit of his Son into your hearts, crying, Abba, Father" (Galatians 4:6).

In the Lord's Prayer, Jesus teaches us to pray, "Our Father." God is Jesus Christ's Father. He is also your Father and my Father, if we are born of the will of the Father.

When Christ becomes incarnated in our hearts, we become born of God. Christ becomes alive in our hearts.

Bible Reading: John 1:1-14
One Year Bible Reading Plan:
  Revelation 14
  Habakkuk

My heart is the manger crib of His love
Expressing the glories of heaven above,
My heart is His temple, He reigns as king;
He makes my whole being rejoice and sing.

Ben Coblentz, Millersburg, OH

. . . Abraham rejoiced to see my day.
—John 8:56

Sin Is a Dread Disease

And their word will eat as doth a canker.
2 Timothy 2:17

Last fall I felt tired and needed more sleep and rest than usual. Unknown to me at that time, there was a dread disease doing its deadly work in my body. Deadly cancer cells were rapidly multiplying, creating a tumor mass and robbing my blood of its energizing red blood cells. Quickly I became weak and anemic. When the cancer was discovered in January, it was progressing rapidly. Unless drastic measures were taken soon, death would certainly ensue, perhaps in only several months. I underwent six months of chemotherapy. Now the doctor's report is that there has been a complete remission of the cancer.

This deadly growth illustrates a spiritual danger we all face. If we allow sin to multiply in us, it will keep growing, making us weak spiritually. It may begin as a small sin: a little unforgiveness, a moment of anger or bitterness, or love for fine things of this world. Unless sin is dealt with, it will grow into something needing drastic remedies, or it will certainly bring us spiritual death.

The only thing that can save us from spiritual death is repentance and the blood of Jesus Christ. If we will humble ourselves and recognize that we have sinned and need Jesus to cleanse us, we can be released from our death sentence. Like cancer, the longer sin is allowed to advance in our lives, the more pain and suffering we will have to endure in order to be healed. But, thank God, healing is possible through our Lord Jesus Christ.

Bible Reading: 1 John 1:1–2:17
One Year Bible Reading Plan:
Revelation 15
Zephaniah

Paul Jantzi, Milverton, Ontario

*The cancer of sin, unless treated,
will certainly bring death.*

Christmas

. . . Let us now go even unto Bethlehem. . .
Luke 2:15

Are you moved by the scene of Christ's birth? Pause with me just a moment, and let us consider the circumstances once more. As we enter the stable, we are met by the odors of animals: a few cattle, several donkeys, and a camel or two are munching on their morning ration of hay. A mouse scurries into the corner as we approach.

Joseph and Mary are standing by one of the mangers, looking on with peace and joy in their hearts. Stepping quietly up to the manger, we see a small bundle, wrapped in swaddling clothes with only a tiny head sticking out. It is the baby Jesus! Is it not a wonder that God, the great Creator, would come to earth in such a humble fashion as this? The story has been told many, many times, but it never grows old.

It is good and proper for us to set aside a day to commemorate the Birth of Christ. It is good to have a day when families gather for sharing and fellowship. However, let us keep the commemoration of Christ's birth in perspective. Let us keep our devotion focused upon the mystery of the Incarnation. "And without controversy great is the mystery of godliness: God was manifest in the flesh, justified in the Spirit, seen of angels, preached unto the Gentiles, believed on in the world, received up into glory" (1 Timothy 3:16). As we go through the day, let us make sure that we serve the Christ and not the flesh.

> **Bible Reading:** Luke 1:26-38
> **One Year Bible Reading Plan:**
> Revelation 16
> Haggai

Henry Yoder, Clarkson, KY

His birth was but a path to Calvary.

The Incarnation of Jesus Christ

Therefore the Lord himself shall give you a sign; Behold, a virgin shall conceive, and bear a son, and shall call his name Immanuel.
Isaiah 7:14

The Virgin Birth of our Savior is disbelieved by liberal thinkers. True Christians see this as a Satanic attack upon a foundational truth. If we should question His Virgin Birth, what might the enemy have us question next? The crucifixion, the resurrection, the ascension, or the second coming? "If the foundations be destroyed, what can the righteous do?" (Psalm 11:3).

God has created human beings in four different ways, each of them special. Consider them:

1) God created the first person without a man or woman involved. God used the dust of the ground and breathed into His creation the breath of life (Genesis 1:7). This was indeed a miracle!

2) God created the second person without the involvement of a woman. What a miracle!

3) God now creates human life using both man and woman. Though we have often seen it, birth still seems almost miraculous to us. "Surely we are fearfully and wonderfully made," the Psalmist cries, and we agree. Each child is a gift of God!

4) God's greatest miracle was the birth of a child to a woman, without a man involved, because the child was the God-Man, Jesus Christ. "Born of the virgin Mary, conceived by the Holy Ghost," declares the Apostles' Creed.

Bible Reading: Luke 2:1-20
One Year Bible Reading Plan:
Revelation 17
Zechariah 1–3

What is the problem? What is there to doubt? Why the skepticism?

Friends, we have a miracle-working God!

Jim Yoder, Leitchfield, KY

God said it, that settles it. The wise man believes it, the fool debates it.

December 27 _____

Godly Wisdom

*But God hath chosen the foolish things of the world to
confound the wise; and God hath chosen the weak things
of the world to confound the things which are mighty.*
1 Corinthians 1:27

In 1 Corinthians 2 Paul gives God all the credit for the powerful sermons he had preached to the Corinthian church. Paul did not try to impress the people with his personal intelligence, but he let the Holy Spirit work in his life.

Do we allow the Holy Spirit to control our lives fully, so that God can fill us with His wisdom? Can He use us as He used Paul, to show His divine power and wisdom to others? When we are asked to teach Sunday school or share a devotional, do we allow the Holy Spirit to reveal His truth to us, or do we rely on our earthly intelligence to explain God's Word?

We need to rely on God and let the Holy Spirit work in our lives as we do the Lord's work. Not only will we receive a greater blessing by relying on God's wisdom, but the people we serve will also benefit from our reliance on God's wisdom rather than on earthly wisdom. We receive godly wisdom by meditating on God's Word, through prayer, and by maintaining a close walk with God.

God reveals to the spiritual man things the carnal man is unable to see or understand. The spiritual man is born again by the Holy Spirit; therefore he is capable of knowing His mind and receiving the teachings of the Holy Spirit (1 Corinthians 2:16).

> **Bible Reading:** 1 Corinthians 2
> **One Year Bible Reading Plan:**
> Revelation 18
> Zechariah 4–6

Joseph Hostetler, Belleville, PA

The Gospel is heavenly wisdom.

Beware of Envy

_Let your conversation be without covetousness;
and be content with such things as ye have._
Hebrews 13:5

Envy is "displeasure at the advantage of another, with a desire to possess the same advantage." Our old carnal nature is basically selfish, desiring to be what others are, have what others have, and do what others do. Even as Christians, we must deal with the sins of envy and jealousy.

Envy caused Cain to become angry and slay Abel after his brother's sacrifice was accepted by God but his own was not. Joseph's brothers envied him after he told them his dream. Later, they sold him to the Ishmaelites to get him out of their way. The Bible says it was envy that moved the Jews to capture Jesus and deliver Him to Pilate. How true the Scripture that says, "For where envying and strife is, there is confusion and every evil work."

In contrast, Jonathan, the son of King Saul, loved David unselfishly. He surrendered all his rights to the throne in favor of his friend David. He even risked his life to protect the one who would be king in his place.

The opposite of envy, jealousy, and covetousness is contentment. Contentment is a virtue that, when coupled with godliness, is great gain (1 Timothy 6:6). Contentment means that we are satisfied with what we have, even though others may have more. It means we work with the abilities that God has given to us, rather than wishing for someone else's gift. When we love others, we rejoice to see them prosper, even if they rise higher than ourselves. Love never envies (1 Corinthians 13:4).

May we, by God's grace, keep our hearts free from envy. Let us be satisfied with our lot in life and serve the Lord wholeheartedly with what He has given to us.

John Glick, Gap, PA

Bible Reading: James 3:13–4:10
One Year Bible Reading Plan:
Revelation 19
Zechariah 7–9

Envy is a sickness that only gratitude can heal.

Satan's Subtle Tactics

For we dare not make ourselves of the number, or
compare ourselves with some that commend themselves:
but they measuring themselves by themselves, and comparing
themselves among themselves, are not wise.
2 Corinthians 10:12

Even though people are departing more and more from the teachings of Christ, it is evident that few are alarmed. I am reminded of Genesis 3:1, "Now the serpent was more subtil than any beast of the field which the LORD God had made." Satan is indeed very subtle, crafty, and cunning. Perhaps his most cunning and alluring lie is the claim that the grace of Christ glosses over our sins rather than enabling us to become free from sinning. He has coupled that lie with another, saying if a person feels okay about his condition, his heart is right, and all is right.

People adapt well to the "follow the leader" syndrome. Other churches are doing it, and the ministry especially approves; so they feel safe in following.

Once a little girl had a bulldog puppy as a pet. One day, her mother found her sitting on the porch, making ugly faces at her little puppy. Mother explained to her that making faces is not acceptable conduct. Tearfully, the little girl replied, "He started it."

They who measure themselves among themselves are not wise. We must not think that we can follow others and get by. Do we think we can excuse our actions by saying, "Someone else started it"? Let us follow Christ, who has gone before us into the presence of the Father.

> **Bible Reading:** Genesis 3:1-13
> **One Year Bible Reading Plan:**
> Revelation 20
> Zechariah 10–12

Melvin Yoder, Gambier, OH

Let us truly set our affection on things above,
not on things on the earth.

A Gentleman Is a Gentle-Man

_And the servant of the Lord must not
strive; but be gentle unto all men._
2 Timothy 2:24a

George Washington and General Lafayette were walking together one morning when they were greeted on their path by a slave. The old man paused, tipped his hat, and said, "Good mo'nin Gen'l Washington." Immediately, George Washington removed his hat, bowed, and answered, "Good morning to you, and I hope you have a pleasant day."

General Lafayette was shocked. When he recovered his composure, he exclaimed, "Why did you bow to a slave?"

Washington smiled and replied, "I would not allow him to be a better gentleman than I." Today's society rarely refers to men as gentle. The "macho attitude" prevails, which permits men to be rude, overbearing, and ungrateful, swaggering around being tough.

Paul wrote to Titus, "Speak evil of no man, be no brawlers, but gentle, shewing all meekness unto all men. . . ."

Gentleness is a fruit of the Holy Spirit, and a character trait of Jesus ruling in our lives. Gentlemen, let's be gentle today.

Kevin Miller, Auburn, KY

Bible Reading: Titus 3:1-8
One Year Bible Reading Plan:
Revelation 21
Zechariah 13, 14

_A real gentleman is a combination of
gentle strength and strong gentleness!_

It Pays to Obey

Behold, to obey is better than sacrifice,
and to hearken than the fat of rams.
1 Samuel 15:22b

Recently, one of my sons was attempting to install a shaft on a piece of equipment, which I knew to be an awkward task to perform. As I came upon the scene, I informed him that I had better do it myself. Now, we know that determination is good, but obedience is far better. Anyway, he proceeded to connect the shaft. Suddenly, there was a howl as he held his pinched finger, smarting with pain. After things subsided I said, "Now that's what we call delayed obedience with instant results." God does not always repay disobedience on the spot, nor is it always harvest time in October. Many are the people who have disobeyed in their youth and reaped a bitter harvest in their later years.

Sometimes later generations have suffered because one person did not learn the virtue of obedience. For example, Balaam disobeyed, and years later lost his life. Because of his counsel the Israelites fell into sin and 24,000 died.

Saul disobeyed by not destroying the Amalekites and their king, Agag. He lost his position as king. But generations later, the Jews were almost extinguished by Haman, a descendant of Agag.

On the other hand, Queen Esther learned obedience in her youth (Esther 2:20) and because of her obedience, God honored her, using her to save the Jewish nation from destruction.

"Behold, to obey is better than sacrifice." And so it is. The obedience of a child is of far more worth than expensive gifts and gushy cards from the disobedient!

Bible Reading: 1 Samuel 15:10-28
One Year Bible Reading Plan:
Revelation 22
Malachi

Stephen Miller, Loyal, WI

He leads best who has learned to follow.

You Can Find Our Books at These Stores:

CALIFORNIA
Squaw Valley
  Sequoia Christian Books
  559/332-2385

GEORGIA
Glennville
  Vision Bookstore
  912/654-4086
Montezuma
  The Family Book Shop
  912/472-5166

INDIANA
Lagrange
  Pathway Bookstore
  2580 North 250 West

Odon
  Dutch Pantry
  812/636-7922

Wakarusa
  Maranatha Christian Bookstore
  219/862-4332

IOWA
Kalona
  Friendship Bookstore
  2357 540th Street SW

KENTUCKY
Harrodsburg
  Kountry Kupboard
  859/865-2211

Stephensport
  Martin's Bookstore
  270/547-4206

LOUISIANA
Belle Chasse
  Good News Bookstore
  504/394-3087

MARYLAND
Union Bridge
  Home Ties
  410/775-2511

MICHIGAN
Fremont
  Helping Hand Home
  231/924-0041
Sears
  Hillview Books and Fabric
  231/734-3394
Snover
  Country View Store
  989/635-3764

MISSOURI
Rutledge
  Zimmerman's Store
  660/883-5766

St. Louis
  The Homeschool Sampler
  314/835-0863

Seymour
  Byler Supply & Country Store
  417/935-4522
Versailles
  Excelsior Bookstore
  573/378-1925

NEW MEXICO
Farmington
  Lamp and Light Publishers
  505/632-3521

**Our books may also be found on many
Choice Books Bookracks**

NEW YORK
Seneca Falls
Sauder's Store
315/568-2673

NORTH CAROLINA
Greensboro
Borders Books and Music
336/218-0662

Raleigh
Borders Books and Music
919/755-9424

NORTH DAKOTA
Mylo
Lighthouse Bookstore
701/656-3331

OHIO
Berlin
Gospel Book Store
330/893-3847

Carbon Hill
Messiah Bible School
740/753-3571

Hopewell
Four Winds Bookstore
740/454-7990

Mesopotamia
Eli Miller's Leather Shop
440/693-4448

Middlefield
Wayside Merchandise Books
and Gifts
15973 Newcomb Road

Millersburg
Country Furniture & Bookstore
330/893-4455

Plain City
Deeper Life Bookstore
614/873-1199

PENNSYLVANIA
Belleville
Yoder's Gospel Book Store
717/483-6697

Ephrata
Clay Book Store
717/733-7253

Conestoga Bookstore
717/354-0475

Guys Mills
Christian Learning
Resource
814/789-4769

Leola
Conestoga Valley Books Bindery
717/656-8824

McVeytown
Penn Valley Christian Retreat
717/899-5000

Narvon
Springville Woodworks
856/875-6916

Springboro
Chupp's Country Cupboard
814/587-3678

Stoystown
Kountry Pantry
814/629-1588

SOUTH CAROLINA
Rembert
Anointed Word Christian
Bookstore
803/499-9119

**Our books may also be found on many
Choice Books Bookracks**

TENNESSEE
Crossville
  Troyer's Country Cupboard
  931/277-5886

TEXAS
Kemp
  Heritage Market and Bakery
  903/498-3366

VIRGINIA
Dayton (Farmer's Market)
  Books of Merit
  540/879-5013

Harrisonburg
  Christian Light
    Publications
  540/434-0768

Stuarts Draft
  The Cheese Shop
  540/337-4224

WISCONSIN
Loyal
  Homesewn Garments
  715/255-8059

CANADA
British Columbia
  Burns Lake
  Wildwood Bibles and Books
  250/698-7451

Ontario
  Brunner
  Country Cousins
  519/595-4277

**Our books may also be found on many
Choice Books Bookracks**

Order Form

To order, send this completed order form to:
**Vision Publishers, Inc.
P.O. Box 190
Harrisonburg, VA 22803
Fax: 540-432-6530
e-mail: visionpubl@ntelos.net**

_____   _____
Name   Date

_____   _____
Mailing Address   Phone

_____
City   State   Zip

Beside the Still Waters   Quantity _____ x $10.99 each = _____

Price _____

Virginia residents add 4.5% sales tax _____

Grand Total _____

All Prices Include Shipping and Handling

All Payments in US Dollars

☐ Check #_____
☐ Visa
☐ MasterCard

Card # ☐☐☐☐ ☐☐☐☐ ☐☐☐☐ ☐☐☐☐

Exp. Date ☐☐☐☐

Thank you for your order!

*For a complete listing of our books,
write for our catalog.*

Bookstore inquiries welcome

Order Form

To order, send this completed order form to:
Vision Publishers, Inc.
P.O. Box 190
Harrisonburg, VA 22803
Fax: 540-432-6530
e-mail: visionpubl@ntelos.net

_____ _____
Name   Date

_____ _____
Mailing Address   Phone

_____
City   State   Zip

Beside the Still Waters   Quantity _____ x $10.99 each = _____

Price _____

Virginia residents add 4.5% sales tax _____

Grand Total _____

All Prices Include Shipping and Handling

All Payments in US Dollars

☐ Check #_____
☐ Visa
☐ MasterCard

Card # ☐☐☐☐ ☐☐☐☐ ☐☐☐☐ ☐☐☐☐

Exp. Date ☐☐☐☐

Thank you for your order!

For a complete listing of our books,
write for our catalog.

Bookstore inquiries welcome

Order Form

To order, send this completed order form to:
Vision Publishers, Inc.
P.O. Box 190
Harrisonburg, VA 22803
Fax: 540-432-6530
e-mail: visionpubl@ntelos.net

_____   _____
Name   Date

_____   _____
Mailing Address   Phone

_____
City   State   Zip

Beside the Still Waters   Quantity _____ x $10.99 each = _____

Price _____

Virginia residents add 4.5% sales tax _____

Grand Total _____

All Prices Include Shipping and Handling

All Payments in US Dollars

☐ Check #_____
☐ Visa
☐ MasterCard

Card # ☐☐☐☐ ☐☐☐☐ ☐☐☐☐ ☐☐☐☐

Exp. Date ☐☐☐☐

Thank you for your order!

For a complete listing of our books,
write for our catalog.

Bookstore inquiries welcome

Order Form

To order, send this completed order form to:
Vision Publishers, Inc.
P.O. Box 190
Harrisonburg, VA 22803
Fax: 540-432-6530
e-mail: visionpubl@ntelos.net

_____ _____
Name   Date

_____ _____
Mailing Address   Phone

_____
City   State   Zip

Beside the Still Waters   Quantity _____ x $10.99 each = _____

Price _____

Virginia residents add 4.5% sales tax _____

Grand Total _____

All Prices Include Shipping and Handling

All Payments in US Dollars

☐ Check #_____
☐ Visa
☐ MasterCard
Card # ☐☐☐☐ ☐☐☐☐ ☐☐☐☐ ☐☐☐☐
Exp. Date ☐☐☐☐

Thank you for your order!

For a complete listing of our books,
write for our catalog.

Bookstore inquiries welcome